ENGAGING MINDS

CHANGING TEACHING IN COMPLEX TIMES • SECOND EDITION

BRENT DAVIS

DENNIS SUMARA

REBECCA LUCE-KAPLER

 Routledge

Taylor & Francis Group

NEW YORK AND LONDON

First edition published 2000
by Lawrence Erlbaum Associates, Inc.

This edition published 2008
by Routledge
270 Madison Ave, New York, NY 10016

Simultaneously published in the UK
by Routledge
2 Park Square, Milton Park, Abingdon, Oxon OX14 4RN

Routledge is an imprint of the Taylor & Francis Group, an informa business

© 2008 Taylor & Francis

Printed and bound in the United States of America on acid-free paper by Edwards Brothers, Inc., Ann Arbor, MI.

Publisher's Note: This book has been produced from camera-ready copy supplied by the authors.

Library of Congress Cataloging in Publication Data

Davis, Brent.
  Engaging minds : changing teaching in complex times / Brent Davis, Dennis Sumara, Rebecca Luce-Kapler. — 2nd ed.
      p. cm.
  Includes bibliographical references and index.
  ISBN-13: 978-0-8058-6287-4 (pbk. : alk. paper)
  ISBN-13: 978-1-4106-1690-6 (e-book : alk. paper)
  1. Learning. 2. Teaching. I. Sumara, Dennis J., 1958- II. Luce-Kapler, Rebecca. III. Title.

  LB1060.D38 2008
  370.15'23--dc22
                          2007019435

  ISBN10: 0-8058-6287-0 (pbk)
  ISBN10: 1-4106-1690-8 (ebk)

  ISBN13: 978-0-8058-6287-4 (pbk)
  ISBN13: 978-1-4106-1690-6 (ebk)

Contents

Chapter 9   Teaching Frames   157
               Historical and emergent conceptions of teaching

Chapter 10   Teaching Challenges   175
               Inclusive and critical perspectives on teaching

Chapter 11   Teaching Conditions   191
               Reframing the pragmatics of pedagogy in complex terms

Chapter 12   Teaching Encounters   209
               The ethical dimensions of a life that includes teaching

               REFERENCES   227

               NAME INDEX   235

               TOPIC INDEX   239

Dedication

To Tom Kieren. Teacher.

Acknowledgments

We would like to recognize those teachers, researchers and scholars who have labored to interrupt the assumptions and norms that frame popular understandings of knowing, learning, and teaching. Only a handful of these persons could be mentioned in the pages that follow, but we acknowledge our work is enabled by an extended network of educators and critics who share the hope that formal education can be more than it is.

More locally, we are indebted to undergraduate and graduate students, colleagues, reviewers, and family members whose careful readings and focused responses to the first edition of *Engaging Minds* have contributed in many and substantial ways to this one. As well, we note the critical assistance of several people who responded to drafts of this version, including Moshe Renert, Juan Carlos Castro, Wendy Nielsen, Gillian Gerhard, Rachel Moll, Valerie Triggs, and Tammy Iftody (at the University of British Columbia) and Ted Christou, Jennifer Davis, Laura McEwen, and Chris DeLuca (at Queen's University).

Most of the new images for this edition were drawn by Jenny Arntzen. The photographs in chapter 12 were taken by Oksana Bartosh. The cover image was created by Loretta Walz, and Dónal O'Donoghue helped us with the graphic design.

We acknowledge the contributions of our editor, Naomi Silverman, whose gentle provocations and skillful interventions helped to bring this work to form.

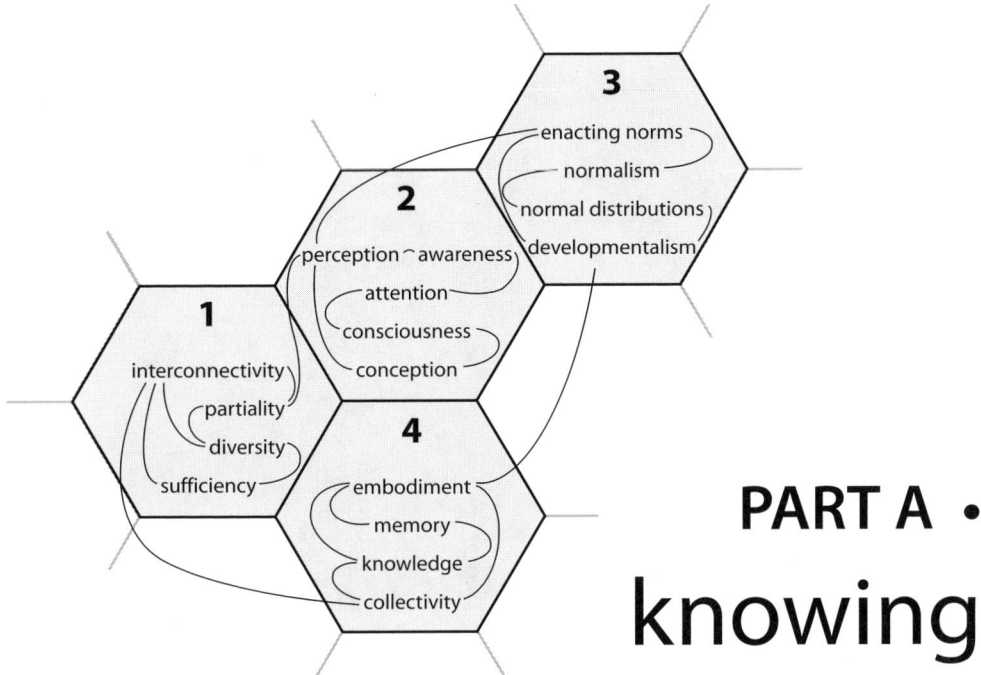

3 enacting norms
normalism
normal distributions
developmentalism

2 perception — awareness
attention
consciousness
conception

1 interconnectivity
partiality
diversity
sufficiency

4 embodiment
memory
knowledge
collectivity

PART A •
knowing

Etymology

The word *know* is derived from the Greek *gnosis*, "spiritual knowledge or deep insight," the complement of which is *episteme*, "everyday know-how." English is unusual in the fact that just one term encompasses these different facets of knowing. Most other languages have two or more verbs to address the range of meanings. For example, the French terms *connaître* and *savoir* and the German words *kennen* and *wissen* are used to distinguish between "being familiar with" (persons or things) and "having mastery of" (facts).

Synonyms

accept, be acquainted with, be able to perform, apprehend, believe, be cognizant of, comprehend, discern, discriminate, distinguish, experience, be familiar with, feel, fathom, go through, grasp, have, master, meet with, be onto, perceive, prove, recognize, remember, savor, see, be sure of, taste, undergo, understand

Antonyms

doubt, forget, ignore, misinterpret, misunderstand

Cognates

agnostic, cognition, cognizance, diagnosis, Gnostic, ignoble, ignorant, incognito, notice, notion, notorious, precognition, prognosis, prognostication, recognize

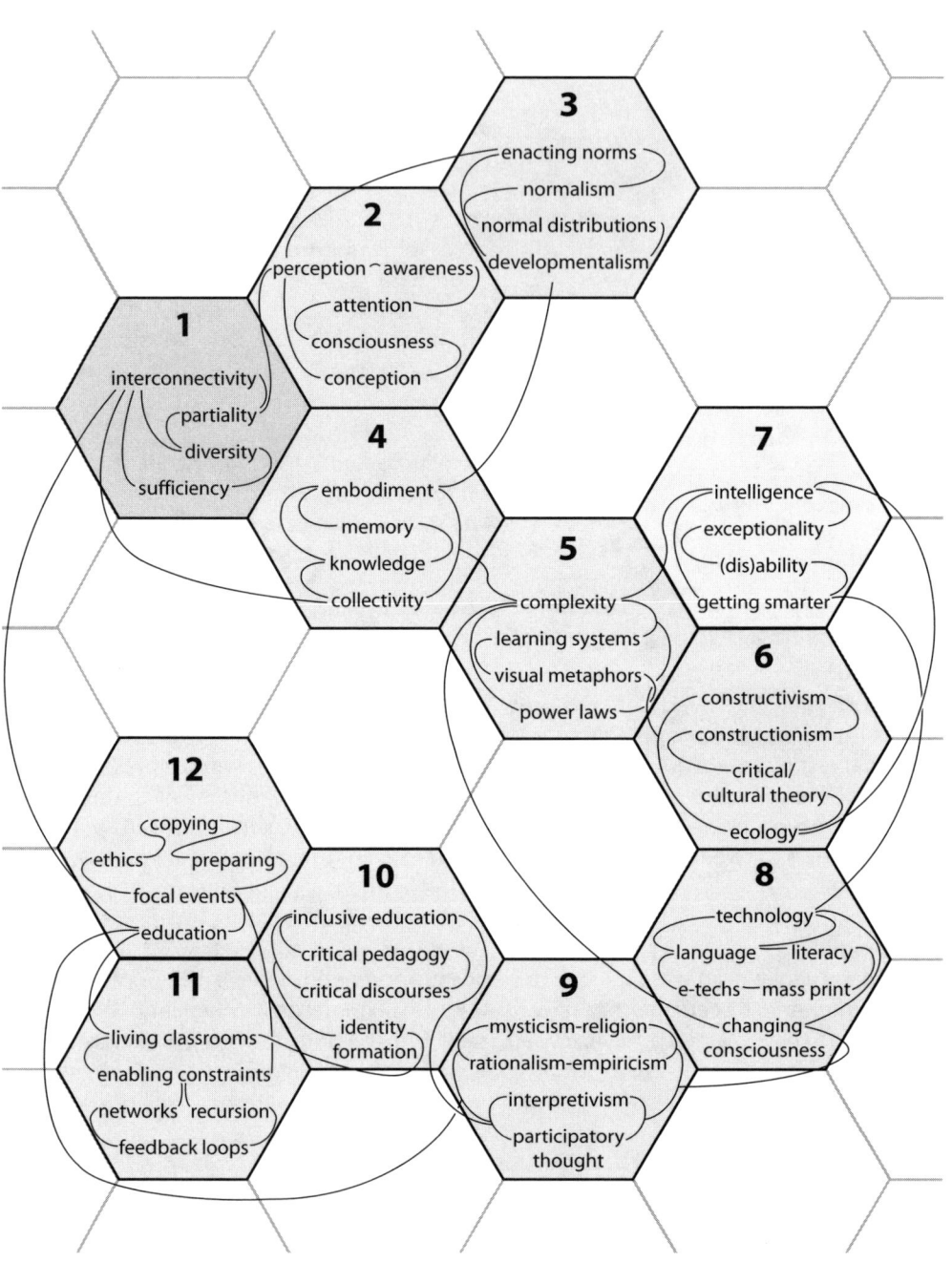

1   Knowing Frames

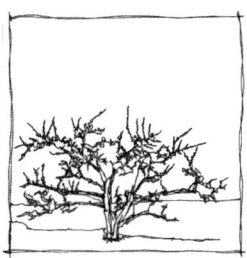

Why is the image of a tree so common in discussions of knowing? We speak of the tree of knowledge and its branches of study. We talk about the seeds of awareness, the roots of understanding, the growth of insight, and the fruit of the labor of learning.

The popular embrace of this organic metaphor is in some ways out of sync with prevailing perceptions of knowledge—which is overwhelmingly discussed as though it were some *thing* out in the real world, waiting to be uncovered and taken in by the receptive mind.

But the tree image presses attentions toward a very different web of associations. A tree is a growing and evolving form. It is a whole in and of itself, but it is also a community of parts, including roots, trunk, branches, bark, leaves, and seeds. And each of these parts is itself a community of cells and other vibrant forms.

Of course, the tree can't be reduced to these elements. Its viability arises in the network of connections among subsystems. Their web of co-activity enables the movement of water and food, the gathering and conversion of energy, respiration, and other life functions. A tree, then, is not so much a thing as a rhythm of exchange.*

As well, the very form of a tree is a record of its flow through time. Its precise pattern of branches on branches on branches is simultaneously unpredictable and familiar. The form is similar to the branching patterns encountered in other trees, in their root systems, in the veins of their leaves, in river deltas, in lightning bolts, and in circulatory systems. Yet it is utterly unique, a still-forming product of the interlocked dynamics of climate, seasons, other living forms, and information once contained in a tiny seed.

Perhaps, then, the prominence and persistence of the tree image in discussions of knowledge has to do with the way it reminds the observer of the patterns that connect forms to one another. The image of the tree of knowledge hints at the vibrancy, the sufficiency, the contingency, the evolving character of knowing.

---

* This phrase is from Neil Evernden, *The natural alien: Humankind and environment* (Toronto: University of Toronto Press, 1993).

1.1 Interconnectivity

This is a book about teaching.

Unlike most texts on the topic, it isn't written from the assumption that definitions of teaching are settled—or even that there can or should be broad agreement on meanings. Instead, it's organized around difficult questions about perception, cognition, action, identity, context, intention, and other issues that contribute to understandings of teaching.

"What is teaching?" is itself a difficult question. In fact, there seems to be only one point of agreement among varied teaching theories, philosophies, and practices—namely that teaching has something to do with prompting learning.

And that point, of course, begs the question, "What is learning?" As tempting as it might be to think that this one has been answered, in fact learning is an extremely complex phenomenon that is not yet well understood. Like the phenomenon of teaching, learning is interpreted in a stunning variety of ways. And, also like teaching, there seems to be little agreement among those interpretations—save for the suggestion that learning is about transforming what is known.

So, then, what is knowing? This is the question that we start with in this book. In Part A we ask: What is knowledge? What does knowledge do? What does it mean to know? What is a knower? It turns out that these are not trivial questions, and emergent answers are presenting some immense challenges to commonsense beliefs.

Part B is focused on learning: What is learning? How does it happen? What is a learner? Why are some learners so much more capable than others? Can intelligence be enhanced? As with the topic of knowing, emergent insights into these issues can be challenging, particulary within discussions of teaching.

Part C deals with that topic. As might be expected, it too offers contrasts to entrenched beliefs and practices. Informed by the discussions of knowing and learning, and seeking to be attentive to the contingencies of time and place, the intention in this section is to present a practicable conception of teaching that is fitted to the world in which we find ourselves.

The titles of the opening chapters in each of the three parts of this book include *frame*, a word that has the same root as *from*. Both terms point to histories and movements, highlighting that perceptions and interpretations are tangled with experience.

We are *framed* by where we are *from*. And, because we are never still, our frames are constantly evolving.

In many ways, the discussions presented here are as much attempts to recover lost or repressed insights about knowing, learning, and teaching as they are attempts to unsettle popular beliefs about formal education. The core themes of complexity, interdependence, emergence, and transformation reach deeply into the history of human understanding. They are evident in the myths and folklore of virtually every culture. However, until only very recently, these matters have been eclipsed for several centuries by insistences on precise definitions, unambiguous classifications, unimpeachable foundations, and irrefutable logic.

Discussions of what it means to educate and to be educated haven't been spared from these desires for universal truths, accurate measurements, context-free methods, and predictable outcomes. In university bookstores and professional libraries, the shelves set aside for texts on education are dominated by thick tomes that speak authoritatively to such well delineated topics as lesson planning, classroom management, evaluation strategies, and questioning techniques. These sorts of instrumental concerns are often broken down even further into specific technical proficiencies, which are then presented as the foundations of good practice.

Most teachers have encountered these categories of "professional knowledge" on the checklists and evaluation rubrics that are used to grade their practices. We, the authors, have a great deal of experience with such artifacts, first as public school teachers and more recently as teacher educators. More than once we have found ourselves in the uncomfortable situation of observing a teacher candidate who seems to be doing everything "by the book"—that is, who is demonstrating a thorough knowledge of how to state clear learning objectives, how to integrate all the required elements of a proper lesson, how to implement an even-handed classroom management strategy—but who is plainly ineffective. Impeccable lessons are crafted and presented, but often in complete ignorance of the contingencies of the classroom. An aim of this book is to explore the roots of this sort of disconnection.

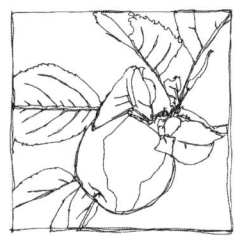

Classic icon of the relationship between teacher and student, one of the more prominent and long-standing emblems of education is the apple.

Caught in a web of provocative associations, the apple is also a symbol that can be used to frame both entrenched and emerging sensibilities in discussions of knowing, learning, teaching (see p. 17).

However, the book isn't principally about implicit beliefs or sedimented practices. Rather, there's a more hopeful purpose. We aim to explore emergent insights into knowing, learning, and teaching for the possibilities they offer to education.

We don't approach these topics by trying to replace one façade of confident assurance with another. Instead, we strive for a more tentative approach to the complexities of existence and education—an attitude that we have attempted to foreground with some playful uses of language. Such phrases as "engaging minds," "knowing acts," "learning positions," and "teaching conditions" are used to flag an emphasis on interrogating habits of knowing while serving as reminders of the unrealized possibilities of knowledge. Interpretable both as noun phrases (objects) and verb phrases (actions), these headings reflect the necessary conditions for knowing—namely the coupled capacities to fix and unfix and to anchor one's step in order to push into the next. In other words, this book is written from the conviction that knowledge is a dynamic phenomenon—hence the use of the gerund *knowing*, which is intended as a reminder that knowledge isn't a thing.

One of the strategies used to avoid the temptation to fix knowledge is to be attentive to vocabulary and to webs of association. By way of familiar example, consider the phrase, "the business of schooling," from which it follows that students are clients, education is a marketable service, teachers are skilled laborers, and knowledge is a commodity. This cascade of entailments can easily be extended. For instance, if one "buys into" the belief that formal education is a business, then it makes sense to demand efficiency, cost-effectiveness, quality control, worker accountability, and resource management—precisely the sorts of notions that arise to justify cutbacks in educational funding, increases in class sizes, reductions in preparation time, and the imposition of standardized tests (for both students and teachers). We could go on.

In brief, how one speaks cannot be separated from how one thinks and acts. Knowing and doing are not different phenomena.

Trees are more than an interesting thematic or a source of provocative metaphors.

For instance, there is some evidence that merely having a view of trees (rather than the usual blank walls of a hospital) hastens recovery of patients. Apparently, plants can also help to reduce anxiety.

There's also evidence that "green time" can help children to focus, especially those with a history of being easily distracted.*

---

* See Jesse Norman, *Living for the city* (London: Policy Exchange, 2006).

Trees, of course, aren't autonomous forms, but aspects of grander systems. For example, to understand why one specimen might produce such an abundance of fruit or why another might generate so many seeds, one must consider the life of the tree in relation to the life of the forest of which it is part. A tree is caught up in webs of exchange, providing shelter and sustenance for many varieties of insect, bird, reptile, and mammal (not to mention more microscopic forms of life). They in turn pollinate its blossoms, distribute its seeds, and fertilize its roots.

The interdependencies extend even further as these living forms participate with others in the interchange of oxygen and carbon dioxide and in the movement of water around the planet—aspects of seasonal patterns and annual cycles that unite ground and sky, organic and inorganic, life and death, past and present, possibility and actuality.

The suggestions that trees are not singular entities and that forests are more than collections of trees are actually fairly new, first proposed by Russian geographer Georgy Fedorovich Morozov* about a century ago. His metaphor of "forest as plant society" foregrounds that these ecosystems give rise to properties that can't be manifest by individual trees.

It is not without irony that the "forest as society" metaphor proposed by Morozov has been reversed in many current discussions of culture and society. Owing in large part to the emergent realization that natural systems are stunningly complex, it is not uncommon to encounter analogies between human social systems and natural ecosystems.

1.2 Partiality

One of the core themes of this text is that knowing always spills over the perceived boundaries of the knower. Humans are not self-contained, insulated, or isolated beings, but are situated in grander social, cultural, and ecological systems.

One rarely encounters such a strong emphasis on knowing and knowers in the most popular "How to Teach" manuals. We believe that failures to address these issues—or, more troublesome, failures to recognize them as issues at all—have supported the emergence of an educational orthodoxy that rests on some shaky foundations and an educational establishment that serves as a place to perpetuate cultural conventions rather than as a site of innovation.

At issue here is the realization that every act of knowing is *partial*—in the twofold sense of "incomplete" and "biased." Knowing entails a selection, and by consequence, a discarding of other interpretive possibilities. Such selections are neither innocent nor benign. Evidence of this claim can be found in the actual impact of modern schooling: far from fulfilling the promises of benevolence and opportunity that are so often mentioned in discussions of formal education, the school has been shown to be wholly complicit in

* Cited in David Suzuki & Wayne Grady, *Tree: A life story* (Vancouver, BC: Greystone, 2004).

the maintenance of an economically stratified society in which particular domains of knowledge, particular cultural traditions, and particular social identities are given priority over others (see chap. 10).

This sort of privileging, in and of itself, isn't the main problem. After all, knowing consists of enacted partialities. Given that human perception and consciousness are limited, it would be naive to hope for a wholesome, unprejudiced knowledge of everything. However, what is troublesome is the failure to notice the existence of these partialities. Such ignorance can allow dangerous complacencies—believing that enough is known, being comfortable with/in prevailing ideologies, not concerning oneself with the ethical obligation to be attentive to other worldviews, not attending to the impact of one's actions on other phenomena.

At the moment, the world is witnessing some extreme consequences of such complacency. Global warming, threats of pandemics, surges in allergies, asthma, and cancers—these and other looming crises are the products of knowing. They have emerged from the ways that humanity (and, in particular, western civilization) has construed its place in the world. And herein lies another problem. At present, humanity doesn't seem to know what to do, since appropriate responses are likely matters of knowing *differently*, not merely knowing *more*.

Returning to the point at the start of this section, knowing always spills past the boundaries of the knower. Knowing is relational; it is not just about ideational associations (as mentioned in the previous section); it also implicates the knower in webs of physical association. Knower, knowledge, and the phenomenon known can't be separated. What one knows, who one is, and what one does aren't distinct issues.

How does formal education configure into these webs? What is the educator's responsibility in contributing to collective capacities to know differently, rather than merely to know more?

This imperative to know differently is a recurrent emphasis in this text. Happily, insofar as educational practice is concerned, there have actually been some promising signs of thinking differently. Recent discus-

Some plant species are *rhizomatic*—that is, they spread through underground shoots. For example, often all of the trees in a poplar grove are parts of a unified organism that are connected by a single root system.

These sorts of rhizomes provide a useful visual metaphor for the interconnections of certain notions. Seemingly distinct (and opposing) ideas can be deeply intertwined, even if their associations remain hidden from view.*

* See Gilles Deleuze & Felix Guattari, *Anti-Oedipus: Capitalism and schizophrenia* (Minneapolis: University of Minnesota Press, 1983).

sions of the nature of knowing, the processes of learning, and the possibilities for teaching have presented challenges to the reductive, fragmenting mentality underlying checklists, linear curricula, rigid lesson formats, standardized evaluation rubrics, and related artifacts. Emerging from such seemingly disparate domains as anthropology, neurology, sociology, psychology, mathematics, computer science, cultural studies, ecology, and biology, there has been a confluence of ideas around the embedded, embodied, and situated nature of knowing. As is developed more thoroughly in the pages that follow, this transdisciplinary movement has helped to uncover some of the self-perpetuating and uncritical associations that are used to structure and defend certain schooling practices.

In the process, the movement has helped to resituate education—not as the means through which western civilization replicates itself, but as a source of hope for the future. Some have gone so far as to suggest that an education that is about knowing differently rather than knowing more may be humanity's best hope.*

* See, e.g., Edgar Morin, *Seven complex lessons in education for the future* (Paris: UNESCO, 1999).
** From Wade Davis, *Light at the edge of the world: A journey through the realm of vanishing cultures* (Washington, DC: National Geographic, 2002).

Small increases in temperature, trace amounts of mercury, a bit of deforestation, moving to a single crop—these sorts of events were once seen as inconsequential on a global scale. The planet, after all, is vast.

One of the important realizations in the past half-century of ecological study has been that triggers and consequences are not proportionately related as seemingly minor environmental changes have contributed to massive ecological disasters. This insight has prompted a great deal of discussion, and it has contributed to some tremendous shifts in popular thinking about the place of humanity in the biosphere.

In particular, humanity seems to be reawakening to the fact that it is one species among many. There has also been a growing awareness of the need for systemic diversity across all levels of biological organization. There must be genetic diversity in a species, a diversity of species in a habitat, a diversity of habitats in an ecosystem, and a diversity of ecosystems around the planet. If the variation in just one of these level is reduced, that level (and, for that matter, all the other levels) can become vulnerable.

This same sort of thinking has been more recently applied to the human realm—the *ethnosphere*.** A remarkable variety of cultural traditions have arisen around the world as humans have adapted their knowing to fit with contexts that include arctic tundra, equatorial jungle, prairies in the middle of continents, mountainous islands in the middle of oceans, deserts, rainforests, and so on. In each case, an emergent society—that is, a system of knowing—has arisen that is deeply rooted to place. Considered together, these systems of knowing constitute the ethnosphere—the collected wisdom of humanity, the multiplicity of ways the world has been imagined, the diversity of understandings of humanity's place in the biosphere.

It might be argued that, in the same way that biological diversity at all levels is needed for the ongoing viability of the biosphere, so social and cultural diversity are needed to ensure the viability of humanity.

1.3 Diversity

As an integral part of western culture, formal schooling has been framed by assumptions about knowledge
and political reality that are overwhelmingly rooted in
Enlightenment empiricism and European imperialism.
These totalizing influences have been so prominent
that they are often taken as "the way things are." In
fact, if and when they are questioned, critiques are
frequently dismissed as overly philosophical or "out
of touch with what teachers really want."

A principal intention of this book is to interrogate
such assumptions and assertions. Throughout, we
look to more recent trends in western thought and to
diverse worldviews in the hope of prompting more
complex understandings of knowing, learning, and
teaching. We're buoyed in this project by our ongoing
work with practicing teachers who, consistently, have
welcomed the ideas as being better fitted to the realities
of their classrooms than the prescriptive and reductive
legacies of empiricism and imperialism.

In contrast to those monolithic frames, one of the
more prominent themes in the perspectives developed
here is diversity.

Diversity is a topic at the center of discussions of
indigenous peoples, whose widely varied knowledges
and sensibilities have been eclipsed by western ways
of knowing. Some insights of indigenous educators
are particularly relevant to the intentions of this text,
and so we discuss them briefly here.* We underscore at
the outset that our purpose in pointing to indigenous
worldviews is not to appropriate others' insights,
but to emphasize the importance of attending to the
knowings that arise in diverse cultures, eras, and
landscapes.

As developed in subsequent chapters (esp. chaps.
5 and 9), empirical science has been the prevailing
attitude toward the production of knowledge in the
western world over the past several hundred years.
The pillars of empirical thought include repeatable
experiments, concise measurements, and predictable
results—elements whose values are clearly evident in
the stunning successes of modern science.

THEORY *versus* PRACTICE?

You need an ex-	You don't have time
plicit and logically	to sort through the
defensible system	logical implications
of beliefs in order to	of every decision,
decide what is best	and so good teaching
to do. Good teach-	is all about sound,
ing is rooted in good	rehearsed, mastered
theory.	**practice**.

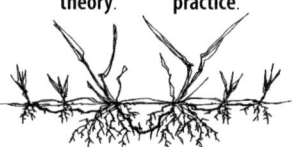

COMMON ROOTS: Anchored to the philosophy of ancient Greece, the realm of
the ideal (i.e., of ideas) is seen as distinct
from the realm of the physical—hence,
theory (how one sees the world) is split from
practice (how one acts in the world).

* For a more comprehensive introduction to
indigenous education, see Linda Tuhiwai Smith,
*Decolonizing methodologies: Research and indi-
genous peoples* (London: Zed Books, 1999).

An unfortunate consequence of the success and subsequent privilege of empiricism has been the tendency to position modern science as monolithic, unified, and representative of all of western knowledge. Indigenous scholars have helped to show that, in fact, western knowledge is much more diverse and conflicted than is commonly portrayed. A more appropriate image than a monolith is a bazaar of artifacts, ideas, narratives, vocabularies, icons, and texts that are drawn from many knowledge traditions and that are manifest in rules, beliefs, philosophies, and practices. These elements are simultaneously stable (held in place by constant rehearsal) and dynamic (undergoing constant modification as contexts evolve).

Even so, the inherent diversity of western knowledge and culture is rarely a matter of explicit awareness. This point is also underscored by indigenous educators, who are often cynical of the motives and methods that infuse western knowledge. For example, the tendency to think of knowledge as a commodity—that is, as a fixed and marketable thing—is a peculiarly western notion, and one that has positioned non-western cultures as sites for domination and exploitation. Another troublesome element of the western cultural archive is the tendency to regard the individual as the basic unit of knowing and sociality, out of which all knowledge and culture arise. These assumptions of independence from others and isolation from the natural world make it difficult, if not impossible, to appreciate worldviews that are rooted in notions of collectivity and connection.

The contrast between individualism and collectivity is perhaps the most significant clash between western and many indigenous belief systems.* The ethics, practices, social structures, and relations of indigenous cultures are often organized around vibrant senses of connection among people and between humans and the more-than-human world. In such contexts, knowing cannot be understood in terms of dispassionate academic exercises or production of goods for sale. Rather, knowing is about who you are and what you are doing, and it unfolds within interlaced sets of political, social, and environmental conditions.

The rhizome image (below and on the facing page) is reused in each chapter to flag beliefs that seem at odds but that share roots. For instance, the common concern of a "theory-practice split" can be traced to an ancient assumption on the nature of reality—a belief that is not really tenable.

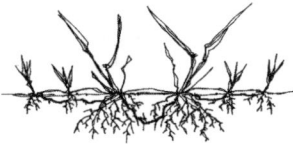

Theory, literally, has to do with how the world is perceived. How we see the world affects how we act; how we act affects how we see the world. In other words, all practice is theorized and all theory influences practice.

* See Gregory Cajete, *Look to the mountain: An ecology of indigenous education* (Asheville, NC: Kivaki, 1994).

Western education has played a prominent and troubling role in these clashes of cultures. For most of its brief history, modern schooling has been organized around the reproduction of a narrow, empiricist conception of knowledge. Indeed, schools have served not only as instruments of the empiricist attitude, but also as tools of Western imperialism.

Over the past few decades, indigenous educators have helped to foreground this issue and open it up to broader discussion. Evidence has been gathered to show how schools have been used to dismiss non-western knowledges and to systematically dismantle indigenous communities by exoticizing cultures and by forcibly separating children from their traditions.* Even though some of these injustices have been interrupted, violence continues through teaching practices and curricula that are infused by a theory of knowledge that is rooted in empiricism and imperialism, and thus organized around an individualistic and commodified conception of knowledge.

It is for this reason that the first section of this book is about knowing. Throughout we attempt to be attentive to what is taken for granted, hoping to point toward a way of knowing that is tentative, evolving, and partial—one that does not position the student as a sponge, a consumer, a mimic, or someone to be colonized, but as a participant. That is, we aim to present conceptions of knowing, learning, and teaching that move away from deeply engrained empiricist and imperialistic attitudes.

Empiricism and imperialism continuously reform themselves, so this project is a matter of ongoing struggle. At the moment, for example, teachers, school officials, and educational researchers are facing demands for "accountability" and "evidence-based practices"—notions that are rooted in empiricist science. More broadly, "globalization" appears to be serving as a new vocabulary of imperialism as multinational corporations seek to overrun economies, communication technologies disrupt local communities, and nations seek to impose ideologies. We join with many indigenous scholars as we seek to develop an awareness of the importance of nurturing diversity

What counts as knowledge?
Different cultures have dramatically different responses to this question. In some, for example, all forms and events are understood to be interconnected. Knowing thus has to do with noticing correspondences and relations—and with being able to appreciate one's position within

* See, e.g., Celia Haig-Brown, *With good intentions: Euro-Canadian and Aboriginal relations in colonial Canada* (Vancouver: University of British Columbia Press, 2006).

in biological and cultural systems. A vital site for this work is teaching.

For us, teaching is not about replication but about creating something new through moments of connecting and reconnecting with one another, with the past, and with the environment. On these interpersonal, temporal, and ecological levels, we further align this work with the scholarship of those indigenous educators who understand education in terms of the-individual-and-the-collective and the-biological-and-the-cultural. It is a sense of education that does not see learners in terms of personal or cultural deficit, but in terms of the possibilities that arise when personal and cultural diversities are brought into conversation. It is an education that is not about controlling and managing, but about engaging.

these webs of association. In some traditions, even things that seem completely opposed are understood to be fundamentally intertwined.

This sensibility is suggested by the pervasive presence of circles, spirals, and dancing motifs among icons and symbols, highlighting notions of connectedness and co-dependence.

Perhaps most importantly, it is an education that seeks to be attentive to the theories that inhabit its practices. As indigenous scholars around the world have helped to foreground in their critiques of empiricism and imperialism, theories contain within them techniques for selecting, organizing, prioritizing, and validating what is perceived and done. Left unconscious, theories can lock knowers into realities that are limited and limiting. Made explicit, theories can help to plan, strategize, and transform.

At the moment of this writing, the one million residents of the city of Vancouver—including the three of us (the authors), who have gathered here to discuss the writing of this book—are under a "boil-water" advisory. There's a small risk the water supply has been contaminated by E. coli bacteria that might be clinging to huge amounts of silt washed into the city's reservoirs during record-breaking rainfalls.

As one might expect, a focus of the media coverage is the question, "Why did this happen?" Opinions vary, but there are two points of consensus. First, the contributing factors are too complexly intertwined to enable a complete understanding of the situation. Second, despite such complexity, humans are likely responsible.

One detail has been getting considerable airplay: sometime in the not-too-distant past, government officials gave in to pressures from the forestry industry to allow the logging of significant areas around water reservoirs. The removal of the trees whose roots held the soil in place, coupled with ever more extreme weather events, set the stage for massive landslides.

And so, even as we discuss ideas that seem far removed from the ground several floors below, we find our thinking to be drawn toward the ecological consequences of human knowing. The slightly murky water that was used to make our coffee, the extra time needed to prepare lunch—these and other details remind us that smooth walls and modern conveniences present only an illusion of separation from nature.

1.4 Sufficiency

Conceptually, the two principal emphases in this book are (1) an interrogation of webs of association that shape understandings of knowing, learning, and teaching, and (2) an integration of current transdisciplinary research, with a view toward articulating possibilities for schooling that are attentive to time, context, and change.

As authors, one of the struggles we have faced in this project is finding ways to structure the presentation of information that are consistent with the sensibilities announced. For instance, when we fix the words in a published document, how can we be sensitive to issues of contingency, context, and the evolutionary nature of human knowledge? In a text that runs from start to finish, how can we highlight the limitations of linear argument?

The first of these two questions has proven particularly troublesome. In the desire to make strong claims, there is a constant danger of stating emergent insights too emphatically—that is, of representing *knowing* as *knowledge*. In the first edition of this book, we thought we had effectively dealt with the issue by being explicit about assumptions, highlighting inconsistencies, using playful vocabulary, and attending to diversities of interpretation. However, as we sat down to discuss this revision, some seven years after the original draft, we were taken aback at the errors and overstatements presented in the first edition. We have attempted to address these matters to the best of our current knowing, but we recognize that we will probably be shaking our heads at much of what we have written when we meet to discuss new insights and possibilities seven years from now.

As for avoiding the pitfalls and limitations of a linear mode of presentation, we have developed several strategies to complexify the text, four of which we will mention here. First, each chapter consists of a pair of interlaced discussions, one more anecdotal and the other more typically academic. These strands were structured to be complementary. With the exception of the selection for this chapter, the anecdotal strands

A *participatory epistemology* is a theory that asserts that all aspects and objects of the world—animate and inanimate—participate with humans

are reports of actual educational and research events, based in classrooms and other schooling contexts, and spanning a range of subject areas.

Part of our intention here was to present examples to illustrate the academic discussions, and another part of the intention was to "present ourselves." We are teachers and researchers who live in particular places, interact with particular people, and hold particular beliefs. As we engage in discussions of knowing, learning, and teaching, we feel an obligation to represent how we are in the world.

This structure of interlaced discussions might also be justified in terms of some recent research into human memory. As developed in more detail in chapter 4, cognitive science researchers typically identify two sorts of conscious long-term memories: *episodic* (event-based, autobiographical, and narratively structured) and *semantic* (fact-based, rote, and often lacking an integrated structure). The former tend to be more stable and more easily recalled than the latter—hence the effectiveness of the ancient teaching practice of embedding factual knowledge in rich images and narratives. This deeply rooted teaching practice (and not the recent cognitive research) prompted us to structure the chapters as we have, but it's comforting to know that cutting edge scientific inquiry supports a pedagogical practice that reaches back into antiquity and stretches across cultures.

Another feature of the writing is the use of the margins. We wanted to take advantage of these spaces to highlight, elaborate, and occasionally digress. This feature is actually prompted by a few pedagogical principles, including the need to provide opportunities to take short rests from the text and the desire to re-emphasize matters of particular relevance.

As for references, in a significant departure from the first edition, we have incorporated footnotes in places where we have felt some readers might want to have access to more information. We have been very selective in this regard, focusing on accessible and comprehensible references that, for the most part, have good reference lists themselves. If you are interested in more detail and in more rigorous discussions,

in the ongoing project of knowledge-production. Knowing about a tree, for example, entails insight into ways that the tree is woven into a grander relational web.

Although most often associated with non-western sensibilities, participatory epistemologies are re-emerging on the contemporary academic scene and are usually associated with a resurgence in interest in ecological and spiritual matters.

you should be able to find them through the citations provided.

This approach to referencing is not typical of academic texts where the more common practice is an extensive bibliography. We wanted to avoid the artifice of authority that sometimes goes along with a long reference list. Our intention is not to impress or validate but to invite others into the further play of ideas. We thus felt it appropriate to constrain choices. Presenting a long list is often no more helpful than presenting no list at all.

Another reason for this strategy is a belief that knowing has a networked structure—a point that is developed in more detail in chapters 4, 5, and 11. We see this book as a node in that network. The aim is thus to use the referencing strategy to provide access to the grander web of knowing, not to attempt the impossible task of presenting a comprehensive mapping of that web.

Finally, a fourth strategy for interrupting linearity is perhaps more subtle. Rather than conceiving of the text in terms of discrete and sequential steps in the development of an argument, our approach to structuring this book has been to think in terms of nested discussions that loop back onto themselves at various levels. This point is perhaps more easily made with reference to the images presented at the start of each chapter. In a sense, each of the twelve chapters, each of the three parts, and the book itself ends up where it begins.

As discussed in subsequent chapters, a nested structure and an iterative (looping back) dynamic are important aspects of knowing, learning, and teaching. We thus thought it would be an interesting challenge—an enabling constraint (see chap. 11)—to organize a text according to some of the principles it presents.

But more importantly, we wanted the text to embody a principle of knowing that is at the heart of the writing. A knower's knowing is subject to constant modification; yet at the same time, one's sense of the world is curiously adequate. In spite of the partiality of knowing, one is typically unaware of gaps in understanding and perception. That is, knowing has a certain sort of vibrant sufficiency.

One of the main themes developed in Part A (on *knowing*) is that most of what we do doesn't spring from *reason*, but from *rehearsal*.*

That is, for the most part, our actions aren't based on deliberate decisions. Rather, they consist of hastily assembled "chunks" of behaviors that are triggered by particular situations.

This sort of immediate coping (versus reasoned action) points to the importance of practice. However, simple rehearsal can give rise to troubling and resilient habits—and so such efforts should include opportunities to interrogate actions through lenses offered by different theories.

* See, e.g., Humberto Maturana & Francisco Varela, *The tree of knowledge: The biological roots of human understanding* (Boston: Shambhala, 1987); Franscisco Varela, *Ethical know-how: Action, wisdom, and cognition* (San Francisco: Stanford University Press, 1999).

In contrast, much of contemporary educational practice is organized around an assumption of static deficiency—that is, a belief that learners are more-or-less fixed beings with inadequate understandings. In such a frame, the task of education is to complete them.

As we will endeavor to develop in the pages that follow, an education that is oriented by the principle of vibrant sufficiency is very different. One must be mindful of how one frames knowledge, since those frames influence one's understandings of learning and teaching. Concisely, knowing frames.

Of course, when the image of a tree is introduced into a discussion of knowing and education, it is almost inevitable that the topic of apples will come up. Newton's apple has become the symbol of sudden insight, Eden's apple is a metaphor for the perils of knowing, the apple image is used more than any other to introduce the alphabet ("*A* is for …"), and the apple on the corner of a desk is a popular reminder of the relationship between student and teacher.

On a grander level of interpretation, the modern apple tree is a sort of living record of recent human history. Most of the apples that are sold in supermarkets are hybrids of Asian and European varieties, reflecting cross-fertilization of not just plant varieties, but civilizations over past centuries. Moreover, in its engineered flavor and texture, as well as in its size and unblemished surface, the supermarket apple bears traces of intertwined historical events and social movements, including industrialization, urbanization, capitalism, and modern science.

It's all there, in a single apple, sitting on the corner of the teacher's desk—a phenomenon that can only be understood when locating it in a complex biological-and-cultural matrix. The apple is indeed an apt symbol of knowing and knowers.

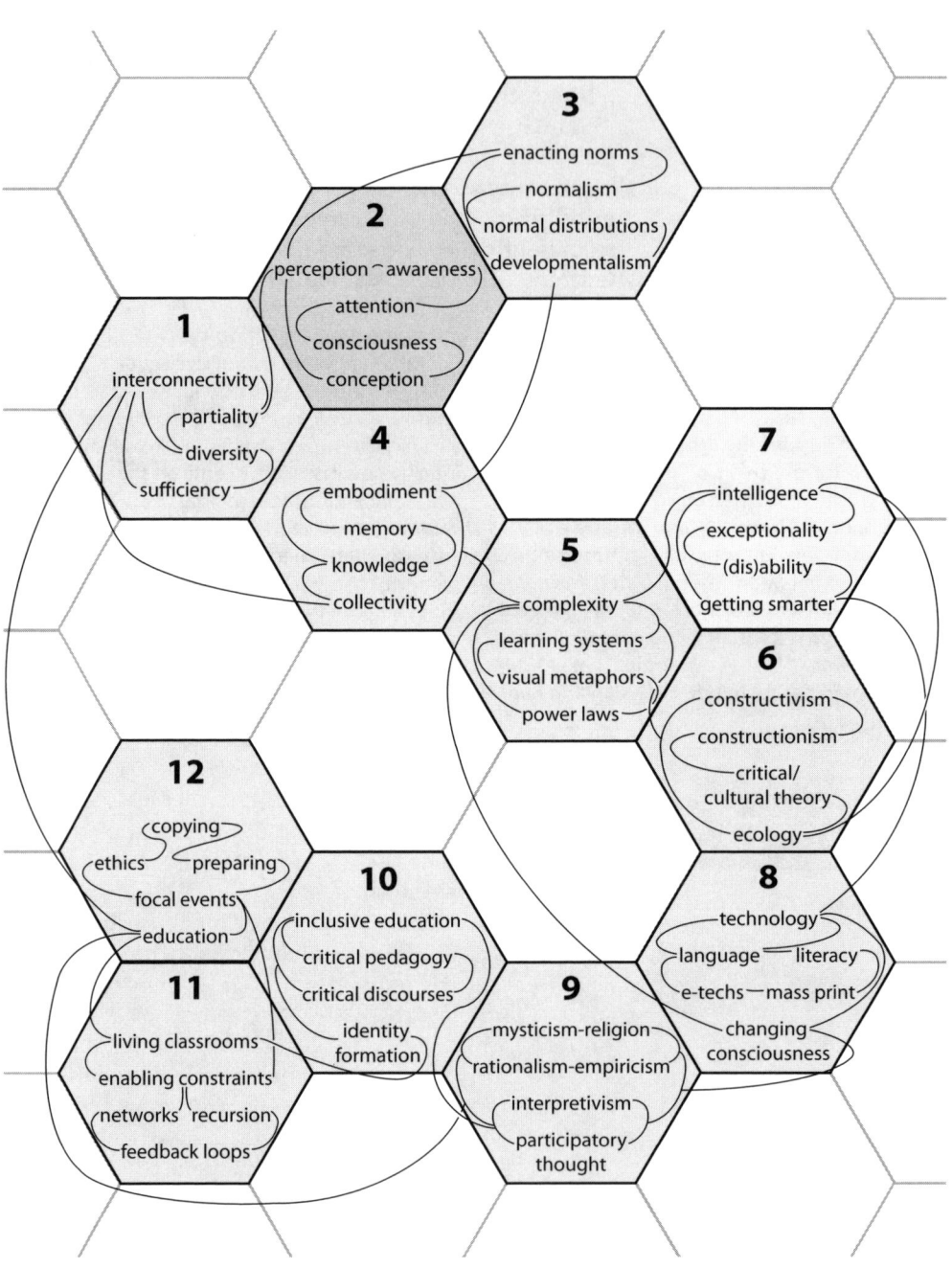

2   Knowing Looks

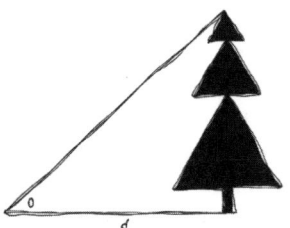

I like to begin my courses for prospective secondary school mathematics teachers with a simple exercise in identifying geometric forms. I ask them to look around and compile a list of as many shapes as they can see—using appropriate mathematical terminology, of course. (To appreciate some of the main themes of this chapter, you might want to take a few minutes to identify some geometric forms within visual range. A typical list has 10 to 20 entries.)

After several minutes, we assemble a master list of all the shapes named. The accumulated result tends to be very similar from one class to the next. It always includes, of course, rectangles (e.g., seen in windows, walls, desks, etc.), squares, and circles. Most of the time there are mentions of triangles, trapezoids, parallelograms, hexagons, ellipses, cubes, rectangular prisms, cylinders, and spheres. And there are always a few unexpected entries: truncated square pyramids, concave kites, and the like.

Part of the purpose of the activity is to highlight just how easy it can be to conduct a quick assessment of what learners already know. I've done almost exactly the same thing in many Grade 7 and 8 math classes—sometimes seeding the room with a few key shapes they're expected to know—and invariably it turns out that just about everyone can identify not just the forms they're already supposed to have learned, but the ones they're expected to learn by the end of the unit. In other words, in just 10 minutes I can find out what needs to be emphasized and what can be taken for granted over the next several classes.

It is a quick and powerful lesson for middle school students and pre-service teachers alike.

2.1 Perception

Why educate?

This question might seem straightforward, but it's actually been at the center of intense debate for thousands of years. And it will likely never be settled. Answers are hinged to beliefs and assumptions on such matters as truth, authority, humanity, and life. There are no simple answers for questions that ride atop such complex issues.

Even though opinions and underlying beliefs can be wildly different, there tends to be one point of agreement: Formal education has to do with one group's desires—conscious and not conscious—to have another group *see* things in the same way. Parents' efforts to educate their children, governments' efforts to educate the general public, and teachers' efforts to educate their students have commonly been interpreted in these terms.

Yet there are problems with the suggestion that education is all about shaping how the world is seen. With regard to the themes and the frames developed in this text, two issues that are often glossed over are, first, the nature of this *seeing* and, second, how one might go about affecting it. Superficially, the discussion here might seem to be about the natures of knowledge and teaching, but more profoundly, the critical issues are perception and causality. Can teachers *cause* learners to change *perceptions* in particular, pre-specified ways? That is, is the project of education, conceived in the terms mentioned above, even possible?

As we develop through the book, the evidence overwhelmingly indicates that the answer to these questions is "No," at least insofar as causality is understood in terms of direct influence.* And, we argue, this realization should prompt educators to rethink the question of what schooling is all about. In this text, we attempt to frame education not in terms of compelling others to see the world in the ways we see it, but in terms of *expanding the space of the possible*. That is, we do not see education in linear–causal terms of achieving preset objectives or re-presentation of established truths, but as a participation in

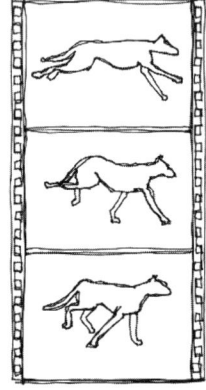

Have you ever realized, a fraction of a second after saying something, that you mispronounced a term or reversed two words?

Such events reveal one of the tricks of consciousness: It disguises the fact that it lags about a half-second behind actual events. That lag is needed for nonconscious processes to sort through, interpret, and select what will become conscious. There is no way of avoiding it—but we are rarely aware of the fact that we're a few frames behind the action.

* There are actually many ways to understand causality. See Alicia Juarrero, *Dynamics in action: Intentional behavior as a complex system* (Cambridge, MA: The MIT Press, 1999).

the ever-unfolding project of becoming capable of new, perhaps as-yet unimaginable possibilities. It is a way of thinking that is mindful of, but not mired in, the past; that anticipates, but does not seek to fix, the future; and that understands that life occurs in the present. Schooling, that is, is not a preparation for life. It is part of living.

In other words, schooling and education are not so much about *shaping* perception to existing frames as *opening* perception to new possibilities—and this is an assertion that requires that we be mindful of what perception is. For instance, if perception is understood as "taking in" or "constructing" facts that exist out in the real world, then it makes sense to organize schooling around established unchanging truths. However, if perception is understood as something more dynamic, complex, and participatory, then education must be rethought. So what does contemporary research say about the nature of perception?

To address this question, a handful of experiments in perception are presented throughout this chapter.* The first involves the image to the left.

With the book about 30 cm (12 inches) from your face, cover your right eye and place a fingertip on the gray dot. Stare at that fingertip with your left eye and maintain that focus as you slide your finger toward the triangle. Without shifting your gaze from the moving fingertip, try to pay attention to what happens to the dot.

It should disappear from view. (If it persists, try sliding your finger a bit more to the right. It might also help to turn the book a few degrees counterclockwise or to vary the distance between your eye and the page. Be sure to focus only on your fingertip.)

Why does this happen? The physiological explanation is simple: Everyone has a blind spot where the optic nerve passes through the back of the eye, leaving a zone with no light-sensitive cells. But that's not the really interesting part.

Try the experiment again, this time attending to what happens with the black line in the middle when the dot falls into your blind spot. For most people, the

---

A "blind spot" experiment. (The instructions begin just beneath the triangle, to the right.)

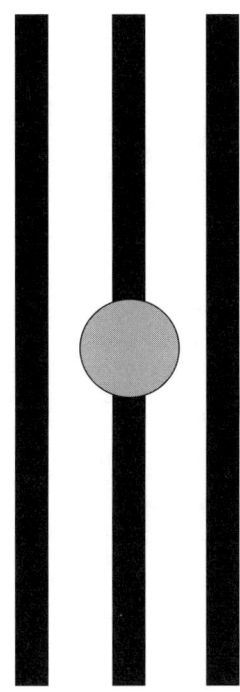

* For more information on the sorts of demonstrations included in this chapter, we recommend Donald D. Hoffman, *Visual intelligence: How we create what we see* (New York: W.W. Norton, 1998) and Donald M. MacKay, *Behind the eye* (Oxford, UK: Blackwell, 1991).

"missing" part of the line seems to be filled it—that is, conscious perception is deceived into thinking there is no gap in the visual field. Of course, this deception is constant. Every functioning human eye has a blind spot yet few humans are aware of holes in the visual field. The intriguing aspect of the experiment, then, is not that there is a blind spot, but that the visual world seems to be seamless and uninterrupted. It's not so much that the hole is not seen, but that we don't see that we don't see it.

Similar issues arise around the phenomenon of blinking. When it's all added up, your eyes are closed for a total of between one and two hours through the course of a day. That is, your eyes are closed for nearly 10% of your waking life due to blinks. Yet the world seems continuous and uninterrupted.

The point? Perception is not merely about gathering information and channeling it to the brain. If it were, we would notice the gaps. Rather, perception is more a matter of negotiating a relationship between current and past experiences. In the cases of the blind spot and blinking, experience has "taught"that there are no holes in the fabric of space and no discontinuities in the flow of time, and so nonconscious processes fill in the blind spots and the temporal gaps with what should probably be there.

The upshot is that eyes are not cameras onto the world, ears are not microphones, and so on. The actual situation is far more complex. For instance, nerve cells run in *both* directions between sense organs and the brain—and *there is more communication from the brain to the sense organ than from the sense organ to the brain*. That means that perception isn't a passive event or a "taking things in." In fact, sense organs actively fish for sensation, making perception more a matter of imposing expectation on experience. (A really convincing way to demonstrate this point is to enter a sensory deprivation tank. When denied continuous contact with an active world, people soon begin to impose sensorial possibilities—that is, hallucinate. A much milder version of this sort of hallucination is thought to occur during sleep.)* So when you're asked to identify something, like geometric shapes, your response

A "fractal card." (The instructions for making this one begin on page 24.)

* For more information on the relationship between sensation and conscious perception, see Tor Norretranders, *The user illusion: Cutting consciousness down to size* (trans. J. Sydenham; New York: Viking, 1998).

might be described in terms of imposing templates onto visual stimulations. Rectangles, circles, and other shapes aren't there; these are distillations from experience that you project onto the world.

For the educator, these assertions raise a critical issue. In a phrase, perception and conception are inseparable. Hence, knowledge shapes perception and vice versa. So what do *learning* and *teaching* mean when perception is perceived as something more complex than taking things in?

The next activity in the introductory session on teaching geometry is making what we call "fractal cards." These are paper-and-scissor creations in which simple iterative processes give rise to surprisingly intricate results. The margin note on the next page provides details on how to make the one pictured to the left.

I usually proceed by highlighting some of the many curriculum topics that might be addressed by these cards. The applicability to the geometry unit is pretty obvious, and connections include identification of shapes, similarity, symmetry, and transformations. As well, it doesn't take much thought to see how measurement topics like perimeter, area, volume, and units of measurement might be taken up. Less obvious, but no less profound, are topics in fractions and other number systems, sequences, series, and limits. Even subtler are mathematical processes like abstraction, generalization, and symbolic representation.

One of the topics I raise in the context of these discussions of curriculum possibilities is the distinction between *mathematics* and *mathematical*. "Mathematics" is generally used to refer to a body of knowledge—that is, a widely accepted collection of concepts and procedures that have emerged through centuries of inquiry. As illustrated by the example of fractal geometry, it is a domain that continues to grow and evolve. "Mathematical," in contrast, is more a reference to a mode of thinking. It involves a noticing of sameness and difference, of pattern and irregularity, of specifics and generalizations, of abstract principles and concrete objects. "Mathematical," true to the meaning of its ancient Greek root *manthanein*, is about learning.

I close that part of the session with the suggestion that it is perhaps the *nurturing of the mathematical*, rather than the *mastery of mathematics*, that should most occupy the math teacher's attentions.

2.2 Awareness

When we open our eyes, do we see the world as it is?

Philosophers and researchers have been occupied with variations of this question for thousands of years. While theories and explanations have differed, overwhelmingly thinkers have converged to the same answer: No.

Recent studies of perception have come to the same conclusion. In particular, they have demonstrated that humans are immersed in a vast sea of sensorial possibilities, only a tiny portion of which ever bubble to the surface of awareness. The evidence actually suggests that, combined, our sense organs can register in the range of 10 million bits of information each second. (This number is based on the estimated total of sensory receptors—e.g., nerve endings in the skin, light-sensitive cells in the eyes, etc.—in a typical human body. Estimates actually vary dramatically from 5 million to 50 million in the texts that we have read. Numbers between 10 million to 15 million are most common.) Of these, it seems a typical person can be aware of only 10 or 20 bits of information every second—that is, a person consciously notes about one out of every million sensory events.

Of course, consciousness *seems* much larger than it is. If you lift your gaze from this text, it is obvious that you are capable of making far more than a dozen discernments. A simple experiment, however, will give some insight into the pace at which such discernments can be made: After reading this paragraph, open the book to a different place, chosen at random. Examine those pages for one second. Then close the book and make a list of the things you noticed. When done, return to this page.

Chances are that your list is fairly brief even if you were familiar with the pages examined—which begs the questions: if consciousness is really so small, why does it seem so much larger? If we humans are capable of perceiving so little information at so slow a pace, why do we feel so aware of so many features of the world?

An analogy between consciousness and a spotlight might help explain this phenomenon. Wherever the narrow beam of a focused light is projected in an otherwise darkened space, the world appears in all its detail. In the same manner, detail is made available to conscious awareness wherever it is focused. At the same moment, however, previously illuminated details are pushed into conceptual oblivion. It is not that they vanish; they are simply no longer present to mind. (This analogy is not meant to suggest that details that are not being consciously noted somehow do not matter. Quite the contrary, the evidence suggests that humans are powerfully attuned to and affected by events and circumstances that may never rise to consciousness.)

Instructions* for making the fractal card pictured on page 22:

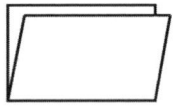

First, fold a sheet of paper in half.

Then, one fourth of the way from the left and right edges, make two parallel cuts. Each cut

should go half the way from the folded edge to the top.

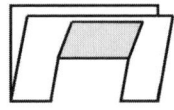

Fold up the flap.

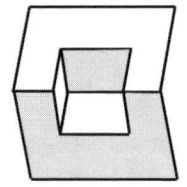

Open the card and push the flap to the inside. (Some folds will have to be reversed.)

Repeat the process on the area marked. (The second iteration will generate two "cells.") Continue to repeat until there are too many

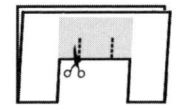

layers of paper to make cuts (typically four or five iterations).

* This graphic is based on an algorithm developed by Elaine Simmt. For further information on this and other cards, see Elaine Simmt & Brent Davis, "Fractal cards: A space for exploration in geometry and discrete mathematics," in *Mathematics Teacher*, vol. 91 (December, 1998), 102–108.

Sense organs differ according to both the amount of information that they can register and the amount of information from each that might become conscious. The following chart gives some rough approximations.

Capacities of Human Sense Organs		
Sense Organ	# of Possible Sensory Events (per second)	# of Conscious Discernments (per second)
eyes	10,000,000	20–40
skin	1,000,000	5
ears	100,000	15–30
nose	100,000	1
tongue	1,000	1

These data help to account for events like being dumbfounded, awestruck, at a loss for words, and so on—since both visual and auditory stimuli alone might consume *all* of conscious awareness. They would also help to understand why non-visual perceptions can be enhanced by closing our eyes.

* For further information on this phenomenon, see Merlin Donald, *A mind so rare: The evolution of human consciousness* (New York, W.W. Norton, 2001). As well, studies of persons with atypical perceptual capacities (stemming from, e.g., autism, region-specific brain injuries, nerve damage, etc.) have helped to foreground what is typically taken for granted, in terms of human co-activity. Oliver Sacks has published many case studies on these matters, including *Seeing voices: A journey into the world of the deaf* (New York: HarperCollins, 1989) and *An anthropologist on Mars: Seven paradoxical tales* (New York: Knopf, 1995).

It's easy to demonstrate this point. Stop to think about a familiar retail area. Is there a dry cleaner? A drug store? You may have regularly walked past such specialty businesses without ever noticing them— until, of course, you needed one (and the spotlight of perception was pointed in the right direction). You can do similar experiments with other senses. What can be heard if you pause from your reading to listen to your surroundings? (Note that you need to pause from reading to pay attention to the sounds of traffic, fluorescent lights, people. Consciousness isn't big enough for you to manage these competing demands.) What can you smell? And so on.

The distinction that's being drawn here is between sensation and conscious perception. The former is vast, the latter is miniscule by comparison. In suggesting this difference, however, it's important to underscore that those sensations that do not impinge on consciousness still play a profound role in shaping what we think and do. Put differently, there seem to be two categories of awareness, conscious and nonconscious. Such disparate schools of thought as behaviorism and psychoanalysis have amply demonstrated the presence and role of the latter. In fact, our attunement to what is around us seems to be mainly nonconscious.

By way of illustration, analyses of videotaped conversations have shown that human interactions involve far more than attending to the words that are spoken. Within such events, speech patterns are precisely synchronized with subtle body movements and are acutely sensitive to events in the surroundings. Yet the speakers are rarely aware of such movements or happenings, let alone the complex choreography of their actions.*

There have been similar studies of parents' actions as they help their children learn language, develop fine motor skills, and become aware of social conventions. Exquisite choreographies of activity emerge as a parent offers subtle cues that maintain a delicate balance between *too much* and *not enough* help. What is surprising in this research, as highlighted in follow-up interviews with parents, is that for the most part they engage in these extraordinary processes without conscious awareness of their actions. When asked about particular prompts and assistance that they provided, parents are rarely able to provide rationales for their actions (beyond obvious and uninformative, "It seemed right," sorts of responses). They are at an even greater loss when asked how and when they learned to teach in this complex, participatory manner.*

In fact, unexpected problems occasionally arise in follow-up interviews. It appears that focusing conscious attention onto specific aspects of these sorts of embodied actions and interactions can actually prompt such engagements to fall apart—in just the same way that a musical recital or an athletic activity can falter when the performer's attention is deflected onto the specifics of the performance. Conscious awareness is often too small to accommodate both an engagement in an activity and awareness of the fine details of one's actions. It is for this reason that it is often reported that exemplary performances and profound engagements correspond to "forgetting" of self.**

Such happenings are not limited to exceptional performances. On the contrary, people are constantly doing far more than consciousness can possibly be aware they are doing. Even now you are performing the very complex task of interpreting the marks on this page, and that is happening without having to devote conscious attention to the shape of each letter or sounding out each syllable. If you had to be aware of the complexity of what you were doing, you wouldn't be able to do it.

There are a number of important implications for educators here. Learning new things, for example, is largely a matter of conscious awareness.*** Enfolding such knowledge into one's life, however, is often a less conscious event. For instance, conscious awareness is usually needed to make sense of rules of grammar, to expand vocabulary, or to discern the standards of acceptable behavior in a new setting. Yet, at some point, such explicit learnings must fade into one's fluid patterns of acting. Having to be conscious of the meaning of each word, the construction of each sentence, or the behavioral code of each setting would be debilitating.

A fractal image is generated by a recursive process—that is, through a series of elaborations in which the starting place of each stage is the output of the previous stage.

For example, the parsley image here is generated by starting with a 3-pronged fork. The first step in the recursive process is to apply three tines to each of the prongs of the original image. The same happens to the new tines in the next step, and so on.

Fractal forms illustrate how surprising detail can quickly emerge from simple beginnings when processes of recursive elaboration are at work.

* See Alison Gopnik, Andrew Meltzoff, & Patricia Kuhl, *The scientist in the crib: What early learning tells us about the mind* (New York: Perennial, 1999).
** See Philip Ross, "The expert mind," in *Scientific American*, vol. 295, no. 2 (August, 2006): 64–71.
*** In fact, some prominent researchers argue that *all* human learning must pass through consciousness. See Donald, *A mind so rare*.

Principles of fractal geometry have been applied in a great many domains, including particle physics, medical research, information science, and movie graphics (to name only a few). Citizens of the western world now encounter fractal images with regularity, especially those who play video games or enjoy movies with many special effects. Fractal geometry has proven useful for generating graphics that can have an eerily real look—trees, mountains, clouds, skin, and other natural forms. In fact, fractal geometry is sometimes described as the "geometry of nature" for exactly this reason.

The next activity in my introductory class on geometric forms is to invite participants to use paper and pencil to draw some fractal images using a few simple rules. (A rule for "fractal parsley" is presented in the margin on the facing page.) It doesn't take long.

Participants are usually surprised at how quickly they're able to generate realistic-looking figures, no matter how talented they are at drawing. Typically, people begin to experiment with variations on a rule soon after learning it. What happens if the tree has four limbs rather than two? What sort of rule might generate a leaf?

I usually end this portion of the class by looking at some familiar natural forms that have a fractal structure. The collection varies, depending on what I can find but usually includes parsley, ferns, cauliflower, broccoli, and kale. As well, I have a collection of images of forms that have tree-like structures (veins, neurons, river valleys, lightning bolts, coastlines, water ripples … the list goes on).

The punch line of this part of the session is usually pretty obvious by the time I get to it: The interpretive tools we have available to us help to open up perceptions, to see things not previously seen, and to notice connections not previously noticed.

2.3 Attention

Moving to the classroom context, what can be said about teaching and learning to teach—and, in particular, about attracting and focusing learners' attentions?

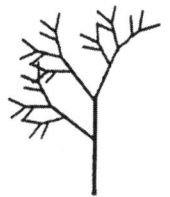 

To begin, educators must consider both the conscious and nonconscious dimensions of topics of study. Given that conscious awareness is so limited, the teacher must delimit information, being careful not to confuse "telling" with "teaching." One must never assume that what is said will actually be noticed by students.

To this end, a popular and prominent guideline within the psychological and educational literature is that no more than six or seven new pieces of information should be introduced in a lesson.* This suggestion is based on the observation that humans, typically, can hold a string of no more than six or seven random digits in mind (hence the 7-digit telephone number).** For longer strings, some sort of chunking is needed to reduce the demands on consciousness. This sort of insight has often been used to support classroom practices that are concerned with "mastery"—that is, practices that focus on isolated skills, repetitive practice, and regular testing to ensure that "chunks" are learned.

* See Steven Pinker, *How the mind works* (New York: W.W. Norton, 1991) for discussions of the research and the ways it has been used and misused within various contexts, including schools.
** First reported by George A. Miller, "The magical number seven, plus or minus two: Some limits on our capacity for processing information," in *Psychological Review*, vol. 63 (1956): 81–97.

Such practices are indeed relevant and effective if education is organized around rote memorization of disconnected facts. However, there is a serious problem with drawing conclusions about what we are able to learn on the basis of how well we can juggle random bits of information. In particular, as recent neurological research has demonstrated, it appears that random information and meaningful information are handled in at least two very different ways in distinct regions of the brain. (See the discussion of memory in chap. 4.)

The point is *not* that rote memorization and repetitive practice are inappropriate. Quite the contrary. Many skills—including the obvious examples of decoding text and counting—must become automatic and transparent before they can be used in the development of more complex competencies. The point is merely that rote memorization without appropriate contextualization may be counterproductive. It might contribute to a student's ability to pass a test, but the material might also be learned in a way that prevents it from being usable in the development of more sophisticated understandings—that is, rote learning might have exactly the opposite effects of what it intends to achieve.

Educators are thus faced with the task of highlighting certain details without decontextualizing them. This task is actually one that parents and teachers (and advertisers) do all the time by repeating key phrases, emphasizing core assertions, returning to orienting themes, checking for comprehension, and so on. Effective teaching may well be neither a matter of ensuring mastery of isolated facts nor of immersing learners in rich settings, but of knowing what's important and having a range of strategies to orient attentions to vital details at appropriate times.

In effect, then, an important aspect of teaching is rendering the familiar strange—about being with learners in the everyday world and prompting attentions to some new aspect, some new way of interpreting the everyday. Teachers have a responsibility to point to the world, to select from the many sensorial and interpretive possibilities that constantly vie for learners' attentions—taking care not to ignore the context that makes an interpretation interesting in the first place.

A figure is *self-similar* if, when enlarged, a well-chosen piece closely resembles the whole. In the case of this fern frond, the portion of the image within each circle is self-similar to the image of the entire frond.

The other fractal images in this chapter, as well as most of the tree images throughout the book, show some degree of self-similarity.

With a few fractal cards in hand, some sketches in notebooks, and some natural forms in view, we have all that we need to begin to make some generalizations about fractals. Four properties that I aim to highlight in this portion of the discussion are recursive elaboration, scale independence, self-similarity, and nestedness.

Recursive elaboration is used to describe the sorts of processes that give rise to fractal forms. A recursion is a repetition, but one that usually gives rise to major transformations, not merely accumulated change. For example, for each of the forms created, every time the rules were applied, a new level of intricacy arose. In contrast, classical geometric forms are constructed through simple elaborations that do not give rise to new levels of detail.

The technical phrase for such levels of intricacy is *scale independence*—which refers to a constant bumpiness of detail, whether you pull in closer or push further away. More technically, a scale independent figure does not become simpler or more intricate when magnified or reduced. For example, a tree is scale independent. As you get nearer to it, new features become evident so that the visual field always seems to be crowded with the same level of detail. (In contrast, forms from classical geometry are not scale independent. For instance, as you magnify a portion of a circle, it gets straighter and straighter, coming ever closer to the simpler form of a line.)

Some scale-independent forms are also *self-similar*—meaning that a well-chosen part, when appropriately enlarged, looks very much like the original whole (see the margin note to the left).

As participants begin to examine the layers of self-similarity that are presented in the fractal cards, fern leaves, and so on, a fourth quality of many fractals becomes evident: *nestedness*. Much unlike classical geometry objects, fractal forms tend to have levels of organization that are nested in other levels of organization.

2.4 Consciousness

A vital part of being "educated" is to be aware of what is being taken for granted and to be able to uncover what has faded into the backdrop of activity.

In this vein, it is important for teachers not only to recognize that consciousness is limited, but also to consider the conditions that contribute to what gets noticed. How is a trickle of perceptions selected out of the torrent of sensorial possibilities? How can we come to terms with the fact that conscious awareness is not presented with "raw data" about the world, but with a distillation, a summary, an interpretation?

A broad range of opinions has been offered in response to these questions. In brief, they vary from the one extreme that perception is strictly a physiological event to the other extreme that all perception is socially determined. Most opinions are somewhere between, positing a shared contribution of heredity and environment. However, even though the most defensible position seems to be one that incorporates the influences of both nature and nurture, the actual story may be far more complex. For instance, now that technologies have been developed to observe working brains in real time, it has become clear that experience affects neurological structure. Bluntly, the brain you have now is different from the brain you had when you started reading this paragraph. Your brain is in the process of establishing new connections. If this is constantly happening, how can nature and nurture possibly be pried apart?

Nevertheless, there is always something to be learned by looking at the evidence that is used to support divergent opinions. And so, in the following subsections, we look at the relative contributions of biology (nature) and culture (nurture) to perception—underscoring that such a distinction is rife with problems.

Biology and Perception. Humans' sensory capacities are species-specific. That is, no other species is attuned to the world in quite the way we are. In general terms, the greater the evolutionary distance between a human and another organism, the larger the variations among sensory capacities and dispositions.

In fact, some life forms have evolved radically different sense organs—so different that we can scarcely begin to imagine how they are attuned to their worlds. Some creatures, for example, are able to "see" heat (certain snakes, in particular). Even more different, some birds may have a fourth, temporal dimension to their sight.* With both eyes on the front of the face, humans (and most predator species) see in three dimensions. Creatures with eyes on the sides of their heads—mainly prey species—have two distinct non-overlapping horizons, each of which is likely seen as two-dimensional. Among insects, it's not clear that the word *vision* is appropriate to refer to their sensitivity to light. Along similar lines, there are inter-species variations among other senses, there are senses that humans lack, and there may well be senses humans haven't imagined (and can't imagine).

In other words, humans are physiologically coupled to their worlds in specific and narrow ways. The world you see when you open your eyes is not the world as it is, in any free-standing, objective sense, since you are only capable of perceiving those aspects that are illuminated by a very narrow part of the electromagnetic spectrum.

Which of these figures is a "kiki" and which is a "booba"?

It turns out that more than 95% of humans, regardless of linguistic and cultural backgrounds, identify the one on the left as the booba and the one on the right one as the kiki. (This result is not dependent on the relationship between the shapes of the letters and the shapes of the figures; it happens in societies without alphabets.**)

Among the implications is the suggestion that perception is biologically rooted, as brains work cross-modally to link the sharp *ki*-sound to the sharp angles and the soft *boo*-sound to the rounded edges.

* See Francisco Varela, Evan Thompson, & Eleanor Rosch, *The embodied mind: Cognitive science and human experience* (Cambridge, MA: The MIT Press, 1991).

** See Vilayanur S. Ramachandran & Edward Hubbard, "Hearing colors, tasting shapes," in *Scientific American Mind*, vol. 16 (October 2005): 17–23.

What do you see here? Two rabbits looking to the right? Two birds looking to the left? A bunny and a bird facing one another? Or facing opposite directions? Something different?

Human consciousness can entertain only one distinct interpretation at a time. We're capable of flipping among different thoughts, but can only consider one at a time.

It appears that consciousness is able to juggle about a half dozen discrete thoughts, but must move back and forth among them. If we stop rehearsing some of them, or if one becomes too dominant, it's likely that a ball or two will be dropped.

* See Gopnik et al., *The scientist in the crib.*
** See Eleanor Rosch Heider, "Universals in color naming and memory," in *Journal of Experimental Psychology*, vol. 93 (1972): 1–20; and Brent Berlin & Paul Kay, *Basic color terms: Their universality and evolution* (Berkeley, CA: University of California Press, 1999).

To complicate things further, one cannot really make sweeping claims about the specifics of human perception. There are dramatic, physiologically-based variations from person to person, ranging from familiar differences (e.g., colorblindness and extreme sensitivity to smell) to quite rare anomalies (e.g., synaesthesia, in which sensory modalities such as sight and taste might be fused—so colors have flavors or vice versa). In fact, you don't have to look far to find variations among sensory capacities: typically, one's own eyes and ears are differentiated, with varied sensitivities to brightness, color, volume, and tone. Not only do we see and hear differently from one another, our own eyes and ears don't match up perfectly with one another. Moreover, sensory capacities and habits change as one grows older, desensitized by aging or lack of use (and sometimes enhanced through practice).

Culture and Perception. It has been argued that the main determinant of perception is cultural context not biological constitution. This sort of claim certainly seems to fit with the realization that perception and conception are inseparable.

Before delving into the evidence, however, it's important to underscore that there do appear to be some culture-independent, biology-based perceptual tendencies. For instance, newborns who are only a few hours old show preferences for vertical lines over horizontal ones and for dots arranged like faces over random images.* In quite a different vein, studies of various societies' strategies for categorizing colors—strategies that are often argued to be linguistically based—reveal that diverse peoples seem to gravitate toward the same broad divisions. In fact, there is a tendency to pick *exactly* the same shades of, for instance, red or blue as the most representative of particular categories.**

But one must be careful not to conflate sensory capacity (e.g., vision or touch) with perceptual ability. Perception implies interpretation, and ability to interpret hinges on experience—meaning that perception is mainly learned. This point has been thoroughly established through case studies of individuals who, through one means or another, have regained some sensory capacity—usually vision—after many years without it. Contrary to what might be expected, the restoration of sight is not always an occasion for celebration. In some cases, the reaction is more toward fear and frustration as the person is suddenly faced with making sense of a barrage of unfamiliar and fluid forms. It often takes years for such a person to learn to discern edges, to track movement, and to notice relevant distinctions—in brief, to see.*

Given that humans learn to see in specific social and cultural contexts, it follows that *what* one learns to see depends in large part on *where* one learns to see—which refers both to the physical structure of one's world (e.g., artifacts, plant life) and the interpretive tools made available (e.g., languages, religions, ideologies). And it is thus that, while the genetic variation among humans is very small, the worlds different individuals perceive can be … well, worlds apart. Even among people who are raised side by side.

So profound are the variations in worldviews and mindsets across cultures, eras, religions, landscapes, and so on, that a good deal of academic discourse in the last half-century has rested on the premise that perception is *entirely* determined by culture. In particular, language is often seen as selecting what is and is not perceptible.**

Clearly, habits of perception tend to flow along the deep etchings of the linguistic landscape. Our language focuses the spotlight of perception on particular details and renders others virtually imperceptible. However, to reduce all perceptual possibility to what has been named seems somewhat simplistic. The situation is probably more complex than that, more a matter of ongoing recursive elaborations than straightforward cause-and-effect.

It's actually not difficult to conduct an experiment into this phenomenon. In fact, the interspersed narrative in this chapter has been developed around one such experiment. As elaborated in the next part of the narrative, when participants are asked to repeat the opening activity—that is, to make a list of geometric forms in immediate visual range—the shift in percep-

What do you see in the figure below? (Try to answer before reading on.)

If you had been told in advance that the image is intended to represent two persons sitting back-to-back, each holding a duck in their outstretched arms, you would likely have seen something like that. Although the image is an accidental inkblot, such pre-interpretation can carve a rut for perception. Every event of language influences perception in this manner, although not always so directly.

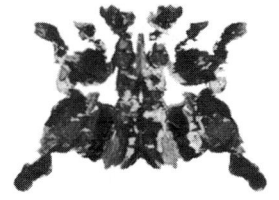

* A classic account of this is offered by Oliver Sacks in his essay "To see and not see," in *An anthropologist on Mars*.
** The extreme version of this opinion is known as "linguistic determinism." See the wikipedia.org entry on the "Sapir-Whorf Hypothesis" for the latest in discussions of the topic.

tions over the course of the activity can be startling. Clearly the introduction of a new vocabulary has a profound effect on perception.

But words do much more than orient perception; they also structure action, catching us in cycles of construction and interpretation that amplify habits of sense-making. Consider, for example, the ways classical geometry has been used to shape our living spaces. Modern cities are built around straight lines, countrysides are parsed into tidy rectangles. In turn, the predominance of these forms contributes to a tendency to interpret other aspects of existence in terms of classical geometry. Think about your educational experience—organized on a rectangular schedule, likely conducted in a rectangular room in a rectangular building on a rectangular block in a rectangulated city. Or look at the classical shapes used to organize this book.

So perception is *constrained* by culture. But at the same time, it is *enabled* by culture. (This notion of "constraints that enable"—enabling constraints—reappears in Part C of the book.) As already developed, consciousness is simply too small to accommodate the fullness of sensation. Language and other cultural tools might be understood as more than means to select some aspects and ignore others; they are also strategies to connect experiences and to compress information so that we can cope with more. As is developed in the next chapter, for example, a word like *normal* collects together an immense range of concrete experiences and abstract qualities, but allows consciousness to operate without being overwhelmed by these sorts of details. In this way, language and other cultural tools enable our capacities for thought and perception even while shutting out most perceptual possibilities.

BIOLOGY *versus* CULTURE?

Humans have species-specific sensory capacities, suggesting that perception is physiological. That is, perception is mainly a matter of **biology**.	Perceptions are learned. In particular, perceptions are largely conditioned by language. That is, the main determinant of perception is **culture**.

COMMON ROOTS: Both positions assume that biological constitution is separable from cultural influence—in brief, that biology determines *what* is perceptible, and culture determines *how* things are perceived.

When I begin to feel that participants have a fairly robust sense of what fractals are and how they might be identified, I quite abruptly return to the opening activity. Using exactly the same phrasing that I did at the start of the session, I ask them to look around and compile a list of as many shapes as they can see—using appropriate mathematical terminology, of course.

The responses this time are typically very different, and so far they have always been punctuated with expressions of surprise—and even astonishment.

For example, it's not unusual to overhear questions and comments like, "Has that tree always been there?" and "Look at the self-similarity in those clouds!"

2.5 Conception

Another surprising quality of human consciousness is that it is always running a little behind the action. It takes some time—about half a second—for nonconscious processes to sort through sensations and to render them meaningful by linking them to other experiences. And so, we are never really aware of what's happening right now. In other words, consciousness isn't a controller, it's more a commentator. It doesn't really initiate action as much as it justifies or contextualizes action that has already been initiated.*

This lag time, coupled with the realization that perceptions and interpretations are pretty much predetermined by biological predispositions and/or cultural discourses, would seem to present a challenge to beliefs about self-control and autonomy. But does the research into perception and consciousness really challenge "freedom of choice"?

The blunt answer is, "Yes." However, there are some important qualifications, and these revolve around rethinking the nature of consciousness—not as a fixed and unchanging form, but as a complex phenomenon that evolves. And education appears to play an important role here.

A preponderance of neurological and sociological evidence supports the conclusion that we are not free to select *directly* what enters consciousness any more than we are free to choose heart rates and body temperatures. However, just as these phenomena can be *indirectly* manipulated (by, for example, engaging in particular physical or imagined activities), consciousness can be indirectly affected. The key is to understand that the role of consciousness is not to *control* but to *orient*. Analogous to a teacher in a classroom or a television station in a community, consciousness plays a vital role in affecting what happens next by shining the spotlight on certain possibilities while ignoring others.

Once something is presented to awareness, we can act on it. That doesn't imply control, but it does present at least some form of choice. Clearly, subsequent events are not *determined by* what is in the spotlight of

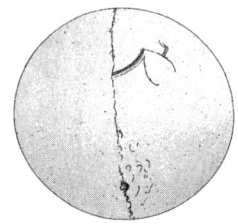

With the invention of the telescope in the early 1600s, two astronomers turned their gazes toward the moon. In England, Thomas Harriot saw a "strange spottednesse." (One of his sketches is above.) In Italy, Galileo saw something quite different. (One of his sketches is on the facing page.)

Why the differences in perception?

Galileo was a trained artist, educated to interpret the play of light and shadow. His education may have enabled him to see the strange spots in terms of mountains and craters illuminated by a distant sun.

There are many similar examples of this sort of insight in the history of western science, demonstrating that one's conceptions and one's perceptions are inextricable.

* For overviews of the extensive research base for this suggestion, see Norretranders, *The user illusion* and Daniel C. Dennett, *Consciousness explained* (New York: Little, Brown and Company, 1991).

consciousness, but those choices are usually *dependent on* what is highlighted. What we perceive matters.

As illustrated by the geometry activity in this chapter's discussion boxes, the teacher can play a pivotal role in orienting attentions in ways that prompt transformations in personal perception and consciousness. Participants in the activity became aware of properties and relationships among, for example, trees and clouds that they'd never noticed before, even though they'd looked at these forms thousands of times over many years.

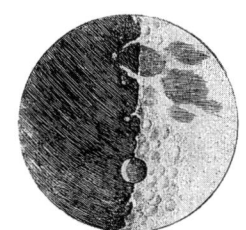

In other words, education might be recast, not so much as helping people to *know* what they don't know, but as *noticing* what they haven't noticed. Education, that is, might be conceived in terms of affecting perception—about pointing to certain aspects of the world in a deliberate attempt to foster different habits of interpretation. So framed, education is about an ongoing expansion of one's perceptual world. It is an unending process of interrogating perspectives, positionings, and points of view. It is all about how knowing looks.

As a teacher, I tend to organize each of my classes around a "big question," and the one that I used when thinking about this geometry lesson was, "What does mathematics do?"

This is quite a different question than "What is mathematics?" or, more broadly, "What is knowledge?" These issues have been the topics of intense philosophical debate over the past several centuries, and sorting through the associated assumptions and assertions is no easy task.

But the question of what mathematics *does* has a much more pragmatic flavor. Certainly a major part of what it does is shape our perceptions ... thereby affecting how we act, part of which is realized in the ways we structure our physical worlds ... which, in turn, further entrenches and amplifies habits of interpreta-tion. And so "what mathematics does" is more a question about *knowing* than a question about *knowledge*.

I try to bring this point home in the geometry session with a brief tour through different world views over the past few millennia, attempting to highlight how prevailing developments in mathematics came to be knitted into cultural forms such as the fine arts and academic argumentation. In particular, I try to direct attentions to a current evolution of sensibilities, in which fractal images and chaotic dynamics are displacing Euclidean forms and cause–effect logic, especially around such complex phenomena as learning and teaching. If we are to understand these phenomena differently, I argue, we must have access to new vocabularies, visual metaphors, and so on.

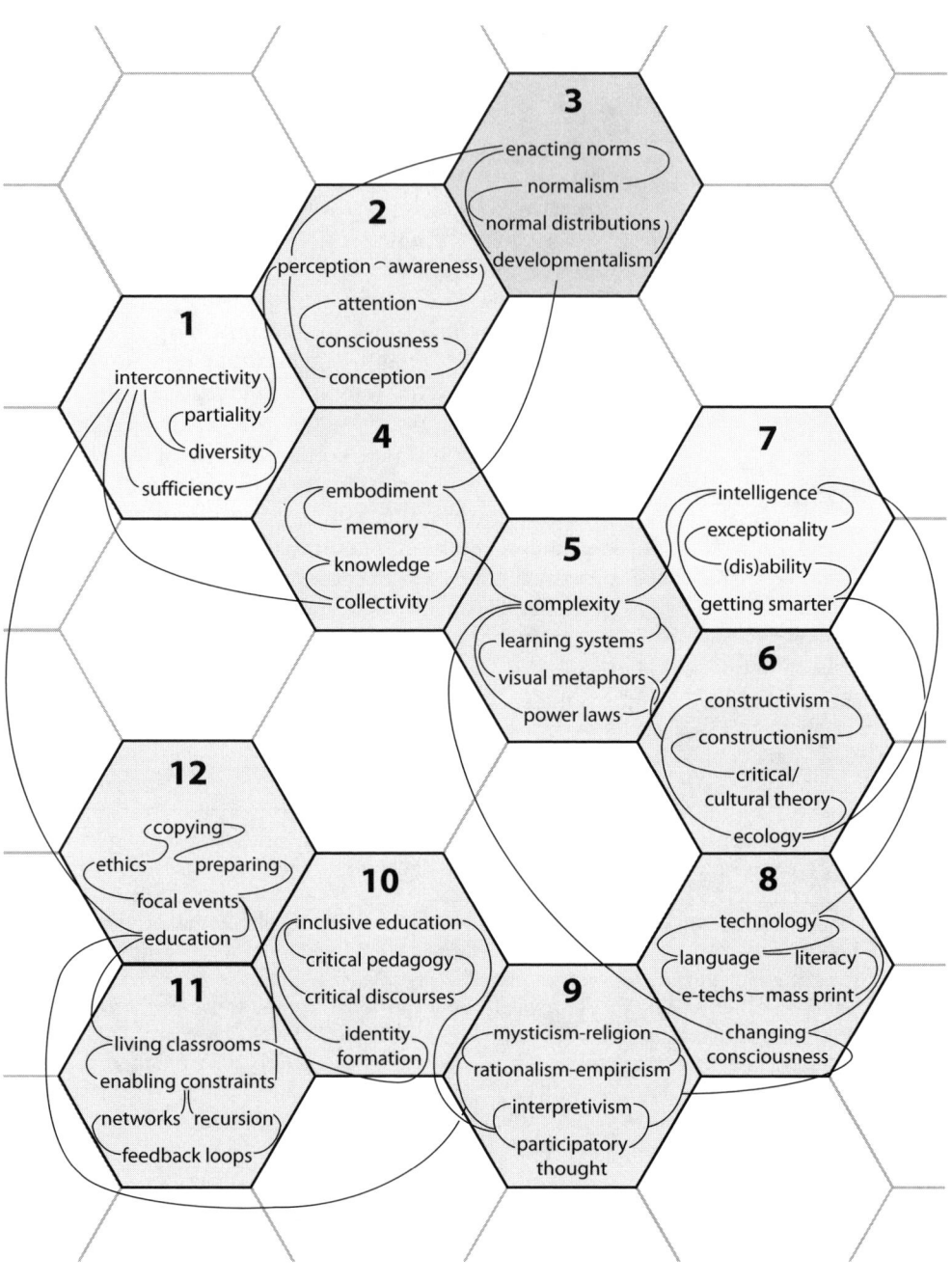

3   Knowing Acts

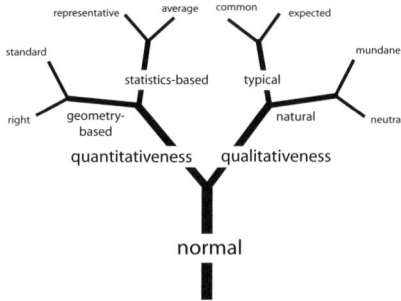

It's a bit surprising how often the word *normal* comes up in discussions of schooling: normal intelligence, normal development, normal behavior, normal routes ... we could go on and on. Of course, the meanings of the term vary across these phrases. Nonetheless, we believe that its pervasiveness points to something important. The interspersed narrative in this chapter is concerned with unpacking a little of what is assumed and asserted when some aspect of education is described as "normal."

The backdrop of these discussion boxes is a study of pre-service teachers' emerging identities and identifications. Reported in greater detail elsewhere,* that research was concerned with uncovering some of the normative structures of teacher education programs, as well as some of the counternormative strategies invented by pre-service teachers as they negotiated those structures.

As the study unfolded, it became clear that the construct of "normal" was even more pervasive than we'd first anticipated. In these dialogue boxes, we point to some of its usages in the context of one particular program, endeavoring to highlight how diverse and often incompatible meanings play profound roles in shaping the educational experiences of teachers and students alike.

But first, picking up on a strand of thought from the previous chapter, it's worth looking briefly at some of the associations that contribute to meanings of the word *normal*. To begin, the word is derived from the Latin *norma*, the "carpenter's square." It entered common usage in English several hundred years ago, in the context of building things. Being close to normal originally meant being close to a perfect right angle. By the early 1800s, it had been taken up by social scientists and used to frame studies of

---

* See The Counternormativity Discourse Group, "Performing an archive of feeling: Experiences of normalizing structures in teaching and teacher education," in *Journal of Curriculum and Pedagogy*, vol. 2, no. 2 (2006): 173–214.

how and to what extent certain behaviors and traits did or did not conform to common standards.

Normal is part of a whole family of terms rooted in Euclidean geometry that, as developed in the chapter 2 dialogue boxes, has permeated western worldviews. This web of associations is a strong one, and it reaches beyond references to physical shapes into conceptual realms—including rightness and wrongness, truth and falsehood, morality and immorality, efficiency and inefficiency. For instance, think about what you might get yourself into if you were to advocate for something other than what's *right, normal, direct,* or *straight*. Antonyms include *bent, deviant, twisted, kinky, queer, warped,* and *skewed*. (All of these words either literally mean or are derived from roots that mean "not straight" or "not flat.") Such terms don't seem to be pointing at good things.

Entry:	normal (adjective)
Definition:	right (literally, "straight"—a notion borrowed from Euclidean geometry)
Synonyms:	correct, direct, erect, even, explained, forthright, just, justified, level, linear, orthodox, perpendicular, plain, plane, rectified, regular, regulated, right, right angle, righteous, rule-following, square, standard, straight, straightforward, true, truthful, upright, upstanding
Antonyms:	bent, deviating, gauche, kinked, queer, sinister, skewed, twisted, warped

3.1 Enacting Norms

At one point in the not-too-distant past, many colleges of education were called "normal schools." This phrase dates from the early 1800s, and it was originally used to signal how teachers were expected to serve as models for others—that is, teachers were positioned as beacons of normality. And even though the phrase is rarely mentioned any more, the suggestion that teachers are to be exemplars or cultural representatives of collective ideals still lingers.

Is this suggestion appropriate? Should we continue to think of teachers as models or representatives? If so, whose ideals should they be modeling, and whose culture do they represent? After all, the role of public education has changed dramatically in the nearly 200 years since the first normal schools opened in North America when cultural groupings tended to be more homogeneous. In a context of rapidly changing demographics, increased social and cultural mobility, and enhanced communications, it would seem troublesome to assume that there is any sort of constant and unified culture to be represented, let alone to hope that an individual could possibly serve as a model.

This issue cuts to the core of what schooling might be all about. One way to frame the issue is to interrogate the ways that education has been conceived and

In mathematics a *normal* line is one that crosses another at a *right* angle.

organized around meanings of the word *normal*—which is one of the intentions of this chapter. A secondary, and complementary aim is to continue the examinations of knowing and knowledge.

To these ends, one of the tactics that was employed in the preparation of this chapter is known as *deconstruction*. This term refers to an approach to investigating habits of association, focusing in particular on the usually-not-noticed aspects of languages, images, ideas, and practices that orient, shape, and enable perception and conception. A goal of deconstruction is to sponsor new possibilities for thinking and acting.

That is, deconstruction isn't really about taking things apart; it's more about bringing forward what is excluded, concealed, implied, or otherwise unsaid or unsayable. It's elaborative, not reductive. In other words, it is concerned with the implicit associations—those invisible structures and connections that constitute most of what we know but that we are usually not aware we know.

For instance, think about the word *normal*. The interspersed narrative in this chapter is concerned with foregrounding some of the associations that render the concept meaningful as well as some of the consequences of these associations, especially for educational practice. One of the intentions of this effort is to highlight that most of human knowledge is not explicit. Rather, it is tacit, implicit, embodied, acted out, enacted. It is manifest in interactions, attitudes, structures, and obsessions.

By contrast, for most of its history, formal educational practice has been organized almost entirely around explicit knowledge—ideas and insights that are available for conscious study. An unfortunate consequence is that the vast webs of association that render those bits of knowledge sensible tend to be obscured if not completely inaccessible. Formal schooling is usually focused on the visible part of the iceberg of knowledge, often oblivious to the submerged mass that enables that tiny portion to poke above the surface.

In some ways, this situation cannot be avoided. As developed in chapter 2, human consciousness is too limited to deal with much. Most of the details have to

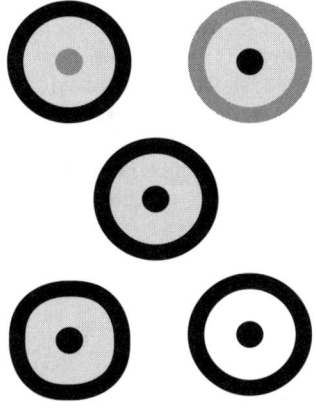

Which figure is the most different? (An answer is provided on the next page.)

be pushed into the conceptual shadows if new insights are to be brought to light—and it might thus be argued that cultural norms serve an important purpose by reducing demands on conscious thought. However, given some of the insidious consequences of certain implicit associations (like the sorts that have collected around the word *normal*), it seems reasonable to argue that formal education must also be attentive to the enacted dimensions of knowing.

To restate this point, using a phrase introduced in the previous chapter, an important aspect of education is rendering the familiar strange—reawakening attentions to entrenched habits of association and exploring alternatives. Ours is a species that is perceptually oriented toward difference. As *biological* beings, we are physiologically attuned to variations and changes, sometimes amplifying subtle differences into major distinctions. As *cultural* beings, we tend to elaborate certain discernments through symbolic technologies and shared interpretive systems. In brief, as *biological-and-cultural* beings, we participate in bringing forth worlds of significance.

(See the previous page for the context of this discussion.)

The middle figure is the most different. Each of the others differs from the "norm" in one way: The upper left has a gray dot; the upper right has a gray border; the lower left is squarish; the lower right has a white background. With no unique trait, the middle figure is the most different, even though it seems the most normal.

This item points to a logical flaw in the conventional notion of *normality*: in a species made up of highly differentiated beings, a truly normal specimen would be truly abnormal.

Within academic circles (including formal education), a major influence on popular interpretations of *normality* is statistics-based research.

This point was driven home for us when we were just beginning our study of pre-service teachers' self-images. As with any research project of this sort, a first step was to find participants. One of our strategies to solicit involvement was to display posters around the Education building to inform students of the study and its intentions. The first person to contact us, however, wasn't a prospective participant but a concerned colleague. A senior professor and respected researcher, he left a telephone message to alert us to "a flaw in the research design." As he explained, "You can't get a representative sample of the student population through a process of self-identification. If you want a valid result, you need to use a random sampling technique."

Representative here refers to a necessary element in the selection of research subjects. To be able to make claims about an entire population based on a study of just a few individuals, one must ensure random selection. However, our study was concerned with personal experiences, not global qualities—so although he meant well, our colleague's advice was inappropriate.

Entry:	normal (adjective)
Definition:	representative
Synonyms:	archetypal, characteristic, classic, classical, delineative, depictive, emblematic, evocative, exemplary, ideal, illustrative, model, presentational, protypal, prototypical, quintessential, standard, symbolic, typical
Antonyms:	atypical, deviant, extreme, outlying

3.2 Normalism

People are different from one another.

But how different?

Clearly, at least part of the response to this question has to do with habits of perception, which as noted in chapter 2 are biologically rooted and culturally elaborated. One relevant point that wasn't much developed in that chapter is that human perception is largely oriented to difference—to the book that's out of place, to the child who's so much taller, to the misspelled word, to the shoes that don't quite match, to the girl in the group of boys. Humans are difference-seeking distinction-makers.

In fact, our perceptual systems are not only predisposed to make distinctions, but to amplify them—and, on occasion, to impose some that just are not there in any objective sense. (The margin activity on this page is offered as simple experiment in this perceptual tendency.) The most common explanation for this predisposition is that it's really useful for survival. Boundaries are the most valuable information in the environment, and so we might expect sight, hearing, smell, taste, touch, and our other senses to be oriented toward fishing out details about edges and exaggerating them. Humans have extended this perceptual tendency into conceptual habit. We are constantly making conceptual distinctions—and often amplifying them. This habit isn't necessarily bad; it's vital, for example, for self-definition and collective identification. Knowing who or what you are is obviously tied to knowing who or what you are not.

However, distinction-making is sometimes carried too far. In point of fact, for instance, humans are virtually clones of one another. Yet, for the most part, when we meet someone for the first time, attentions are usually focused not on extensive and profound samenesses, but on few and superficial differences—on, for example, slight differences in height or accent or skin tone.

In a realm as complex as human perception, this tendency toward what Sigmund Freud called the "narcissism of minor difference" often contributes to some

The rectangles above are all uniformly shaded, but each looks lighter where it touches a darker block and darker where it touches a lighter one. (If you cover a border with a pen, you'll notice that neighboring blocks aren't as different as they seem.) This illusion demonstrates that perception doesn't make absolute judgments; it compares.

The diagrams on pages 56, 110, 111, and 154 employ the same illusion. Part of the point is that there are no cut-and-dried distinctions among the phenomena identified in those images.

profound problems. As noted in chapter 2, perception is not a simple process of gathering information. Rather, it is about making associations between immediate experiences and prior events—a process over which we have no direct control. And not all of the associations we make are appropriate or productive.

On the collective level, many of these nonconscious associations are embedded in language—as we endeavor to highlight with the example of the associations of *normal* in this chapter's dialogue boxes. On the individual level, a number of psychologists have been looking at the biases instilled by nonconscious association-making. One seemingly simple tool that has been created to examine implicit associations—appropriately called an Implicit Association Test (IAT)*—is revealing. An Implicit Association Test is intended to provide insight into nonconscious connections. A test consists of a list of items, and your task is to assign each entry to the category to which it belongs by marking the appropriate column. It's important to do it as quickly as possible and not to worry about errors.

If you haven't already tried the IAT items in the margins of this page and the next, now would be a good time. The following discussion will be much more meaningful if you've done them.

If you are like the majority of people in the western world, you should have noticed a difference between the first and second tests. The latter is harder for most, simply because the associations of maleness-and-business and femaleness-and-home are much stronger than the associations between maleness-and-home and femaleness-and-business. And while it's easy to offer critique, the phenomenon shouldn't be surprising. Males account for about 90% of the executives in major corporations, and females continue to be responsible for a disproportionate amount of domestic labor. So when the category is "Male or Home," there's often a conceptual hiccup when pressed to answer quickly. (To be clear, the point is *not* that the situation is somehow justifiable; rather, at issue is the presence of an embodied bias.)

Implicit Association Test designers have created a few tests that provide even more revealing insights

An Implicit Association Test

Assign each word to the appropriate category by checking one of the boxes. (*Do the one on this page first.*)

Male or Business		Female or Home
☐	Ralph	☐
☐	Anna	☐
☐	Curtains	☐
☐	Office	☐
☐	David	☐
☐	Stapler	☐
☐	Peter	☐
☐	Fax	☐
☐	Gloria	☐
☐	Debra	☐
☐	Kitchen	☐
☐	Accountant	☐
☐	Playpen	☐
☐	Lara	☐
☐	Bathroom	☐
☐	CEO	☐
☐	Parents	☐
☐	Darren	☐
☐	Sarah	☐
☐	Michael	☐

* See Anthony G. Greenwald, Debbie E. McGhee, & Jordan L.K. Schwartz, "Measuring individual differences in implicit cognition: The Implicit Association Test," in *Journal of Personality and Social Psychology*, vol. 74, no. 6 (1998): 1464–1480. Visit http://www.implicit.harvard.edu for several computerized examples.

Another Implicit Association Test

Assign each word to the appropriate category by checking one of the boxes. *(Do the one on the previous page first.)*

Male or Home		Female or Business
☐	Dinner	☐
☐	Donna	☐
☐	Kevin	☐
☐	Manager	☐
☐	Timeclock	☐
☐	Garth	☐
☐	Gord	☐
☐	Becky	☐
☐	Domestic	☐
☐	Salary	☐
☐	Personnel	☐
☐	Ellen	☐
☐	Linda	☐
☐	Vacuum	☐
☐	Copier	☐
☐	Neil	☐
☐	Sofa	☐
☐	Mary	☐
☐	Overtime	☐
☐	Tom	☐

into prevalent (but not necessarily conscious) associations. Some of these are available online (see the footnote on the previous page). These computerized examples have the advantage of timed feedback to provide more precise information on the strengths of personal associations around gender, race, class, and other categories. A warning, however: the results can be disconcerting.

It's not all bad news. IAT researchers have also found that if people are presented with strong examples prior to taking a test—of, for example, Oprah Winfrey and Martha Stewart before doing a gender/business test like the ones to the right—reaction times change. While humans have no direct control over the associations made, it is clear that indirect influences can profoundly affect what is assumed to be normal.

It seems reasonable to argue that formal education can play important roles in excavating and challenging some common implicit associations. In this sense, an important part of formal education is the interrogation of conceptions of normal, noting that refusing to engage in these sorts of critical examinations might be construed as a tacit agreement to participate in the perpetuation of enacted prejudices. Ignoring implicit associations is, arguably, the same as accepting them.

One of the prominent worries of the pre-service teachers in the study had to do with the selection of age- and grade-appropriate activities. Most of them were assigned to practicum settings with learners that were at least 10 years younger, and they simply weren't confident that they would be able to identify and develop tasks that were suited to their students.

As we tried to unpack this worry, we encountered a number of concepts that were drawn from theories of human development—including references to stages of emotional, social, moral, physical, and conceptual development.

At first the concern seemed overblown, and we tried to suggest that, in fact, such "stage theories" were based on averages, not absolutes. We pointed out that it was probably more important to attend to what students had been doing, their interests, and their contexts when selecting topics and tasks, and not to be overly concerned with some abstract notion of what they might or might not be able to do.

It was only sometime later that we noticed the way the conceptions of *normal* had been used in these discussions: "How can I keep track of all the *standards* for fourth grade students?" "What should a *normal* child be able to do?" "What do I do about the students who are below *average*?"

There are indications in these sorts of statements that a few statistics-based constructs had become something more than intended. Calculations of average measures were being treated as though they were *normative*. In other words, participants seemed to be interpreting *averages* as *norms*—that is, as absolute prescriptions rather than context-specific, constantly shifting indicators.

Entry:	normal (noun)
Definition:	average
Synonyms:	center point, mean, median, medium, middle, middle part, middle position, midpoint, norm, par, standard
Antonyms:	anomaly, maximum, minimum, variant

3.3 Normal Distributions

In the mid-1800s, there began a pronounced movement in some of the social sciences—in particular, sociological and psychological research—to ultilize quantitative research methods. The shift is often characterized as a blatant attempt by researchers in the humanities to place themselves on a par with the physical sciences, but that assessment may be a little harsh. It occurred at a time when the prevailing opinion was that measured phenomena enabled stronger research claims, and so the embrace of quantification likely had more to do with implicit associations than explicit desires.

A major component of this movement was the broad application of statistical methods, particularly those associated with the bell-shaped "normal distribution." To give a bit of background, normal distributions present two important pieces of information: the *mean* (i.e., the arithmetic average or an indication of where data points cluster) and the *standard deviation* (an indication of how data points spread out). The shape of the curve highlights how, for certain phenomena, most data points gather around a middle value, and so "average" events are much more likely than "extreme" ones. In brief, the likelihood of encountering an anomaly drops precipitously as one moves further from the mean. Many everyday phenomena—the sizes of potatoes, human heights, shoe sizes, gasoline prices—seem to obey normal distributions.

The original impetus for the development of the normal distribution, almost 200 years ago, was the study of errors in celestial measurements. When astronomers tried to plot their observations and calculations, they simply could not generate the smooth curves that were predicted by Newton's laws of motion. The reason was simple: All measurements incur errors.

Human communication relies on assumption, familiarity, pattern, expectation, and so on. The respondant, above, for example, assumed that the first person (1) is looking for his keys, (2) used them the evening before, (3) wants some help finding them, and (4) might have left them in a garment. None of this information was explicit.

Such events hint at how much of "what's said" isn't said at all. Meaning, that is, is mostly about implicit associations, not explicit articulations.

Mathematicians at the time assumed the errors in measurement to be random—some results were too high and some were too low; most were quite near actual values, but a smattering were way off. After considerable examination of different clusters of data, French researchers led by Pierre-Simon de Laplace and Siméon-Denis Poisson realized that errors are always distributed in the same way. There are consistently more small errors than large ones, and this variety follows a predicable pattern. When plotted on a graph, the sizes of errors produces a particular bulging shape that was dubbed the "error curve," then the "distribution of errors curve," then the "normal distribution of errors curve," and ultimately the "normal distribution." At about the same time, German mathematician Carl Friedrich Gauss was conducting an independent study of the curve and named it the "Gaussian distribution."

In fact, mathematicians were already familiar with this curve, as probability theorists who studied random events had previously noted that predictable results arise from a large enough pool of random events. For example, if you and 99 friends each flip a coin 100 times, the combined results will always generate something that looks like the normal distribution (and with even more results, you'll get a more precise fit to the mathematical curve).

The normal distribution began to move from the natural sciences into the social sciences in the early 1800s as researchers started to examine social statistics (e.g., birth and death rates) and, later, human dimensions (e.g., height and girth). This work was anchored in the assumption, borrowed from the physical sciences, that variation is linked to error. That is, for instance, rather than interpreting differences in height in terms of a natural diversity, they were seen as departures from an ideal standard.

By the mid-1800s, social science researchers began to apply the normal distribution of errors curve to personality characteristics and behaviors in addition to physical measurements. This movement was based on the assumption that "average behavior" was "normal behavior." The resulting social physics gave rise to the

A "normal curve" (or "bell curve") illustrates how many naturally occurring phenomena vary. The shape of the curve highlights how data points (i.e., measurements) can cluster around an average (the mean, μ). As one moves away from the mean, the probability of particular measurements decreases sharply (e.g., really small potatoes and really immense potatoes are much less likely than average-sized potatoes).

With this curve, "normality" is defined in terms of nearness to the mean. Typically, those points within one standard deviation of μ (the dark grey region in the figure) are considered the most normal.

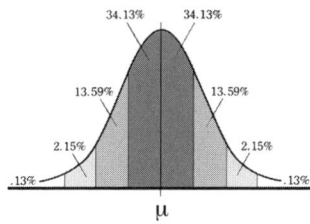

concept of the "normal man" whose physical dimensions (height, weight, foot size, etc.), moral attributes, aesthetic sensibilities, intellectual capacities, and so on represented a level of perfection to which all should aspire. (It bears emphasizing here that the bulk of the research into normality was conducted on males. Typically women were either ignored or, more often, regarded as smaller or lesser versions of men.)*

Sensibilities have changed somewhat since the 1880s. Usually, average is not seen as ideal in quite the same way. In particular, some deviations from the mean (e.g., taller, higher IQ, smaller waist size) are seen as desirable and superior. At the same time, however, deviations in the other direction are sometimes seen as undesirable or as indications of flaws or weaknesses.

With the broad application of the normal distribution in the social sciences, it should come as no surprise that educators also embraced the construct. At the moment, assumptions anchored in the mathematics of the normal distribution underpin such emphases as common curricula, homogeneous classrooms, uniform teaching methods, age-appropriate routines, and standardized achievement testing. All of these rest on the assumption of a "normal child," and all of them contribute to the entrenchment of that assumption within educational structures.

Although a fiction—there are no statistically normal children—the notion of the normal child has become a pervasive and largely transparent part of educational discourse. Somewhat ironically, one does not often encounter direct assertions about normality. Rather, statistics-based conceptions about normal are most obvious in a proliferation of labels that point to the extremes of the normal distribution—ones that assume a center without actually mentioning it. These labels include *abnormal, challenged, delayed, disabled, disordered, dysfunctional, handicapped, hyperactive, maladaptive,* and *retarded* (and, on the more culturally positive side of the curve, *advanced, gifted,* and *talented*). Each of these assumes and asserts a standard, predetermined, and measurable norm. (We return to the topic in chap. 7.)

More recently, and partly in response to negative connotations of many of these labels, more neutral-

"Grading on a curve" was first suggested in 1908 by Max Meyer.** It caught on quickly and continues to be popular, even though evidence clearly indicates that norm-based grading increases competition and reduces cooperation. Under norm-referenced pressures, students tend to see one another more as hindrances than as helpers, and discourse tends to be more about individual rights than social responsibility.***

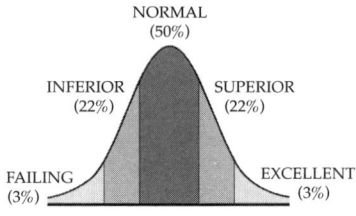

* See Michel Foucault, *Abnormal: Lectures at the Collège de France, 1974–1975* (eds. Valerio Marchetti & Antonella Salomoni; trans. Graham Burchell; New York: Picador, 2004).
** Max Meyer, "The grading of students," in *Science,* vol. 28 (1908): 243–250.
*** See Barbara Rogoff, *The cultural nature of human development* (New York: Oxford University Press, 2003)

sounding phrases like *differently-abled*, *exceptional*, and *special* have been taken up. This shift has been accompanied by imperatives to accommodate students with diverse needs in regular classrooms. (The two most prominent of such efforts are known as *mainstreaming* and *inclusive education*—see chap. 10.) Unfortunately, challenges to assumptions about normal ability, normal development, and normal behavior have been rare-to-nonexistent. Difference and diversity have been overwhelmingly cast as qualities to be "tolerated," "managed," and "ameliorated," rather than appreciated, embraced, and fostered.

This tension has prompted a seemingly irresolvable debate over whether educational efforts should be focused on the center of the normal distribution or on the extremes. On the one hand, a focus on normal children is seen as more efficient and economical, but it sets up risks of boredom and alienation for those students who aren't situated under the hump of the bell curve. On the other hand, a focus on exceptionalities is seen as more humane, but resource-intensive.

These positions appear to be diametrically opposed. But, in fact, they don't span the full range of possibility—in large part because they're both rooted in assumptions of normal distributions and normal developmental trajectories. Throughout this book, we are attempting to foreground, interrupt, and offer alternatives to such assumptions.

INDIVIDUALIZED *versus* NORMED?

Each human is unique. Formal education should foster individual gifts and talents. Instruction should thus be **individualized**.	How, what, and when we teach is informed by studies of the development of typical children. Instruction should thus be **norm-referenced**.

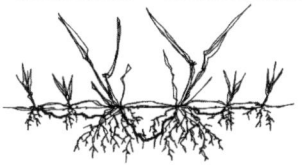

COMMON ROOTS: Proponents of both sides of this debate tend to assume that individuals are fully autonomous and, hence, that one must choose between serving the interests of the individual and serving the needs of society.

Given research and educational cultures that cast normal as *representative*, a mathematized sensibility that equates normal with *average*, and a societal habit of associating normality with *rightness*, we weren't surprised that pre-service teachers seemed to be preoccupied with fitting in—that is, with being seen as normal by both their future colleagues and students.

It was probably to be expected, then, that most of the volunteers for our study were people whose appearances and identifications placed them at odds with the mainstream. The group included members of religious minorities, gays and lesbians, and persons with "body issues." Worries around these sorts of identifications came to a head right before they began student teaching. A phenomenon emerged that group members came to call the "pre-practicum make-over." Wardrobes were adjusted, tattoos were covered, earrings were removed, hair was cut. As one person explained, "I loved my long hair ... but I got it cut for the practicum—to be *fashionable*." That is, to fit in, to be perceived as normal.

It's not hard to underscore the normalizing powers of a desire to be fashionable. Just try to wear garments several years out of date, pants that are too short, patterns that are mismatched, or items that are perceived as gender-inappropriate. The pressures to be normal through being fashionable are quickly apparent.

Entry:	normal (adjective)
Definition:	typical
Synonyms:	accepted, accustomed, acknowledged, agreed, allowed, approved, authorized, button-down, card-carrying, chosen, common, commonplace, conventional, correct, current, customary, decorous, endorsed, established, everyday, expected, fashionable, formal, general, habitual, in, in vogue, inoffensive, kosher, legit, ordinary, orthodox, plain, popular, predominant, preferred, prevailing, prevalent, proper, recognized, regular, ritual, routine, sanctioned, square, standard, stereotyped, straight, suitable, traditional, typical, unremarkable, usual, well-known
Antonyms:	abnormal, exotic, foreign, irregular, out of sync, passé, questionable, radical, strange, uncommon, unconventional, uncustomary

3.4 Developmentalism

The word *developmentalism* is used to refer to any theory or model that presents a sequence of stages through which a person is expected to progress on the route from birth to death. A number of developmental hierarchies have been proposed over the last century, and some of the most prominent ones are represented in the margins of the next several pages.

Developmentalist theories are generally founded on extensive observations, and the better ones take into account issues of physical traits and cultural contexts. However, although many authors of these theories have gone to great lengths to underscore that stages are fluid, contextual, and complex, there has been an overwhelming tendency to interpret development in terms of linear progressions from incompleteness (i.e., childhood) to wholeness (i.e., adulthood). In fact, educators, educational researchers, and policy-makers have been among the worst interpreters of these theories, possibly because simple images of ladders and staircases fit with the linearized structures that are already in place in schools.

Perhaps the most significant problem here is that the two main categories of developmental theories—namely those focused on *physical* development and those concerned with *conceptual* development—tend to be conflated. For the most part, physical development is remarkably stable across humans (assuming that basic nutritional and psychological needs are met), owing in large part to the fact that the genetic variation

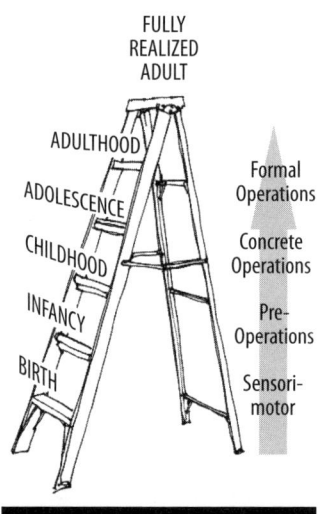

A Linearized Interpretation of Jean Piaget's Stages of Intellectual Development

among us is very small. For that reason, it is possible to make some broad statements about development. For example, the neuronal density of toddlers tends to be two to three times higher than that of adults.* That density declines steadily through childhood, but increases again in early adolescence, and then begins to decline again.**

An awareness of this sort of information is vital for educators. For example, such details help to account for young children's abilities to learn language so quickly (a capacity that most people lose by adolescence), for changes in behavior during teenage years, and for diminished ability to remember among most adults. In brief, the different tendencies and abilities that are manifest at different ages are largely genetic in origin—learned at the species level rather than the cultural or individual levels.

But this is where the problems with developmental theories arise. First, as reliable as theories of physical development are, there are always exceptions. Second, as one grows, personal experience and culture become ever more important to physical development. Factors such as nutrition, opportunity, education, deprivation, and even environmental contaminants can play critical roles in one's physical unfolding.*** Third, given the relative stability of physical development across most humans, there is a tendency to assume that conceptual development unfolds in a similarly predictable way.

For that reason, images of simple vertical structures are predominant in the educational literature, supporting such problematical principles as:

- developmental progressions of conceptual abilities are similar for everyone—regardless of personal experiences and cultural contexts;
- there are definite and discernible endpoints to these progressions;
- stages of development are discrete and non-overlapping;
- the stages are sequenced, so as one enters a new stage, one transcends the previous stage.

Research has demonstrated clearly and consistently that these and other assumptions are inappropriate.

ADJUSTED ADULT

EGO-INTEGRITY
GENERATIVITY
INTIMACY
IDENTITY
INDUSTRY
INITIATIVE
AUTONOMY
TRUST

A Linearized Interpretation of Erik Erikson's Stages of Psychosocial Development

* See Gopnik et al., *The scientist in the crib.*
** See Leslie Sabbagh, "The teen brain, hard at work," in *Scientific American Mind*, vol. 17, no. 4 (August/September 2006): 20–25.
*** See Rogoff, *The cultural nature of human development.*

But they are persistent, and they seem to be hinged to difficulties with the word *normal*. When used in the context of these theories, "normal development" refers to calculated averages for specific subpopulations—that is, *not* to the way things are supposed to be, merely to the way things were for the groups studied. Indeed, as studies have been extended to include more females or representatives from diverse cultures and social classes or more engaging tasks, the results are sometimes dramatically different. This shouldn't be surprising, given that significantly different interpretive strategies are sometimes employed across different social groups and cultures. (See chap. 9 for a brief introduction to some of these interpretative frames.)

To re-emphasize, *normal* in discussions of development does not mean "universal" or even "in general." Here *normal* means "on average, for the subjects examined." There's a big difference. Many of the original studies for the most prominent models (like the ones presented in the margins here) were based on specific subgroups (e.g., male undergraduate students, or children of well educated, upper class professionals).

Another significant difficulty has to do with the assumption of linearity (recall the connection made in this chapter's first dialogue box). As evidence has accumulated,* it has become clear that one does not progress sequentially through developmental levels. A staircase or ladder image is inappropriate. Rather, a particular stage is better thought of as an *elaboration* of preceding stages—all of which are still available to the individual. For instance, with reference to Piaget's frequently cited theory of intellectual development, it is commonly thought that most adults in a modern and western society think at the "formal operations" level. That means that they are able to use fairly sophisticated abstract reasoning skills to make sense of situations. However, it turns out that most adults find it easier to learn a new mathematical concept *concretely* and *sensorially* through physical manipulation of concrete materials than *formally* from an abstract explanation. In other words, it's not that western adults *do* operate at a formal level; it's that they *can* operate at a formal level. They have a broader spectrum of strategies

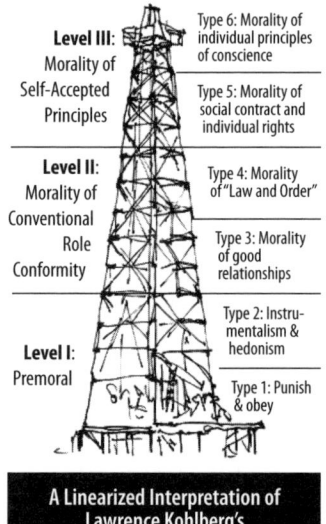

Level III: Morality of Self-Accepted Principles

Type 6: Morality of individual principles of conscience

Type 5: Morality of social contract and individual rights

Level II: Morality of Conventional Role Conformity

Type 4: Morality of "Law and Order"

Type 3: Morality of good relationships

Type 2: Instrumentalism & hedonism

Level I: Premoral

Type 1: Punish & obey

A Linearized Interpretation of Lawrence Kohlberg's Levels and Types of Morality

* See J.E. Stone, "Developmentalism: An obscure but pervasive restriction on educational improvement," in *Education Policy Analysis Archives*, vol. 4, no. 8 (April, 1996). Available through http://epaa. asu.edu/epaa/.

and responses to use as they move through diverse experiences. There are no linearities or hierarchies when it comes to thought and development, merely increasingly varied ways of responding to different situations.

This point is supported by neurological evidence that demonstrates that brains simply don't change much as people seem to shift to more sophisticated modes of thinking, question-posing, moral action, and so on.* Instead of a massive and sudden rewiring, it seems that observed stages are "emergent" phenomena—that is, events that arise gradually in the interactions of a great many other events. For example, in the first few years of life, the child is occupied with learning what to attend to. As useful discernments are learned, attentions become more focused on organizing and making associations among perceptions—and this shift is usually marked by a sharp increase in language use and an equally pronounced reduction in abilities to make fine-grained discernments among sounds. (These changes are associated with, although not caused by, changes to neural density at different ages, as noted above.) So conceived, different stages likely arise from needs to cope with too much information—from knowing too much—not from sudden triggerings of innate mechanisms at pre-programmed moments. It's likely more about emergent need than natural unfolding. A vital point here is that "development" is not about progressing to a prespecified (adult) endpoint. Rather, it is about flexible and appropriate adaptation to the immediate situation. That is, *conceptual development isn't about the future. It's about the present,* as conditioned by past experience and biological predisposition.

Recent thinking thus suggests somewhat different images might be more appropriate to describe development, ones that involve recursive cycles and feedback loops. One simple possibility is a cyclist moving over a varied terrain. Depending on the demands of the moment, the cyclist will shift gears—in effect, selecting the most contextually appropriate manner of dealing with a particular landscape. Similarly, we readily "shift" from one mode of thinking/acting to another in response to new or difficult situations. A cyclist with

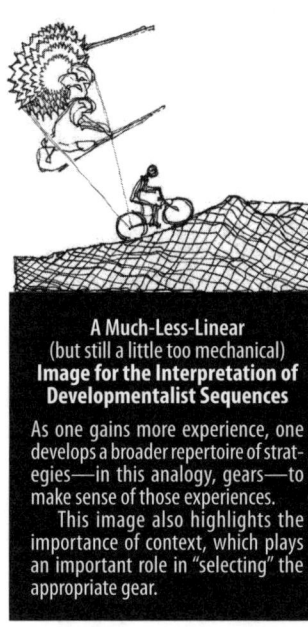

A Much-Less-Linear
(but still a little too mechanical)
Image for the Interpretation of Developmentalist Sequences

As one gains more experience, one develops a broader repertoire of strategies—in this analogy, gears—to make sense of those experiences.

This image also highlights the importance of context, which plays an important role in "selecting" the appropriate gear.

* See, e.g., Mark H. Johnson, *Developmental cognitive neuroscience: An introduction* (London: Blackwell, 1997).

only one gear would be at a distinct disadvantage. But a cyclist who can switch between lower gears (simpler strategies) and higher gears (more sophisticated, farther reaching strategies) would be able to deal with much more varied circumstances.

This image is supported by findings in neurology. The brain prefers to operate at the most familiar, habitual, and efficient (i.e., nonconscious and automatic) level that it can.* This preference for efficiency would explain why it sometimes appears that we progress through distinct levels or stages: as more encompassing and efficient strategies arise, the brain gives them priority over previous strategies until, of course, situations are encountered that are so unfamiliar that earlier strategies (i.e., "lower gears") are called for. The suggestion here is that as one's experiences are broadened, in effect, one develops "new gears"—that is, strategies that are more encompassing and flexible. This manner of recursive elaboration, reminiscent of the growth of a fractal image (see chap. 2), seems to be a much more powerful way to interpret development.

To recap, development should not be thought of as a linear, predetermined progress through clearly defined stages. It might be better considered as a process of recursive elaboration, moving to ever more sophisticated ways of interpreting experience. So understood, the most critical aspect of the teacher's role is not provision of information, but participation with learners in the development of strategies to interpret that information. In other words, the calculated norms that are presented in developmentalist theories should be regarded as rough sketches of emergent possibility. Norms based on arithmetic averages are certainly indicators, but they are not absolutes or universals.

This suggestion represents a dramatic departure from the most common way that developmentalist theories are deployed in educational institutions. As hinted by such phrases as "developmental readiness," "age-appropriate routines," and "norm referencing," these theories have often been deployed to justify practices of teaching the same thing at the same time in the same way to a group of people who might have little more in common than their year of birth.

It might be tempting to think that the meanings of words like *normal* and *right* are simply too diverse and diffuse to make any strong claims about their impacts on habits of knowing.

But that is precisely the point. When a notion comes to be so pervasive and so engrained that it seems utterly nonsensical to think otherwise, it might be time to try to think differently. Words are never neutral or innocent. Just think about some of the entailments of a seemingly benign imperative like "LOOK RIGHT" or "BE NORMAL" when invoked by traffic guards, politicians, fashion merchants, religious leaders, statisticians, …

… or teachers.

* See Pinker, *How the mind works*.

So what does this say about formal curriculum, teaching practices, and schooling structures? Should conceptions of *normal, norms, normal distributions, normalism*, and so on be abandoned?

Once again, even if it were possible to leave such notions behind, it wouldn't be a good thing. In order to respond appropriately in a complex world, humans must continuously draw on embodied *prejudices* (a word that means, literally, pre-judgments). These biases, in effect, constitute *most* of what we know.

However, such knowledge should not be understood in terms of collections of facts that exist either out in the world or inside our heads. Rather, such knowledge is about established (but mutable) patterns of action. As the intertwining examples of normalism and developmentalism demonstrate, what is taken for granted is more powerful than what is made explicit.

In more pithy terms, what we know is inseparable from what we do. Knowing acts.

Perhaps the most pervasive examples of imperceptible normative structures in the schools where our research participants completed their practicum experiences are the images, icons, and practices of Christianity, which exist in even the most explicitly secular settings.

One Muslim participant in the research was particularly attuned to an array of cultural norms that were simply unavailable to us as researchers. In fact, we found ourselves dismissing her concerns as "the way things are." In particular, she was distressed at the posters and activities that surrounded observations of November 11 (Remembrance or Veteran's Day) at the school where she was doing her practicum. During that time, she encountered practices and artifacts that we simply did not notice, including the suddenly ubiquitous form of the cross. When she first brought the issue to our attentions, we realized not only that we had been oblivious to these normative forms, but that even when made aware, we were tempted to treat them as innocuous. Indeed, we later wondered privately if this person might be "a little overly sensitive."

Such is, of course, one of the most insidious aspects of normative practices. They conceal themselves as not just the "way things are," but "the way things should be." After all, what is so offensive about being asked to color a picture of a cross in art class? What could be so troublesome about two *normal* line segments—that is, mathematically speaking, two lines that form a right angle?

Entry:	normal (adjective)
Definition:	natural
Synonyms:	automatic, blind, everyday, flavorless, immersed, imperceptible, invisible, lost, mundane, mute, neutral, oblivious, reasonable, scentless, silent, taken-for-granted, thoughtless, transparent, unconscious, unheard, unmindful, unnoticed, unseeing, unseen, unthinking, voiceless, "way things are," wordless
Antonyms:	counternormative, deconstructed, mindful, thoughtful

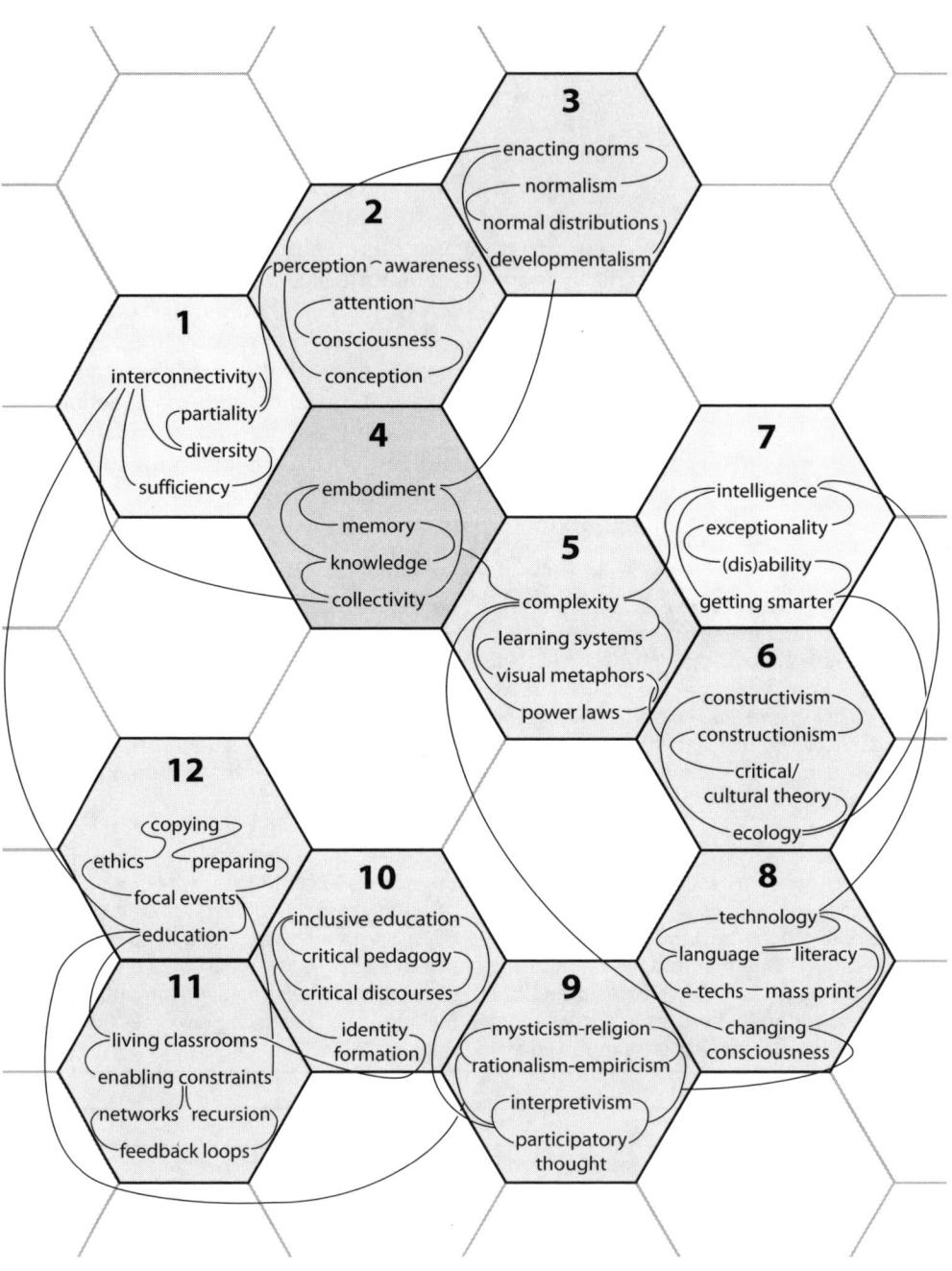

4   Knowing Structures

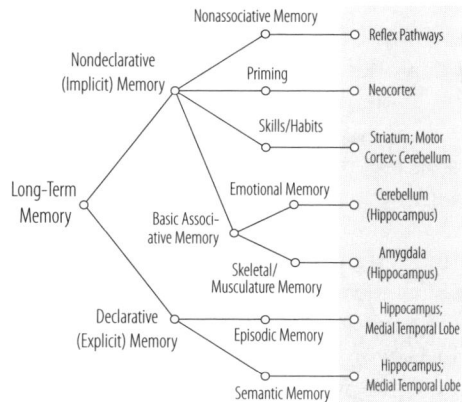

By any account, it was a strange circumstance for a school.

The building itself had been at the physical center of the community for nearly 20 years, and many of the parents of current students had attended through their elementary grades.

But, this year, the school wasn't at all the same. Only one member of the previous year's teaching staff had returned. Owing to a long-standing series of complaints and tensions that had been reported in prior years, the school board had decided that the most expeditious thing to do would be to start the year with a clean slate. All of the "new" teachers were experienced and accomplished, appointed by a principal who had been given free reign to select and invite strong people.

Yet it was clear that there were issues. Even in November, nearly three months into the term, the staff still hadn't gelled. Other than scheduled meetings, teachers spent little time interacting with one another. Even more obvious was the tremendous social gulf between school personnel and community members. Teachers worried aloud that parents were suspicious—and the worry seemed to be justified. Parents weren't volunteering to help out; they rarely accompanied their children into the building; they seldom communicated with teachers.*

Among the many issues presented in this situation are the manners in which individuals pull together into collectives. In this chapter we investigate this topic, focusing in particular on the nature and emergence of "knowing bodies."

---

* For a more detailed account of this event and the surrounding research study, see Brent Davis & Dennis Sumara, "Cognition, complexity, and teacher education," in *Harvard Educational Review*, vol. 67, no. 1 (1997): 105–125.

4.1 Embodiment

One of the interesting features of discussions of knowing and knowledge is the prevalence of notions of bodies: a body of knowledge, a social corpus, the body politic, embodied knowing, and so on.

For the most part, these bodies are treated as vibrant and evolving forms, ones with stable patterns and coherent identities, but with somewhat porous boundaries and the capacities to adapt. Further, many of these bodies seem to be nested in one another. Culture, for example, comprises different social groupings, which in turn comprise individuals.

In fact, this manner of description can be extended in both the micro- and macro- directions, as illustrated in the (very partial) figure below. Each layer or body can be simultaneously seen as a whole, a part of a whole, or a complex compilation of wholes. In other words, there's a sort of scale independence. Indeed, there's a sort of self-similarity. Each layer/body can be described in terms of the co-activities of relatively autonomous agents, and this co-activity is what gives rise to the next level of organization. Of course, these nested bodies don't much resemble one another in

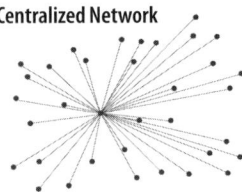

Centralized Network

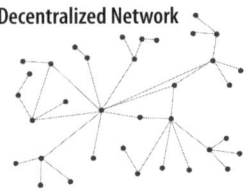

Decentralized Network

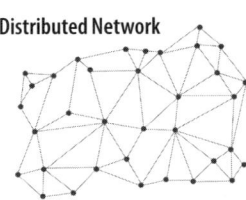

Distributed Network

Three types of network structures, drawn on identical sets of dots (nodes), are shown above.

The *centralized network* (top) allows for rapid communication, but is only as robust as the center hub. The *distributed network* (bottom) is tremendously robust, but communications can be hampered. The *decentralized network* (middle) combines reasonably efficient communication with relative robustness.* It is the "fingerprint" (i.e., the implicit structure) of complex unities, such as each phenomenon/layer identified in the nested diagram to the left.

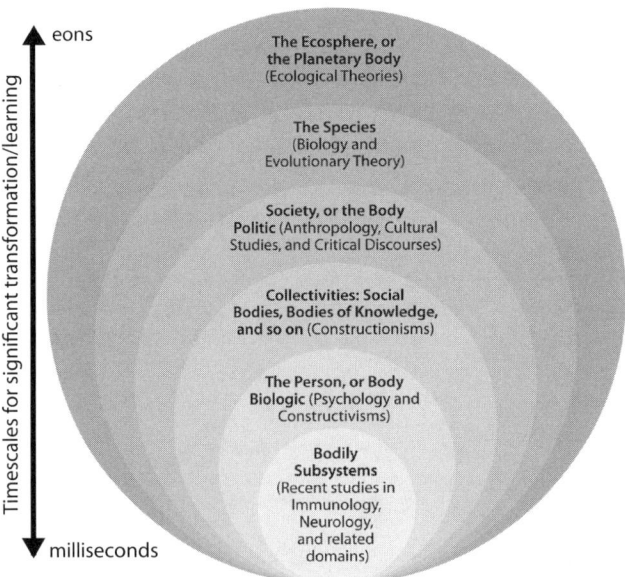

* For introductions to network theory, see Albert-László Barabási, *Linked: How everything is connected to everything else and what it means for business, science, and everyday life* (New York: Plume, 2002) and Duncan Watts, *Six degrees: The science of the connected age* (New York: W.W. Norton, 2003).

knowledge-as-object

acquire insight
grasp a concept
hold an opinion
exchange ideas
toss out thoughts

knowledge-as-food

digest an idea
ruminate
raw data
food for thought
appetite for learning

knowledge-as-edifice

the basics
build on ideas
solid foundations
construct knowledge
structure an argument

knowledge-as-liquid

flow of ideas
drowning in details
immersed in thought
thirsting for knowledge
soaking up information

The question, "What is knowledge?" isn't an easy one to answer. Yet, without having to give it any thought, we all use phrases like the ones above. In each case, a conception of knowledge as some sort of physical object is suggested—even though, on reflection, most would admit there are problems with these sorts of metaphors.

Nevertheless, much of classroom practice is developed around the assumptions that knowledge is some *thing* and, hence, teaching is a matter of delivering, relaying, or transmitting. Alternative interpretations are explored in this chapter.*

* For discussions of the metaphoric roots of abstract thought, we recommend two books by George Lakoff & Mark Johnson: *Metaphors we live by* (Chicago: University of Chicago Press, 1980) and *Philosophy in the flesh: The embodied mind and its challenge to western thought* (New York: Basic Books, 1999).

terms of their superficial physical appearances. But they do have some profound similarities, both structurally and dynamically.

Structurally, all of the systems mentioned in the nested circles illustration are examples of *decentralized networks*. A decentralized network is one of three main types of network (see the margin illustrations on the facing page for brief descriptions of the others). It consists of clusters that combine into grander clusters, and this sort of structure is manifest in all living systems and in ecosystems. In fact, it appears that decentralized networks are not just useful for describing the relations within physical systems. They can also be used to make sense of the structures of associations in systems of ideas—for example, to describe the structures of association among concepts, metaphors, and other connections that constitute a collective body of knowledge or to describe an individual's mind. Memory, language, culture—these and other enacted bodies of knowing appear to be instances of decentralized networks. In other words, structurally speaking, knowing bodies are fractal, not Euclidean.

In terms of system dynamics, the ongoing developments of each of these knowing bodies can be described in terms of evolutionary processes. At every level, knowing is seen as a complex process of co-evolution—that is, of agents (whether species, societies, social groups, persons, cells, or ideas) adapting to and affecting one another and their dynamic circumstances. Put differently, an implication of this conception of knowing bodies is that phenomena such as personal cognition, collective knowledge, and social interaction are tightly interrelated.

Unfortunately, such descriptions can be difficult to appreciate, especially by English-speakers. The prevailing metaphors for knowledge in English are related to physical artifacts, not the evolving relations among interacting agents. Knowledge is popularly characterized as an *object*, as *food*, as parts of *buildings*, and as a *liquid* (see the sidebar to the left).

Educationally speaking, this web of associations is not very useful. Clearly, no physical substances enter learners as they learn, so learning obviously can't be about *taking things in*. By consequence, teaching can't possibly be about *delivering, relaying, transmitting,* or *getting things across*. Rather, as suggested by what is known about the networked structures and evolutionary dynamics of knowing bodies, events of learning are about constant co-adaptations of interacting parts—an ongoing structural dance.

Recognizing that the teaching staff wasn't really coming together as a community, the school's principal undertook to define a shared project. Her reasoning was simple: despite their deep professional similarities, members of the group had no shared history, no collective memory. She was thus happy to take up our suggestion to organize a reading group around a piece of young adult fiction, Lois Lowry's novel, *The Giver*.* Entirely by coincidence, a core thematic in Lowry's book is collective memory—more precisely, what happens to a society when its citizens lose access to its history.

The story was discussed over the course of three meetings. In the first two, discussions were focused on the unfolding story. Quite provocatively, Lowry leaves many narrative threads dangling in the story, and so considerable attention was given to presentation of personal interpretations and questions.

But this changed dramatically in the third session when, midway through the meeting, someone suggested that the school staff had much in common with the society in *The Giver*. Both seemed to be suffering from a certain dysfunction, born of lack of shared memory. The ensuing discussion, while ostensibly about the book, was actually more about the importance of commonalities—how group identities, intentions, and plans must be anchored in some way to shared pasts.

Significantly, with the shared reading of *The Giver*, an important and powerful site for collective identifications was established.

4.2 Memory

The topic of individual understanding has been at the center of discussions of education for millennia. And quite understandably so.

An interesting twist was added to discussions in the late 1980s, when the modifier "taken-as-shared" started to be used to describe subjective meanings, interpretations, and understandings.** The suggestion was that all personal sense-making is rooted in unique sets of individual experiences—and so, while one person's understanding of, for example, addition, might be *compatible* with another's, it can never be *identical*. Differences are seen as inevitable, but we can still work together, because most of the time we naïvely assume that everyone else thinks the same way we do. Generally speaking, then, we ignore idiosyncratic differences and proceed on the delusion that subjective interpretations are the same—we *take them as shared*.

* Lois Lowry, *The giver* (New York: Bantam Doubleday, 1993). The book is the first of a trilogy that includes *Gathering blue* and *Messenger*.
** See, e.g., Paul Cobb, "Multiple perspectives," in *Transforming children's mathematics education: International perspectives* (eds. Les P. Steffe & T. Wood; Barcombe, UK: Falmer Press, 1990): 200–215.

At first glance, this reasoning seems compelling. And neurological, psychological, sociological, and anthropological studies have all supported the idea, so long as two assumptions are made. The first is that all knowing happens inside the the individual. The second has to do with the use of *shared*.

In the phrase "taken-as-shared," the word *shared* is intended to mean "identical"—which is actually quite a departure from broadly accepted usages. By contrast, dictionary definitions focus on dividing, apportioning, distributing, and jointly contributing. These meanings are reflected in common applications, including sharing rides, meals, expenses, stock market assets, and responsibilities. Given that understandings are contextually bound—that is, influenced by common experiences and coming to form in a collective language, one might argue that all meanings are quite literally shared.

To really make sense of this suggestion requires that we think across different levels of complex organization—one might refer to such transphenomenal thinking as a sort of *level-jumping*. On the level of brain-based activity, the claim of sharing seems problematical. How can something that seems hermetically sealed be shared? However, if one jumps to the level of social activity, it becomes much easier to argue that we all play a part in the creation of our shared realities. Shared worlds do not entail identical internal dynamics.

This line of thought is actually pointing to a much bigger issue, one that is at the heart of discussions of education. Overwhelmingly, *individuals have been seen as the fundamental particles of knowing*. Most classroom organizations, curriculum structures, examination regimes, and teaching practices—even the ones that claim to be oriented toward collectivity—frame their goals in terms of the development of individual competence. Ultimately, understanding and insight are not often treated as phenomena that can be shared; they're usually seen as brain-bound and necessarily idiosyncratic.

It might be easier to make sense of the complexity of the issues about knowers and knowing by looking at a more focused aspect of understanding—namely memory—which is by no means a simpler phenomenon, but at least it's better researched. To help orient

The second word of this chapter's title, *structure*, can be defined in some very different ways, depending on the context in which it is invoked.

For instance, in discussions of building things, it calls to mind notions of foundations, platforms, rigid frameworks, hierarchies, planning, and so on.

In contrast, when used by biologists in such phrases as "the structure of an ecosystem," it refers to an ever-evolving relational web that is both reasonably stable and subject to sudden change.

The latter is closer to its original meaning. Linked to *strew* and *construe*, *structure* is used to describe how certain forms (e.g., living and knowing ones) arise in ways that can't be predetermined, but that aren't entirely random.

your reading, the following map links some of the
principal types of memory that are mentioned in the
paragraphs that follow. This mapping presents only
a small subset of the types of memory that might be
discussed. They have been selected for their immediate relevance to discussions of education. (In fact, like
a fractal image, any one of the nodes in the conceptual network will "explode" into much more detail
if examined more closely. For example, the *long-term
memory* node is illustrated in more detail in the graphic
on the title page for this chapter—where some of its
subcomponents are also linked to the brain regions that
researchers currently associate with them.)*

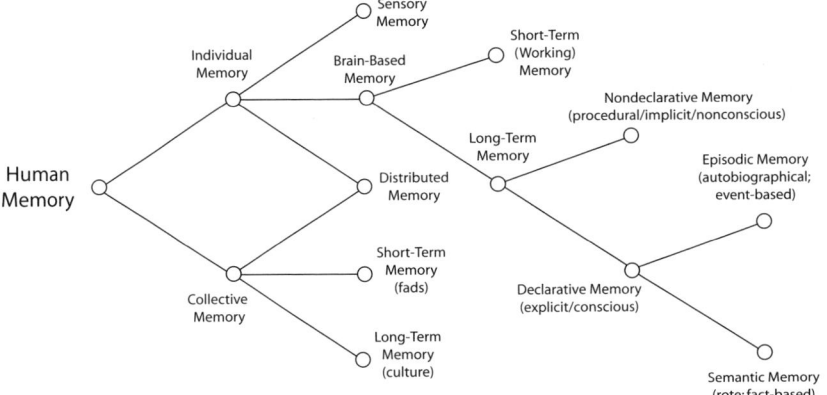

Perhaps the easiest place to begin is with different
categories of **individual memory**, starting with one
sort that is readily demonstrated. The activity in the
margin on the facing page presents an exercise with
sensory memory. This sort of memory tends to be very
short lived, operating at the intercellular level. In brief,
when clusters of cells are activated simultaneously,
they can establish and maintain a level of co-activity
for a short period. *These sorts of sustained patterns of
co-activity among agents are, in effect, the memories of
the system.* (That is, memories aren't stable states, but
vibrant patterns of interaction.) In the example given,
sensory cells in the eye retain a memory of the leaf.
Other examples include ringing in the ears after a loud
noise and lingering pain after a sharp jab. To be clear,
although these sorts of sensory memories might be intense enough to bubble to the surface of consciousness,

* The graphics on pages 55 and 60 are based on
information provided in Joseph LeDoux, *Synaptic
self: How our brains become who we are* (New York:
Viking, 2002) and gleaned from wikipedia.org.

"Sensory memory" is a category that's not often mentioned in discussions of knowing. You can test out the visual version by staring intensely at the dot in the middle of the leaf for 20 seconds and then shifting your gaze to an open white space.

You should see a distinct after-image as collectives of retinal cells continue to be activated—demonstrating how perceptions and memories are about relationships and patterns of activity among active cells.

Whether or not particular sensations are consciously noticed, our sense organs have a sort of memory of any sufficiently intense stimulation. Usually, these fade in a few seconds as the activity of the stimulated cells fades.

* See Jeff Hawkins, *On intelligence: How a new understanding of the brain will lead to the creation of truly intelligent machines* (New York: Times Books, 2004).

they are not formed in the brain. They operate at the cellular level in highly localized regions where particular types of sense-receptor cells are concentrated.

The example of sensory memory is also useful for talking about **brain-based memories**. They too exist in the interactions of different agents, in this case neurons and neuronal clusters. Through technologies that provide real-time portraits of brain activity, we know that specific memories are not highly localized, as was once thought, but tend to involve activations of several different areas of the brain. That is, personal memories might be described as decentralized networks within the grander decentralized network of the brain.*

Short-term memories are a little like sensory memories. They tend to be very short-lived (typically, 15 seconds to a few minutes), and once they've faded they don't much affect subsequent neuronal activity. Sometimes called "working memory," this is the type of recall that we use to keep track of phone numbers, where we are in a conversation, and names of new acquaintances. Short-term memory amounts to what we have "in mind" at any given moment, and in terms of capacity it is amazingly consistent across humans. Whether classic underachiever or Nobel laureate, most people can juggle 6 or 7 items in short-term memory.

By contrast, **long-term memories** are stabler patterns of activity among neurons and brain regions. They are able to resist fading because they are associated with actual changes to brain structure. Just as particular memories are distributed across clusters of neurons, particular clusters of neurons are associations that can be related to many different memories—which means that we have little control over the associations that come to be formed. Memories spill into, subsume, and trigger one another in complex and unpredictable ways, and this can be considered either a curse or a blessing. On the one hand, it means that memory can be volatile and unreliable; on the other, it opens the door to interesting and innovative associations.

Long-term memories can be either nondeclarative or declarative. **Nondeclarative memory**, which is also known as "procedural memory" and "implicit memory," has to do with how-to knowledge. In particular, nondeclarative memory includes skills and procedures that can be used without conscious thought—walking, touch-typing, reading, playing the piano, and so on. Typically learned over a long time and involving much practice, such skills are very durable, but hard to put into words (e.g., try explaining to someone how to ride a bicycle). We simply do them. But imagine how hard it would be to explain how to read to someone who has never encountered the phenomenon.

Declarative memory is the sort of long-term memory that is the focus of most of formal education, since it refers to the memories that can be consciously recalled and readily stated—declared. Two types of declarative memory have been identified: episodic and semantic. **Episodic memory** (or "autobiographical memory" or "event-based memory") has to do with the memory of experiences. Typically, these sorts of memories include associations of times, places, people, and emotions. (As will be discussed later, the sorts of emotional associations can greatly affect the quality and vividness of the memory.) Given the rich associations, these memories tend to be readily recalled and relatively stable. **Semantic memory** (or "rote memory" or "fact-based memory") is more dictionary-like and deals with disjointed bits of information rather than richly contextualized events. That is, these bits of information are remembered in isolation and are not always readily connected to other memories. Such memories can be vivid and accurate. However, in contrast to episodic memory, semantic memories tend not to have many associations, and for that reason they can be notoriously difficult to recall, easy to forget, and subject to interfering with one another. This is especially the case when dealing with largely meaningless, multi-step procedures. A popular strategy to improve semantic memory is to "ride atop" episodic memory by, for example, using mnemonic tools or associating items on a list with rooms in a house—or interweaving narratives and fact-based accounts in chapters.

Because these two categories—that is, episodic and semantic memories—are both so prominent in formal education, it's worth re-emphasizing the contrast. Episodic memories are parts of vast webs of association and unfolding narratives. These associations tend

Saying something out loud—like repeating the name of a person you just met—can greatly enable memory, even if done only once.

Why?

Part of the reason is that the activity of the brain "mirrors" the activity

of the rest of the body. The physical interactions of the body parts associated with an articulation are reflected in the interactions among neurons and brain regions (which are the starting places of memories).

Hearing or thinking a word has a similar, but generally less pronounced effect on brain processes, which means that opportunities to verbalize are important for learning. Neurologically speaking, being able to say things out loud—to recite, to explain, to repeat, etc.—is often a far more powerful learning strategy than listening quietly or doing work in silence.

Among the unfortunate aspects of this phenomenon is that saying something incorrectly (e.g., getting a name or a number fact wrong) can set up an unwanted but resilient resonance pattern among neurons. Be careful what you say!

to make for a more nuanced, more accessible set of recollections than do semantic memories. Compare, for example, your memory of something you learned rotely (perhaps an arithmetic procedure or how to use a piece of machinery) to a memorable classroom event. Chances are that the latter is much richer in detail, even if it unfolded over a considerably shorter period of time and happened only once. An upshot is that, in fact, humans can learn much more than six or seven things in a lesson (i.e., the famous limit on consciousness, as discussed in chap. 2). But details are best learned when they are lodged in an already-established matrix of experience and interpretation.

Often discussions of varied types of memory end here, but there are many other varieties that need to be considered. It starts with the realization that not everything we know is bounded by our skin. Individuals make use of a variety of **distributed memory** systems to offload some of the demands on mental systems. Obvious examples of such tools include written notes and other symbolic representations. Less obvious examples include uses of categories and strategies for organizing objects, such as a file for unpaid bills or a case for pens. These strategies are more pervasive than you might think: as mentioned in chapter 2, most of what we need to remember about the world is left in the world.

Even more subtly, knowledge is invested in tools, in language, in customs, in the structures of homes and cities, and in one another. In other words, there is a sort of **collective memory** of which we are all part. As with each of the systems mentioned so far, collective memory arises in the sustained co-activity of agents. In this case, one might say that we are each neurons in the collective's memory. That is, the same sorts of processes seem to be at work at the individual and collective memory levels. In fact, there are analogous phenomena to short- and long-term memories on the social and cultural levels. **Fads**, for example, very much resemble short-term memories. They occupy attentions for a brief period and then fade rapidly, usually having little or no enduring impact. **Customs**, by contrast, are stable patterns of co-activity that are molded into the structure of a collective.

As mentioned, this manner of discussion could be taken much further, in both micro-and macro-directions. Cells have memories. So do plants. So do species. And ecosystems. And so on. To re-emphasize, memories are patterns of co-activity among agents that come together into more complex collectives—patterns that are reasonably stable, but subject to change. In this way, *all* complex phenomena have memories. They all have means to embody their histories.

Returning to the issue of "taken-as-shared," this understanding of the phenomenon of memory helps to highlight the troublesome assumption that individuals are seen as fundamental particles of knowing. When one pulls back to examine other levels of co-activity, it becomes clear that meanings, understandings, and interpretations are indeed shared—which is not to say identical among individuals, but distributed across collectives and their memory systems.

A futuristic novel, *The Giver* deals with some provocative topics, including eugenics, euthanasia, and burgeoning sexuality. The question of its appropriateness for elementary school learners prompted a shift in the topic of discussion, from *reading* to *teaching reading*—and with this, the identifications in the group shifted even more dramatically from individual concerns and observations (*I*-statements) to collective ones (*we*-statements). Participants commented that the book couldn't be taught, since "it deals with sex," "it's too violent," "it'll be too controversial," and "parents will be up in arms."

In other words, the group rather abruptly cohered around an imagined other—specifically, the relative unknown of the community served by the school. The families of the community were the *not-us* to the emergent *us* of the reading group.

Of course, this consequence gave the principal even further cause for concern. The study group had had its desired effect—teachers had clearly begun to identify with one another as a group. However, this identification was defined in terms of an even more troublesome distinction, one between the school and the community.

A radical proposition was put forward: What if the parents were invited to read the book as well? Perhaps the novel could have a similar effect in helping to prompt senses of collectivity among teachers and parents.

There was some nervous discussion around the suggestion. Not everyone thought it was a good idea, especially in these early stages of establishing relationships with a community. What if the novel were indeed seen as too controversial? Surely that could only serve to further alienate the school staff.

Despite such objections, eventually there was agreement that invitations should be extended. Some weeks later, a group of a dozen parents gathered in the same room to discuss their readings with the teachers. The session began tenuously and with some obvious discomfort. However, when attentions were turned to the novel, an animated conversation quickly took over. Anxieties and imagined identities dissolved over the course of the hour—on the parts of teachers and parents alike.

At the end of the hour, something surprising happened. As a unity, the parents insisted that *The Giver* ought to be taught in the 5th and 6th grade classes. This insistence was tellingly phrased in the language of collectivity: "*Our* kids need to read this." "*We* should teach it."

4.3 Knowledge

So, if a system's *memory* is understood in terms of stable, discernible, and mutable patterns of co-activity among sub-agents, then what is *knowledge*?

As with many of the topics addressed in this book, questions around the nature of knowledge have been at the center of philosophical debate for thousands of years—with no signs of any sort of emergent consensus. Clearly, any attempt to offer a concise definition is doomed. And so, rather than trying to say what knowledge *is*, the strategy here is to explore what it *might look like*.

Knowledge and memory are complementary notions. Briefly, whereas memory points to the internal dynamics of a complex unity, knowledge points to the dynamics of the unity-in-context. Or, in terms of the nested systems diagram on page 56, memory refers to the dynamics within a given circle/system, knowledge refers to how that circle/system fits in a grander circle/system. That is, knowledge has to do with situated fitness. An agent *knows* if it can maintain its fitness or viability in a given context.

Another way of making this point is to talk about what it means to make an error. Specific interpretations and physical acts are only considered errors when they interrupt the flow of activity in which the agent is acting. All of us harbor certain notions and do certain things that seem perfectly reasonable to us, but that would be inappropriate in certain settings. But these interpretations are not errors until they are shown not to fit, because for something to be wrong it has to be manifest in a way that threatens the viability of the knower or the knower's understandings.

An example might help here. Consider the following interaction between a student and his teacher, which was recorded during a math lesson. It began when the teacher noticed that Sen was staring off to the side:

> "Sen, what are you doing?" the teacher asked.
> "Thinking," he answered.
> "What are you supposed to be doing?"
> "Working," Sen sighed, shifting back in his seat and picking up his pencil.

SUBJECTIVE *versus* OBJECTIVE?

Knowledge is an internal phenomenon that arises as the individual makes sense of idiosyncratic experience. Hence, truth is always **subjective**.	With regard to questions of truth, it is what's external to us that matters. To be counted as knowledge, claims must be **objective**.

COMMON ROOTS: Both perspectives share convictions that there is a stable, unchanging reality; individuals end at their skin; knowers are self-contained—and so the internal (mental, subjective) is insulated and isolated from the external (physical, objective).

At first glance, this exchange might seem unsettling. Surely "thinking" is an appropriate activity in a mathematics class. Hasn't the teacher made an error?

There are two ways of answering this question, depending on which level of activity is examined. Within the Sen-and-teacher system, there was no break in the flow of activity. So, on that level, there was no error.

However, there was a rupture on the level of the Sen-teacher-observer system, one that revolved around incompatible meanings of *thinking*. Likely Sen meant (and the teacher heard) "day-dreaming." But that's not what was heard in the grander system.

To repeat, specific actions and interpretations only become errors when appropriately contextualized. In the same way, an agent's stable and discernible patterns of activity are only seen in terms of "knowledge" when considered within an appropriate situation. Knowledge is not some sort of object that is locked inside a head or that is lying in pools out in the world; rather, knowledge is a potential to action—meaning that knowledge is *embodied* (there must be an actor) and *situated* (there must be a context for the action). Bodies know, and that's what makes them part of grander knowing bodies. Knowledge, then, is about relationship.

An immediate implication of this sort of claim is that, under certain circumstances, groups of people can be considered as knowing bodies or intelligent agents. Indeed, there is a good deal of compelling research to support the notion that crowds can be intelligent.* Society, for example, provides a living example of how a collective can be vastly more intelligent than the most intelligent agent in the collective. The same phenomenon can be observed in much smaller social groupings. The following are among the insights that have been gleaned in studies of intelligent groups:

- Productive and innovative groups tend to be decentralized. In particular, decisions about local problems should be made by the people closest to the problems, who are likely to have the most intimate knowledge. They are also the ones most affected by whatever decisions are made. By contrast, rigid and hierarchical organizations with centralized decision-making

In modern and western settings, *spirituality* is often defined in terms of disembodiment, of beyond the physical, of denial of the worldly, of "belief" rather than "evidence."

For these reasons, the topic is rarely addressed by "serious" educational researchers. However, with the development of nested and collective accounts of knowing, the topic is starting to gain much broader attention—in part because these accounts cast us as part of a larger whole. There *is* a grander corpus, a higher unity according to these theories, and we are each part of it. Whether one chooses to think in terms of God, of a higher power, of One-ness, or whatever, there is now a legitimate

* For an accessible overview of some of this research, see James Surowiecki, *The wisdom of crowds: Why the many are stronger than the few and how collective wisdom shapes business, economies, societies, and nations* (New York: Doubleday, 2004).
** This NASA image of Earth was downloaded from Visible Earth (http://www.digital globe.com/).

basis—an embodied way—to address matters of spirituality.

For many, this situation is new. For others, it is more a remembering—a recalling that matters of the spirit are, literally, matters of breathing, of constant connection to and exchange with the rest of the world. The notion that humans exist in webs of relations is an integral aspect of many idigenous epistemologies, including some that are organized around what English-speakers might call *pantheism*—that is, the belief that the spirits of all animate and inanimate forms intermingle throughout the physical realm and over the courses of many human lifetimes.

Elements that are central to many of these orientations include a sense of the ethical responsibilities that humans have within the web of relationships. With the emergence of more ecological sensibilities, these forms of spirituality have recently come to be seen by others as crucial to the survival of the planet.

structures are likely not only to make less appropriate decisions, but also to enact them much more slowly.

• Consensus is often a bad idea when it comes to intelligent co-activity. It can demand compromise, which can lead to lowest-common-denominator solutions that are designed to avoid offence rather than prompt novelty. So long as opinions aren't so polarized as to fragment the group, it is usually best to have some disagreement to force people to be explicit.

• Groups in which people are allowed considerable autonomy, the opportunities to specialize and obsess, and freedom to change their minds tend to be smarter—that is, more flexibly adaptive—than groups in which roles are rigidly specified.

Given these sorts of insights, and returning to the narrative presented in this chapter's dialogue boxes, the reasons that made the reading group an effective activity become apparent. It was a decentralized structure in which individual participants could represent their own interpretations and concerns. As these were made to bump up against the articulations of others, points of convergence and divergence began to be revealed. In the end, two sets of good decisions were made. First, the collective of teachers elected to extend the group to include parents. Subsequently, the teachers-and-parents group chose to involve children in the reading of a provocative book.

This sort of happening is illustrative of what might be called a "win-win logic." Within a well-structured and smart collective, outcomes can benefit *both* the individual *and* the group. It needn't be the case of one or the other, as is often suggested by the persistent and prominent debate over whether formal education should be serving the interests of students or of society. Complexity thinking would suggest that this is a false dichotomy. The issue to bear in mind is that knowledge arises at all levels of complex co-activity, and so that individual interests can be entertained at the same time as collective concerns are addressed. (This topic is addressed in greater detail in several of the subsequent chapters.)

Arrangements were made to use *The Giver* in the 5th and 6th grades English language arts classes. Because the teachers felt that the novel was somewhat complex and that some of the students might find it overly difficult, they read it aloud in class over the period of one week. Following each chapter, students were invited to talk about what they had noticed. For example, after reading chapter 1, the children were asked to identify passages that had caught their attention. This task sponsored an interesting discussion of the associations and interpretations that they were making with the text and, as well, provided evidence of how individual readings are always idiosyncratic.

In one class, during the discussion at the end of the first chapter, one student theorized that the community in the story must be enclosed in a large plastic dome that prevented travel, limited interactions with other communities, and maintained a constant climate. While this idea is not in any way presented in the novel, its inclusion in the group discussion rendered it part of the shared understanding of the text. Through the subsequent weeks devoted to reading and interpreting the book, many references were made to the dome. It became part of the common sense—so much so that that the class soundly rejected the teacher's suggestion that domes, in fact, were not a part of the story.

There were many other examples of unsupported, but nonetheless shared and resilient interpretations. Another emerged around "release," a euphemism used in the book to refer to someone being put to death. Not wanting to accept that possibility, an elaborate scheme involving sedation, clandestine trucks, and inter-community transfers was proposed and endorsed.

These sorts of shared insistence foreshadowed some other strong identifications that developed in the group. Long after the reading of *The Giver*, the teacher noted students' use of phrases from the book, such as "stirrings" to refer to emergent sexuality, or "celebration of sameness" to critique incidents of racist behavior in the school.

4.4 Collectivity

It's one thing to assert that "collective cognition" or "collective intelligence" is a possibility. It's quite another to explain how it happens, especially when it seems that whatever is happening in each of our brains is happening in isolation. One person's cortical structures cannot connect to someone else's.

Or can they?

It turns out, with regard to brain and bodily activity, that humans routinely synchronize actions with one another. For instance, a common, everyday conversation turns out to be a complex event of linked consciousnesses, although participants in a conversation are rarely aware of it. On the bodily level, slowed videorecordings of such interactions reveal an intricate choreography of precisely timed action. Participants' speech patterns are synchronized with subtle body movements that are acutely sensitive to events in the surroundings. The choreography is so tight that a conversation can properly be described as a coupling of individuals' attentional systems. This coupling is reflected on the level of brain activity, as participants in a conversation, quite literally, get in tune with one another.* In brief, while there might not be a physical linkage between the two bodies, they do act as a single cognitive system—with some significantly enhanced capabilities. Ideas can be sustained for a longer time, a greater variety of interpretations can be introduced, a broader pool of experiences can be drawn on. Two heads can be *much* better than one.

Insights into why this happens are more recent, and current explanations focus on a discovery that some describe as one of the most important in the history of neuroscience: mirror neurons. These neurons are located in many parts of the brain—including the centers for language, empathy, and pain—and they fire not only when we perform an action, but when we observe someone else perform an action. (In fact, they can fire when we read about, hear about, or think about an action. Exactly the same mirror neurons fire as would if you were to perform the action yourself.) In other words, everything we see someone do, we mimic in our minds. We mentally imitate every action that we consciously observe, from jumping jacks to crying. It's a phenomenon that helps to explain why we yawn when someone else yawns and why we are so susceptible to emotional manipulations by moviemakers and others who select an array of responses through skillful storytelling, imagery, and sound. Moods and laughter are as contagious as yawns.

Mirror neurons are already active at the moment of birth. Newborns have been shown to imitate simple gestures such as sticking out tongues.** Such immediate copying capacities point to the role of mirror neurons in the development of more complex activities such as learning to walk, talk, and play games. In fact, it appears that mirror neurons play a role in learning almost everything from first grimaces to the most refined physical skills. They also figure prominently into the learned capacity to focus attentions on what someone else is looking at—a vital capacity, given the sea of sensorial possibilities in which we are immersed. Being able to couple attentions in this way helps us to

Why are yawns contagious?
The answer has to do with mirror neurons. They also help to explain phenomena such as infectious laughter, bullying, "group think," and "mob mentality." In brief, we each have clusters of neurons that fire when we are made aware of an action. (See the next page.)

This phenomenon of covert mental (and, often, overt physical) mimicry has been exploited by the entertainment industry to manipulate affective responses. It's the reason behind laugh tracks and tearful scenes. You can test it out yourself by showing an extreme emotion (e.g., elation, dread, contempt) to someone.

* See Donald, *A mind so rare*; Norretranders, *The user illusion*.
** See Gopnik et al., *The scientist in the crib*.

piggyback on one another's perceptual capacities, thus amplifying our own.

Mirror neurons also play an important role in perceiving others' intentions, which is of course an important part in establishing and maintaining social relations. Mirror neurons enable us, literally, to share the emotional import of others' experiences as we tap into the emotional content of their expressions. In particular, mirror neurons play an important part in what neuroscientists and psychologists have come to call "mind reading"—that is, the capacity to anticipate not just what someone will say, but how they're feeling. The evidence suggests that many of these details are actually written in the expressions on our faces. (Conversely, an inactive mirror neuron system might account for certain dysfunctions, including difficulties in language learning and autism.) In other words, there is a profoundly biological component to human language, sociality, and culture.*

In brief, studies of mirror neurons have underscored the importance of imitation and rehearsal in learning. However, it would be naive and reductionist to suggest that these activities, as supported by mirror neurons, are the only components to learning. Other mechanisms arise at the level of human interaction, including the desire to fit in. In fact, it appears that the need to identify with a social group is so strong that the major influence on the development of one's "personal preferences" on music, recreational activities, ideology, worldview, and so on is neither genetics nor parents, but peer group. A rationale for this observation is that the child's main task is not to become a successful adult, but to be a successful child—to fit in, to be part of the group, not to stand out. Your parents were right: it matters who your friends are. Who you become depends a great deal on whom you hang out with.**

This phenomenon is more complex and subtle than the phenomenon of "peer pressure," which is usually used to refer to conscious choices. It is more a matter of adopting shared sets of implicit associations around common likes and dislikes. In particular, a common enemy can be an enormously powerful enabler of social cohesion. On the negative side of things, however,

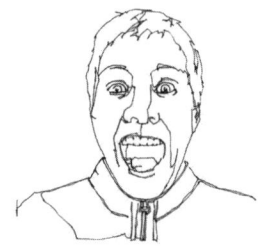

What is this person feeling? And how do you know?

Over the past decade, we've learned a great deal about how we recognize emotions in others. It has to do with mirror neurons.

Mirror neurons have been observed in primates, most mammals, and some birds. A mirror neuron is one that fires *both* when you perform an action *and* when you see it being performed. In fact, you don't have to see a perfor-

---

* For further information of the research into mirror neurons and its implications, see Beth Azar, "How mimicry begat culture," in *Monitor on Psychology*, vol. 35, no. 9 (October 2005): 54–57; Michael Arbib, "From monkey-like action recognition to human language: An evolutionary framework for neurolinguistics," in *Behavioral and Brain Sciences*, vol. 28 (2005): 105–167.

** See Judith Rich Harris, *The nurture assumption: Why children turn out the way they do* (New York: The Free Press, 1998). This book is not uncontroversial, given its challenge to the deeply entrenched belief that personality is largely determined in the pre-school years—meaning that the principal social influences are popularly thought to be parents.

mance: mirror neurons will fire if you're told about an action, read a description, or imagine it. Hence the name: a mirror neuron *mirrors* behaviors, including facial expressions.

That means that when we see someone grimacing in disgust, we mentally (and often physically) rehearse or imitate it, thereby gaining access to how that person is probably feeling. Hence, mirror neurons enable social co-activity by helping us to "mind-read." (In fact, malfunctioning mirror neurons may be a principal factor in autism.) Such mind-reading is rooted in biology (newborns imitate facial expressions) and elaborated by experience (adolescents aren't nearly as good at reading emotions as adults).

Given that they enable us to copy one another, mirror neurons are likely vital to meaning-making.

implicit associations that run too deeply can support the emergence of what is commonly known as a "mob mentality," which is the flip side of collective intelligence. When diversity of opinion is suppressed, when interactions are shallow, and when a common focus of action arises, crowds can do decidedly stupid things. Most of us have experienced at least a minor form of this phenomenon, swept up in the emotional tide of the crowd at a baseball game, in a church, or at a political rally. How easily subjective awareness can be subsumed by collective action can be shocking.

Many of these points were brought to life in the classroom context during the reading of *The Giver*, described above. In particular, there were moments of both shared intelligence and collective delusion. With regard to the latter, the resilience of certain shared, but unsupported interpretations of certain events and passages is telling. The critical element in the interpretations was *not* a fit with the text but interpersonal coherence.

As for moments of collective intelligence, one of the final activities in the unit of study around *The Giver* was a discussion of the role of literature in our society. Among the issues discussed by the 5th and 6th grade students was the nature of a literary text. Was a novel different for having been read?

"Obviously," was the shared response. The story isn't a static artifact. It is something that can only exist within the fabric of relations of those who participate in its telling. And so while the physical artifact of the book might look unchanged, its place in the collective is different. It and all around it have been reconfigured.

A complex insight from a group of 11- and 12-year-olds, demonstrating a deep awareness that we are profoundly social beings. While that sociality might be rooted in our biology, something more complex arises in the space of knowing structures.

Various accounts of the happenings in the school among the teachers, with the parents, and in the classrooms have been prepared and presented over the past decade. For the most part, when researchers and educators listen to or read about this event, they seem to have ready appreciations that it was unique and could never be repeated.

Every now and then, however, someone requests more detail so that they might "replicate the study." To us, this request seems odd. The events at the school could never be imitated, particularly as one looks across the layers of interacting systems (e.g., teachers; teachers-and-parents; teachers-and-parents-and-children) and the unique circumstances (e.g., a transplanted teaching staff, a community with little transience).

So the event cannot be replicated. But the attitude of mindful participation with others around matters of shared concern can be. Taking care to allow interpretive space for others, structuring events for genuine interaction around shared artifacts, letting individuals focus and even obsess about things they find personally compelling—these are the ingredients of a profound and memorable *collective* educational event.

On this count, it is worth underscoring that although the event around the reading of *The Giver* is recounted here as a collective phenomenon, it was triggered and fueled by self-interest. The principal, for example, saw it mainly as a means to establish better community relations. Many of the parents saw it as an opportunity to become more integrally involved in their children's schooling. Most of the teachers saw it as a site to develop teaching ideas. The impetus for the event was a complex product of this mix of motivations, and for that reason alone the event can never be replicated. Someone else's desire for a similar event can never substitute for these sorts of internal dynamics. The "personality" of the emergent collective was every bit as unique and idiosyncratic as that of any individual. Such is the nature of complex bodies.*

* For further details on this research, see Dennis Sumara, Brent Davis, & Delores van der Wey, "The pleasure of thinking," in *Language Arts*, vol. 76, no. 2 (1998): 135–143.

PART B · learning

Etymology

The word *learn* appears to be related to a primitive Germanic word, *liznojan*, "finding or following a track," and to an Old English word, *læst*, "sole of the foot." The word is rooted in imagery of path-following or path-making.

Synonyms

acquire, apprehend, apprentice, ascertain, assimilate, attain, be taught, be trained, become able, become versed, catch on, comprehend, cram, detect, determine, dig up, digest, discern, discover, drink in, find out, follow, gain, gather, get, get down, get into, get the hang of, grasp, grind, hear, imbibe, improve mind, incorporate, ingest, latch onto, master, memorize, pick up, pore over, prepare, read, receive, review, see, soak up, specialize in, study, stumble on, take in, train in, uncover, understand, unearth, wade through

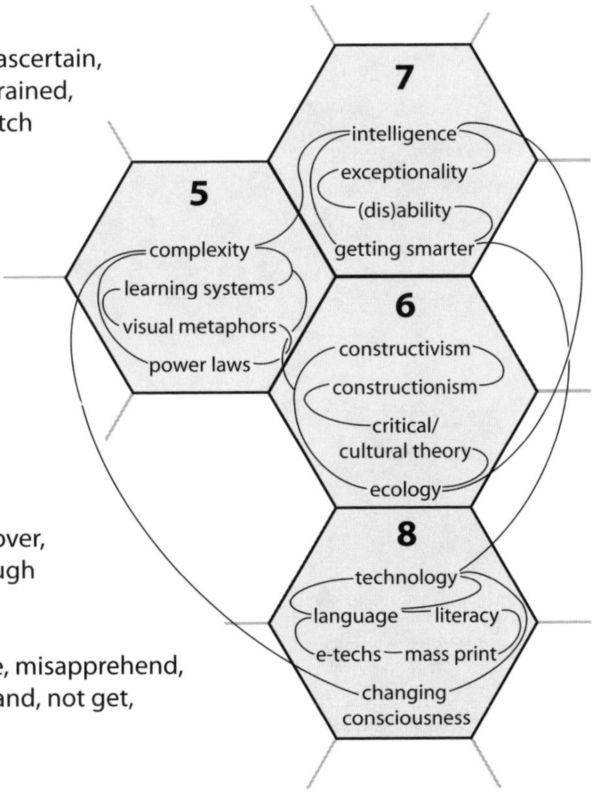

Antonyms

confuse, disregard, forget, ignore, misapprehend, miss, miss the point, misunderstand, not get, overlook

Cognates

last, lore

5
- complexity
- learning systems
- visual metaphors
- power laws

7
- intelligence
- exceptionality
- (dis)ability
- getting smarter

6
- constructivism
- constructionism
- critical/cultural theory
- ecology

8
- technology
- language — literacy
- e-techs — mass print
- changing consciousness

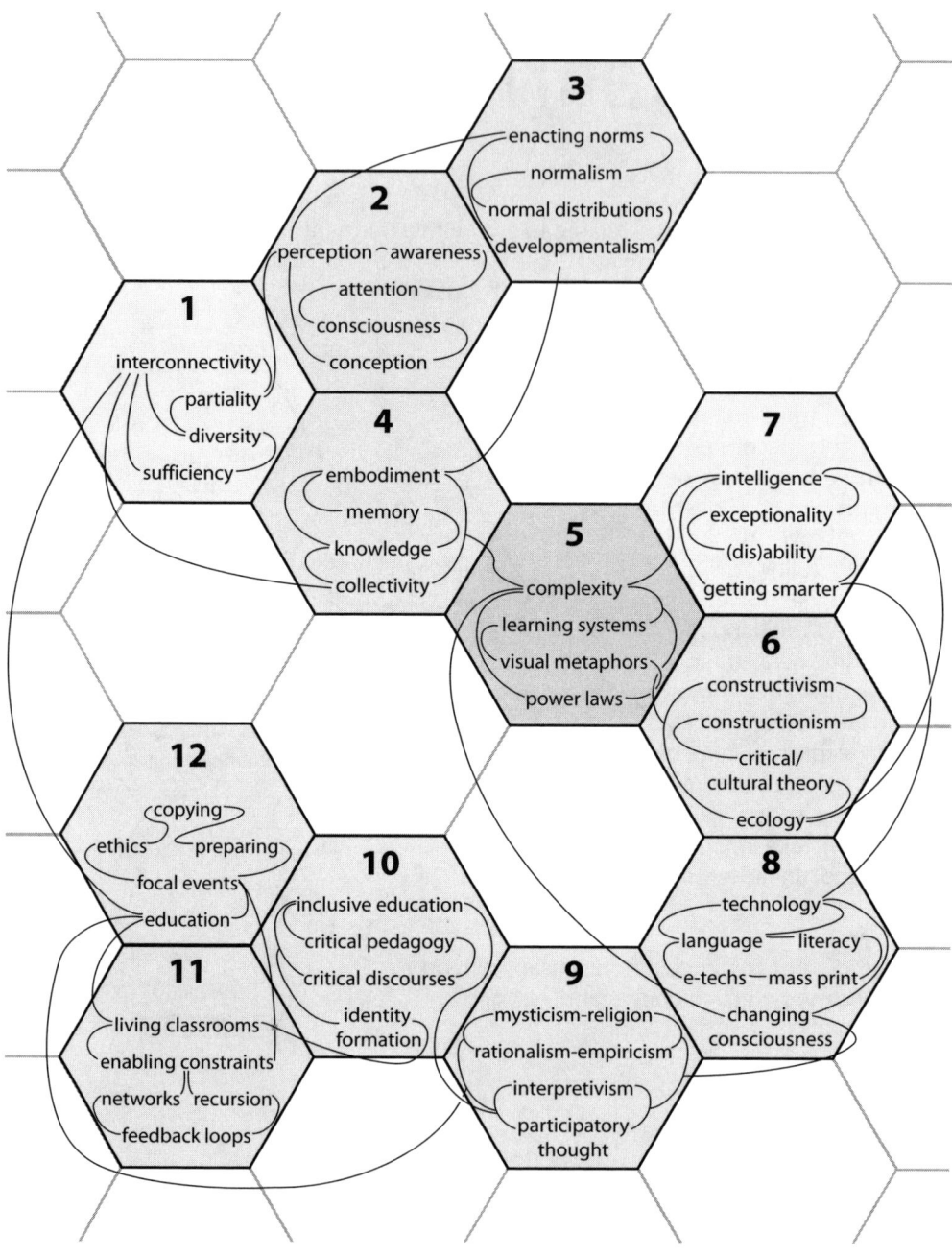

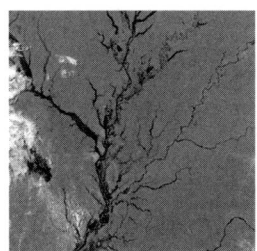

*

This Grade 3 unit on fractions began, as most of my units do, with a few activities intended to tap into childrens' prior experiences with mathematical processes. The opening tasks involved paper-folding tasks—different ways of making halves, to be specific.

I picked that activity because I was confident that my students had all had rich and extensive experiences of cutting, subdividing, assembling, sharing, and so on—and that they had at least a preliminary knowledge of fraction notation. Experience had taught that most also arrive with a cluster of understandings of various relationships among fractional amounts (e.g., four quarters make a whole, a half is more than a third), but that these are never universal and are often anchored to diverse contexts (e.g., music notation, shares that depended on family size, and so on).

My preliminary intentions, then, were to provide opportunities for students to show what they already knew and to develop a reference point that was common to everyone. A shared activity fit the bill. The common experience of folding gave us something we could all talk about, in the process highlighting what was already understood and what still needed to be studied.

5.1 Complexity

One of the major shifts in educational thinking over the last several decades has been a rejection of machine-based metaphors and an embrace of more organic notions. This is especially obvious around the topic of learning. Through much of the 20th century, learning was framed in cause–effect terms, which in turn supported mechanistic approaches to teaching and curriculum. But that framework began to change in the 1970s and 1980s with a shift toward more holistic, contingent, and exploratory conceptions of learning.

This change actually coincided with a broad, transdisciplinary move toward what is now known as "complexity thinking" (or "complexity theory" or "complexity science"). Over the four chapters in this section, some of the core principles and major implications of complexity will be developed as they pertain to the topics of learning, ability, and technology.*

Complexity thinking began with a rejection of the centuries-old assumption that any event can be described in terms of mechanical interactions. The overarching belief, which rose to prominence in the 1600s, was that the universe is a grand "clockwork" and, hence, *everything* can be understood by breaking it down. This attitude underpinned the rise of analytic science, with its quest for universal laws, fundamental particles, and basic truths.

Complexity theorists agree that machines like clocks and refrigerators, as well as physical systems such as billiard ball collisions and chemical reactions, are indeed the predictable sums of their parts. With a thorough knowledge of the motions of the pieces, one can predict the behavior of the whole.

However, while this analytic attitude has been proven effective in the scientific and technological innovations of the industrial age, the approach has been almost useless in efforts to understand and predict phenomena that include large-scale economies, ecosystems, and brains. The reason for the breakdown was not immediately clear, but once it was articulated, it contributed to an intellectual convulsion across disciplines. In brief, certain systems aren't made up

The terms *complicated, holist,* and *complex* are being used here to refer to three different mindsets.

A *complicated* theory is one that reduces phenomena to basic components, root causes, and fundamental laws. In this view, a full understanding of a clock would arise from a detailed knowledge of each of its parts.

A *holist* view of a clock would see it as a functional whole, something that is more than the sum of its parts. This includes an appreciation of the interdependencies of its parts.

A *complexity* theory embraces both complicated and holist views, but also argues that an understanding of a clock demands an attention to the fact that the clock is embedded in social and natural environments, which compels considerations of the roles that a clock plays in shaping social lives, the historical conditions that supported its invention, the materials involved in its construction, the effects of its use on the natural environment, and so on.

* For an overview of the history and key principles of complexity thinking, see Steven Johnson, *Emergence: The connected lives of ants, brains, cities, and software* (New York: Scribner, 2001).

of inert particles, cogs, switches, or microchips, but are themselves collectives of dynamic systems. For example, societies emerge from but cannot be reduced to citizens. Each human citizen arises in, but is something more than the interactions of a cluster of bodily organs. Those organs, in turn, comprise and surpass collectives of living cells. It goes on.

These are *complex* systems. They can never be reduced to their parts because they are always caught up with other systems in a dance of change. Compared to *complicated* (i.e., mechanical) systems, *complex* unities are more spontaneous, unpredictable, irreducible, contextual, and vibrantly sufficient—in brief, they are adaptive. Because complex phenomena transform themselves, tools like Newtonian mechanics and statistical regression are of little use to understand them.

Of course, there are some forms that are difficult to identify as complicated or complex. In particular, some recent technological developments, especially in robotics, render the distinction a fuzzy one.* Nevertheless, the separation of *complex* phenomena (e.g., knowing, learning, and teaching) from *complicated* phenomena (e.g., most mechanical systems) is useful when making sense of how to deal with each. The table below summarizes some of the key differences that are developed in greater detail in various places in this book. (Note that these distinctions aren't absolute, and they're getting hazier as technologies advance.)

As any hound breeder will confirm, a group of dogs is something different than just a *collection* of dogs—that is, the whole is different than the sum of its parts.

Rather, several dogs together will form a *collective* (more often called a "pack") that has a coherence and a set of behavioral traits that are qualitatively different from those of any dog on its own. More is different.

The same is true of many mammalian species, including humans. Unfortunately, many of the theories that have been used to orient thinking about human activity are rooted in the assumption that the individual is the basis or the fundamental particle of all activity—paying no attention at all to transformations that arise when humans are gathered together.

In fact, in discussions of education, the words *individual* and *learner* have usually been treated synonymously. That's not the case in this book, where *learner* is understood in terms of any complex, adaptive unity.

Complicated (mechanical)	Complex (learning)
physics (Newton)	biology (Darwin)
machine metaphors	ecosystem metaphors
linear imagery	cyclical imagery
input/output flows	feedback loops
efficiency-oriented	sufficiency-oriented
goal-oriented	growth-minded
reducible	**incompressible**

* See Philip Ball, *Critical mass: How one thing leads to another* (New York: Farrar, Straus and Giroux, 2004).

Notably, there is no unified or universally accepted definition of a complex system—simply because

various definitions tend to be hinged to the phenomenon that is of most interest to the person offering the
definition. For example, biologists tend to talk about
complexity in terms of living systems, physicists in
terms of non-linear dynamic systems, and economists
in terms of micro- and macro-economies.

And so the definition used in this text shouldn't be
too surprising: *Complex systems are systems that learn.*

We had spent our entire first session on half-folds. With piles of scrap paper in the middle of each group's table, I asked students to fold pages in half in as many different ways as they could imagine. As might be expected, the first two folds that were made by every group were lengthwise and widthwise. After a few minutes, other possibilities appeared as students folded along diagonals by matching up opposite corners.

But then the tone changed. Other folds were attempted, but they started to prompt arguments as a few individuals debated whether the resulting pieces were really halves.

"Do the halves have to be the same size?" one student asked, opening the door to a brief exchange around the mathematical definition of "one half" and the less rigid interpretations of one half that often come up in day-to-day life. Even though the notion of bigger and smaller halves was familiar to everyone there seemed to be no difficulty appreciating that mathematics would not allow for such variations. Only equal parts were permitted when working with fractions.

That comment prompted a worry: "Is a half that is made by folding a piece of paper lengthwise the same as a half that is made by folding it widthwise?"

I decided to take a vote. To my surprise, the class was almost evenly split among the opinions that the widthwise fold was biggest, the lengthwise fold was biggest, and the two were the same size. Seeing an opportunity for exploring processes of mathematical argument and justification, I asked, "Pretend that you have a friend who thinks that the squarish half [i.e., folded widthwise] was larger than the longish half [i.e., folded lengthwise]. How would you prove to him or her that the two pieces were the same size?"

It took only a few minutes of discussion among themselves before Kim's group offered, "You could cut the halves in half. Both kinds of half can be made out of two half halves." That is, both a half-cut made lengthwise and a half-cut made widthwise can be shown to cover the same area as two identical fourths—an argument that most everyone agreed would convince an uninformed friend.

5.2 Learning Systems

A complex system is a system that learns—a learner.

So, what's a learner?

In this and subsequent sections, this question will
be answered in different ways—first an example, then
an examination of some qualities of learning systems,
then a look at the dynamics of learning, and then a
few explorations of the images that are associated with
complex learning systems. On to the example …

Sometime in the late 1970s or early 1980s, zebra mussels—tiny, but prolific mollusks—were introduced into the Great Lakes in North America. No one is certain how it happened, but it likely occurred when a cargo ship purged its ballast tanks after delivering a shipment from Europe. Having no natural enemies, the mussels thrived, quickly spreading through all of the Great Lakes. As their population grew, many ominous predictions were made about irreversible environmental disaster. The mussels, it was asserted, would almost certainly upset a fragile and delicate balance.

But, in fact, none of those dire predictions came to pass although there have been some major consequences. Perhaps the most publicized consequence is the several billion dollars price tag required to clear mollusks from underwater grates and valves. A lesser-known consequence is that the mussels have actually helped to clarify the turgid waters of the Great Lakes, straining out large amounts of suspended matter as they pump water through their systems.

So why no ecological disaster?

The ecosystem hasn't collapsed simply because the web of life in the Great Lakes does *not* exist in a delicate balance. Far from it. As with most ecosystems, it is not static and optimized, but vibrantly sufficient. That is, it is a dynamic, diversified, robust, ever evolving, and constantly learning system. And zebra mussels have now been incorporated (i.e., literally, *embodied*) by/into that system. Put differently, the relational web, the specific qualities, and the response patterns of the lake ecosystem have changed. *The system has learned* in a manner that is dynamically similar to the ways that humans, immune systems, societies, species, and other complex unities learn.

In fact, the Great Lakes ecosystem is likely even more robust now than it was prior to the introduction of the zebra mussels. It turns out that most cases of invasive species contribute to a win-win situation. The species gains a new habitat, and most often the host ecosystem increases in biodiversity.*

As will be developed in chapters 6 and 7, this sort of increase in diversity is vital to understanding human learning and ability.

When patterns such as the flocking of birds, the foraging of ants, or the functioning of brains are observed, it is often assumed that there are centralized controllers.

Most often, however, there are no such controllers. Rather, the observed patterns are *self-organized*. There are no leaders, nor is there any general plan inscribed in the heads of individuals. Instead, such collective activity emerges from a mass of local interactions as each participant responds to its nearest few neighbors.

This realization has prompted a dramatic shift in discussions of complex learning systems.

* For a discussion of the generally positive impacts of the introductions of new species, see Alan Burdick, "The truth about invasive species: How to stop worrying and learn to love ecological intruders," in *Discover*, vol. 26, no. 5 (May 2005): 34–41.

With at least a preliminary agreement that a half is a half is a half, I felt that the class was ready to examine more complicated folds. To start the next day's class I asked, "What would happen if I folded two times to make fourths ... and then folded again?

What I had expected was that everyone would answer, "You'll get eighths," thus setting the stage for my planned lesson on combinations of folds. What actually happened was that, although a handful of students were willing to argue that three half folds in a row would produce eighths, the majority of students who were willing to put forward their opinions felt that the product would be sixths.

I was surprised by this response, but I wasn't dismayed by it. It did, after all, show that these children were thinking in terms of patterns and relationships. One fold generated two pieces, two folds led to four pieces. It seems quite reasonable to expect that three folds would result in six pieces, four would generate eight, and so on.

A quick experiment to check the hypothesis demonstrated that a different pattern was at work, though. It wasn't that each successive half fold increased the total number of sections by two, but that each such fold doubled the number of pieces.

Kim was among the most vocal in expressing her surprise at this result, but seemed to resolve the issue to her satisfaction by the end of the day. Her journal entry for that class included a comment about the event, noting that "every part gets folded"—that is, the number of sections doubles when a new half-fold is made. Alongside she drew a series of diagrams, showing a sequence of folded pages.

5.3 Identifying Complexity

Given the difficulty in offering a one-size-fits-all definition of a complex phenomenon, the most common strategy for deciding if something is or isn't complex is to look for particular characteristics.

For example, phenomena such as the Great Lakes ecosystem, an economy, and a brain share some important qualities. For starters, they all seem to have stable boundaries and identities, even though they're constantly exchanging matter and information with other systems as they adapt on the fly. One might say that complex unities are stable patterns in the stream of matter or activity, and these stabilities give rise to the *appearance* of stable identities and fixed boundaries.

Complex unities maintain their coherences without the help of a supervisor, overseer, director, or master organizer. They are self-organizing and self-maintaining, as illustrated in the example of the Great Lakes "learning" to accommodate zebra mussels. In this sense, learning is a constant restructuring of internal relations in order to maintain sufficient coherence.

On this topic, exactly *what* is learned (i.e., exactly how internal relations are restructured) is determined by the system, not by the event that triggers the learn-

If, over the years, a ship were to be rebuilt piece-by-piece so that every bit was gradually replaced, would it still be the same vessel? If not, at which point would we say that it was a different one?

What about the case of a human, whose body is constantly regenerating? The pancreas and the stomach lining, for example, actually replace themselves every 24 hours. Over 100,000 skin cells are replaced every minute. (The dust in our homes consists mostly of bits of ourselves that have fallen off.)

The point? Complex learning forms may appear to be fixed, but in fact they are only stable patterns in the flow of matter and/or activity.

ing. This is a point that bears repeating since it has profound educational implications. In somewhat different terms, the learning system determines what will be learned, not the event or experience that prompts learning to happen. Much in contrast to complicated (mechanical) systems that can be *caused* to respond in specific ways by external forces, the way that a complex (learning) system adapts to a new situation is rooted in its biological-and-experiential structure—its embodied history. For instance, if you nudge a brick, you can pretty much control the outcome by adjusting the force accordingly. However, if you nudge a person, her or his structure will determine the response. (Some of the finer details of this point, especially as they pertain to schooling, are addressed in the next chapter.)

These qualities of self-organization, self-maintenance, and self-determination reflect the fact that complex unities operate far-from-equilibrium. This realization actually comes as a challenge to some popular theories of living and learning systems, which assume that dynamic systems seek states of equilibrium.

In fact, complicated (mechanical) systems do. But complex (learning) systems do not. For complex systems, equilibrium is death, whereas operating far-from-equilibrium forces them to explore their spaces of possibility—to tinker with new patterns of acting, to modify internal relations, and so on. Such explorations help them evolve new structures and new ways of working.

Returning to the first point in this section, "far-from-equilibrium" does not mean "unstable." Complex unities are stable patterns in the streams of matter or activity, but that doesn't mean they are balanced or unchanging. As demonstrated in the Great Lakes example, to maintain stability in the flux of existence, a complex unity must be capable of flexible response to emergent circumstances. Had the Great Lakes system been in a state of equilibrium when zebra mussels were introduced—as many assumed it to be—the result certainly would have been disastrous. Fortunately, it was already operating far-from-equilibrium … just as you are at this moment. And just as the Grade 3 math class is through the narrative in this chapter.

Perceiving some potential for the added development of the concept at hand, I pressed the issue a bit further. How many pieces would there be if we made another half-fold? If we did it a fifth time? What if we did it ten times?

I set the students to work on these tasks and the second surprise of the lesson occurred. I expected everyone to continue the doubling pattern that I'd just highlighted. But, to my surprise, only a few students adopted this approach. Everyone else began to fold and unfold, count and recount, assigning one another the tasks of determining the totals for four or five or ten folds.

It took only a few minutes for frustration to set in. The pieces of paper began to refuse the creases and the folded sections became too numerous to count accurately. In the hope of assisting students in their efforts, I drew a chart on the board. Although my initial intention was simply to provide a means to collect the emerging responses, I realized that this recording tool could also be used as a generative device as I was drawing it. That is, the chart proved useful in helping learners notice and extend the pattern that was at work here.

The pace at which the number of pieces increased was surprising to many. Even after a quick discussion of the logic behind the doubling pattern (and a double-check on the calculations), a few students announced their doubt. Given that the paper refused to cooperate beyond six or seven folds, a pair of skeptics (Kim was one of them) took out pencil and ruler and began to draw in the folds rather than actually making new creases. Though less-than-perfectly divided, a page covered with lines that marked out 1024 "sort of" equal parts was soon ready for display. In the meantime, others in the class experimented with extending the pattern with larger pieces of paper while a few others played with different number patterns they'd noticed.

Happy with the thinking that I saw happening, I prepared a few questions that I thought might help to extend the investigations: What would happen if we did third-folds instead of half-folds? How many half-folds would it take until you were in the millionths range?

The first question didn't generate much interest, but the second one did. So, the balance of that class was spent in folding, cutting, drawing, and shading efforts, all aimed at isolating "about one millionth" of a sheet of newspaper (which turns out to be slightly smaller than 1 mm x 1 mm) and about one millionth of one panel of the chalkboard.

5.4 Complexity Imagery

As is likely already apparent, complexity thinking is explicitly organized around a particular set of visual metaphors. Over the next several pages, the intention is to highlight several images that have been deliberately selected as alternatives to popular, but troublesome Euclidean forms. These alternatives are intended to uncover and interrupt some deeply entrenched notions and implicit associations.

These entrenched ideas include straight lines, discrete regions with fixed boundaries, and normal distibutions (as discussed in Part A). The proposed alternatives are drawn from fractal geometry. In presenting them, we offer some further critiques of popular perspectives, particularly as they pertain to beliefs about knowing, learning and teaching.

Directed Progress *vs.* Expansive Growth. A brief exercise: *Think about why you're reading this book, here and now, in relation to your personal history.*

If you think about it long enough, you'll likely come to the realization that everything in your life has unfolded to bring you to this place and this moment. Everything leads you to here and now—your biological predispositions, your family and friends, your schools and teachers, your society and culture. If you had to, you could probably map out the path that brought you from birth to here.

One way of interpreting such a trace is that you were fated to be here, either by the laws of physics or by some grand overseer.

Another interpretation is that the path that unfolded is actually just one of many possibilities, arising in a complex web of interconnected events—some deliberate, some accidental, some known, some unknown. In particular, the image of a line connecting birth to where you are now probably seems a bit simplistic.

One of the recurrent themes in this text is that there is something deeply troublesome about the tendency to describe living and learning in terms of movement along a line—or, to extend the web of association, in terms of directed movement, ascent, building up, accumulation, acquisition, or progress.

In contrast, complexity thinking describes learning in nonlinear terms. For example, one suggestion is that living involves ongoing selection from among the possibilities that are presented. The associated image is more tree-like as possibilities branch out into new possibilities and you move along (see the sidebar). In retrospect, it's easy to specify the choices and decisions that brought you here and now, but it would be a mistake to interpret the end result of those decisions as progress along a line. Rather, it is more about moving into and through an evolving space of possibility.

In terms of describing the dynamics of learning, a recurrent theme in this book is that cycles are more useful than lines or, to extend this particular web of associations, learning is better characterized in terms of recursion, iteration, feedback loops, folding back, elaboration, and growth.

Evolution is sometimes discussed as a steady upward progression toward perfection.

Recently, an alternative has arisen—one that is based on *adequacy* rather than *optimality*. In this frame, evolution is a creative process that is prompted by and that contributes to dynamic and evolving landscapes of possibility. The guiding image is not an upward climb toward a pre-given goal, but a drift or flow that leads to a grand diversity of viable possibilities.

This possibility-oriented (vs. goal-driven) interpretation is the one that infuses discussions of complexity.

An upshot is that learning is a decidedly playful phenomenon. In fact, virtually every principle presented in this book could be construed as some variation of the assertion that play is the key element in any event of learning.

The meaning of *play* that underpins this claim is a broad one. In popular terms, play tends to be contrasted to work, and so it is often associated with distraction, purposelessness, and disorder. However, a careful look at the many ways that the word play is used suggests that this understanding is not just narrow, but misleading. Such usages as "stage play," "word play," "child's play," and "play of ideas" might be interpreted to suggest that the opposite of play is not *work*, but *rigidity* or *motionlessness*. In this sense, a vital quality of all living forms is play and, conversely, a likely indicator of an inert (or dead or equilibrated) form is lack of play.

With this interpretation in mind, it's not surprising that play is frequently mentioned as an important element in workplace satisfaction. People, it seems, are more content and engaged when their work allows or calls for creativity, innovation, problem solving, and other occasions for flexible response. In contrast, careers that are defined by fixed and narrow responsibilities (i.e., ones that aren't playful) tend to be regarded as undesirable and "dead end." (It might be interesting to use this contrast to think about some of your teachers and the pleasure—or lack of pleasure—they find in teaching.)

In this sort of context, play is *the possibility of movement*. So understood, ideas can be playful (i.e., they can prompt different interpretations; they can be combined and blended into new, creative possibilities) just as a child's physical explorations of the world are playful and just as the path that you followed to arrive here had play in it. Similarly, the lesson described through this chapter was a playful one. The account provided might project a sense of linear progress, but in the moment of engagement, it was much more about selecting from among the possibilities that presented themselves—that is, about expanding the space of the possible by exploring the current space of possibilities.

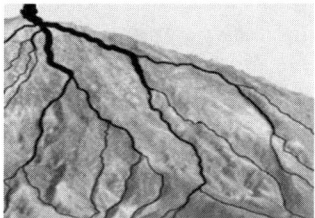

The term "phase space" is used by complexity thinkers to describe the range of possibilities for a complex learning system. Phase spaces are fractal, and they're typically drawn in a tree-like manner, often resembling the range of paths that a drop of water might follow as it runs down a mountain face. (Recall that the roots of the word *learning* meant something like path-making or path-following.)

Of course, phase spaces are dynamic. As specific turns are taken or particular choices are made, new horizons of possibility arise.

Although never explicitly stated, the unit to this point was focused on multiplication and division of fractions. Wanting to move into topics associated with comparing and combining fractional amounts, the next week I introduced "Fraction Kits" consisting of red wholes, orange halves, yellow fourths, green eighths, and blue sixteenths.

Kim was a bit disappointed when she opened her envelope. "There aren't any purple pieces in here," she protested.

I responded pragmatically: "There are only five different kinds of pieces, so I only used five colors. I was done before I got to the purple paper."

"You could add a different kind of piece," Kim offered.

"I think that would just get too confusing," I answered, not wanting to expand the kits before we'd had a chance to examine some of the relationships that they were intended to illustrate.

Kim acquiesced. Or so I thought. We were well into an orienting activity of identifying some of the relationships among the pieces (framed in terms of "trading" certain parts for other parts) when Kim came up to me and asked if it would be all right if she were to make her own purple thirty-seconds. I agreed and promised a sheet of purple if she reminded me at the end of the school day. She didn't forget.

Euclidian Shapes *vs.* Fractal Forms. Another way to make the point introduced in the previous section (about descriptions of learning) is to suggest that the Euclidean images, such as lines, arrows, and finite regions, are not very useful for illustrating the dynamics of learning. Rather, this phenomenon seems to call for more nuanced, scale-independent images, such as fractal forms.

As introduced in chapter 2, fractal images are created through recursively elaborative processes—a sort of feedback loop in which the output of one stage becomes the input of the next. These processes are constantly transformative, yet they preserve a "memory" of the previous stages.

Different fractal images are suited to describing various aspects of learning phenomena. In particular, a tree-like fractal image, based on branches branching into branches, is useful for characterizing emergent spaces of possibility, as suggested in the previous section. A more networked structure, created as nodes collect into grander nodes (as introduced in chap. 4) is useful for characterizing both knowledge-producing systems (including brains, social groupings, and the network of internet users)[*] and the systems of knowledge produced (such as language, mathematics, and science).

These sorts of images share a nested structure (see the image on p. 56), reflecting the manner in which

SIMPLE *versus* COMPLICATED?

If we could measure what every particle is doing with complete certainty, we could calculate everything that has happened and will happen using **Newtonian physics**. For phenomena with many parts, calculations must be based on gross averages. That is, to understand complicated phenomena, we use **statistical analysis**.

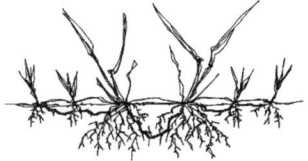

COMMON ROOTS: Newtonian mechanics and statistical regression are both organized around the assumption that the universe and everything in it is machine-like and therefore ultimately predictable and manipulable.

[*] See William H. Calvin, *How brains think: Evolving intelligence, then and now* (New York: Basic Books, 1996).

learning systems are embedded in other learning systems. For example, in terms of brain organization, neurons cluster into minicolumns, minicolumns into macrocolumns, macrocolumns into cortical areas, and cortical areas into the cerebral hemispheres. Each of these levels of organization has its own particular coherence, and is simultaneously a subsystem of a grander learning agent, a learning agent, and a collective of learning agents. Subsequent nested, overlapping, and interlaced systems include social collectives, disciplinary realms, legal systems, economies, cultures, species, and the biosphere. In some sense—and to varying extents—each of these systems is implicated in any classroom event, such as the account presented in this chapter.

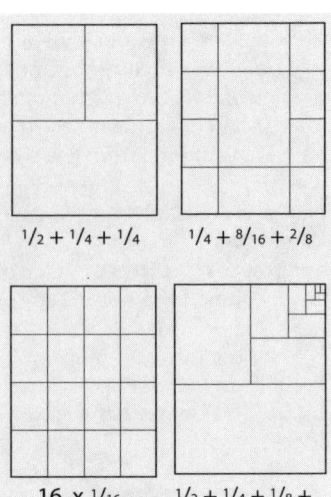

$\frac{1}{2} + \frac{1}{4} + \frac{1}{4}$ $\frac{1}{4} + \frac{8}{16} + \frac{2}{8}$

16 x $\frac{1}{16}$ $\frac{1}{2} + \frac{1}{4} + \frac{1}{8} + ...$

Over the next few lessons, we continued to explore the relationships among the pieces in the Fraction Kits, focusing mainly on questions that asked students to find different ways of assembling a particular amount (e.g., What are some of the ways you can cover one fourth of a page?), of comparing amounts (e.g., Which is greater, $\frac{3}{4}$ or $\frac{13}{16}$?), and of combining pieces (e.g., What do you get if you put together $\frac{2}{4}$ and $\frac{1}{16}$ and $\frac{1}{8}$?). In every instance, I started the explorations with a few sample questions and then, upon a brief discussion of how they might be answered, invited students to make up their own questions.

Most students chose to approach the task by reorganizing and trading pieces, making what appeared to be more or less random arrangements of pieces that covered a whole page.

(A few examples are illustrated above.) On my prompt, they also wrote addition and multiplication statements to describe and record what they had done.

Other students didn't use the kits at all, choosing instead to list addition statements (for example, $\frac{1}{2} + \frac{1}{2} = 1$, or $\frac{3}{4} + \frac{2}{8} = 1$). Kim offered a solution that went beyond the pieces and the chart: "You can make a whole by adding one half to one fourth to one eighth to one sixteenth to one thirty-second to one sixty-fourth .... Well, you just keep doing that forever."

One learner, Alex, invented a strategy for recording these combinations that was not only faster, but that could be used to generate *every* possible combination of pieces. He created a table (a small portion of which is shown below) to systematically list all possibilities.

Normal Distributions *vs.* Power Law Distributions. As discussed in chapter 3, one of the more prominent mathematical constructs within discussions of education is the normal distribution. Its familiar bell-shaped curve is used to illustrate the manner in which, for many phenomena, data points cluster around a central mean and taper off rapidly in a predictable way on either side of that value. For example, the average height of an adult woman in a specific geographic

1	$\frac{1}{2}$	$\frac{1}{4}$	$\frac{1}{8}$	$\frac{1}{16}$
1				
	2			
	1	2		
	1	1	2	
	1	1	1	2
	1	1		4
	1		4	
	1		3	2
	1		2	4

region might be 1.7 m. Most adult women would be within a few centimeters of that height; a few would be slightly further from the mean, and a very small number would be still further. But no one would be 0.3 m or 21 m tall.

The sensibleness of such examples is one of the reasons that many researchers across domains have tended to assume that virtually all variable phenomena must obey a normal distribution. It is only recently, with the study of complex dynamics, that this assumption has been revealed as untenable. For instance, consider the questions, "How powerful is a normal earthquake?" and "What is the average wealth of a person on this planet?"

These queries actually make little or no sense. On the matter of earthquakes, it turns out that minor tremors are pretty much constantly occurring, and these are so frequent and numerous that if they were to be averaged with more major events, a "normal quake" or "representative quake" would be imperceptible to unaided senses. On the matter of net worth, wealth is so disproportionately distributed in the world that a simple average provides absolutely no useful information.

Earthquakes and wealth—along with market fluctuations, skirmishes and wars, moon craters, fads, ecological disasters, human heart rhythms, forest fires, avalanches, city sizes, internet hubs, epidemics, election results, and other complex phenomena *including learning events*—aren't normally distributed at all. Rather, they follow power law distributions.

Power law distributions are useful for describing both the structures and the dynamics of complex learning systems. Structurally, as illustrated by the nested image on page 56, as one moves from grand learning systems (like the biosphere) through smaller learning systems (like species, individuals, bodily organs, or cells), numbers increase exponentially. Each level of organization introduces a new multiplier and so, with reference to the figure in the margin, there are innumerable cells (on the left of the curve) that cluster in varied ways to give rise to relatively few grander learning systems.

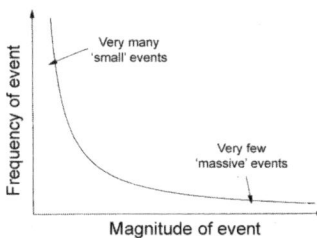

A graph of a *power law distribution* illustrates that, for certain phenomena, there is a very high likelihood of a minor event and a very much smaller probability of a really massive happening. Such events include avalanches, power outages, skirmishes, and shifts in worldviews—all of which are complex events.

With regard to the dynamics of complex phenomena, power law distributions are evident in the fact that there is a very high likelihood of minor events (these can actually be pretty much constant) and a very much smaller probability of really massive happenings. For complex (i.e., learning) events, there is no such thing as a "normal" or "typical" happening, fragment, member, or adaptive instance. There are no normal-sized cities, there is no representative historical moment, there are no typical catastrophes, there is no average insight, there are no characteristic learning episodes.*

This point shouldn't be surprising. What may be a little unexpected is an assumption that researchers had been making for nearly two centuries: the bell-shaped normal distribution could be applied to any measurable phenomenon, including all those mentioned in the preceding paragraphs. This situation has been especially true in discussions of schooling.

However, it would be unfair to say that educators have been oblivious to power law distributions. For example, it's long been known that there is no such thing as a normal question—an insight that was developed by Benjamin Bloom in his "hierarchy of question types" (see the sidebar).** Bloom illustrated his insight with a pyramid, which actually approximates a power law distribution—that is, there tend to be very many lower-level, knowledge-seeking questions and very few, higher-level evaluation sorts of questions.

On its own, this is probably an important intuition. Unfortunately, it has tended to be taken up in a mechanistic rather than an organic way. For decades, educators have been encouraged to pre-select questions from all levels in their efforts to structure efficient routes through topics and subject areas. In other words, one Euclidean image (a pyramid of questions) has been linked to another (a linear lesson).

Reinterpreted in complexity terms, one might think in terms of a power law distribution of questions being linked to a non-linear branching structure. In this structure different levels of questions would be expected to emerge, provided that the contexts were sufficiently rich and were structured in ways that allowed ideas to interact.

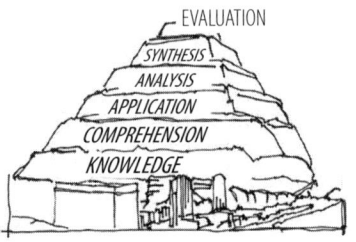

First published in the 1950s, "Bloom's Taxonomy of Question Types" is used to classify questions according to their difficulty and frequency. The simplest and most common questions are at the bottom; the rarest and most complicated are at the the top.

The pyramid shape is meant to suggest that one must build to higher level questions, and it has been used to underpin lesson planning strategies that begin with many repetitive exercises and move toward one or two more demanding questions at the end.

This mechanistic interpretation is unfortunate but not entirely inappropriate. Genuine inquiry seems to obey this sort of dynamic of questioning.

* For an accessible introduction to power law distributions, see Mark Buchanan, *Ubiquity: The science of history . . . or why the world is simpler than we think* (London: Phoenix, 2000).
** See, e.g., Benjamin S. Bloom, *Taxonomy of educational objectives, Handbook I: The cognitive domain* (New York: David McKay, 1956).

The teaching event presented in this chapter can be used to illustrate this point. Most of the questions and tasks were relatively simple, but they were sufficient to prompt higher-level questions and insights. On this count, the range and non-linearity of questions posed might actually be taken as one piece of (necessary, but not sufficient) evidence that the classroom community was a complex knowledge-producing unity.

Prompted by these events, I wondered what might happen if the strategy of using a chart were introduced to the rest of the class.

After calling for the students' attention, I presented my version of Alex's idea, being careful to represent the chart only as a recording tool. I was hoping that students' use of the charts might support understandings of the relationships among fractional amounts, and so didn't want them to treat it in an instrumental way.

The idea was readily taken up. A sort of friendly competition quickly emerged as one group of students posed the challenge of generating a longer list than Alex's. Unhappy with the challenge, Alex soon convinced them that he had already generated the complete list until a member of the second group, Lynn, suggested that it might be possible to use subtraction as well. (Negative numbers hadn't been addressed, and in fact the topic was several years away in the formal curriculum.) Several new possibilities were quickly generated before Lynn added, "Hey, we can use parts of pieces too!"—noting, for example, that a combination of 3 fourth-pieces and a half of a half-piece covered the whole page. Not long after that, a group thought to combine negative fractions with fractions of fractions, giving rise to even more diverse (not to mention conceptually sophisticated) combinations.

Over the course of this 50-minute block, then, these 8- and 9-year-olds were adding, subtracting, multiplying, and dividing fractions although my original intention with this activity was only to give them a little practice with some basic additive relationships—reminding me that students' learning always spills beyond the teacher's intentions.

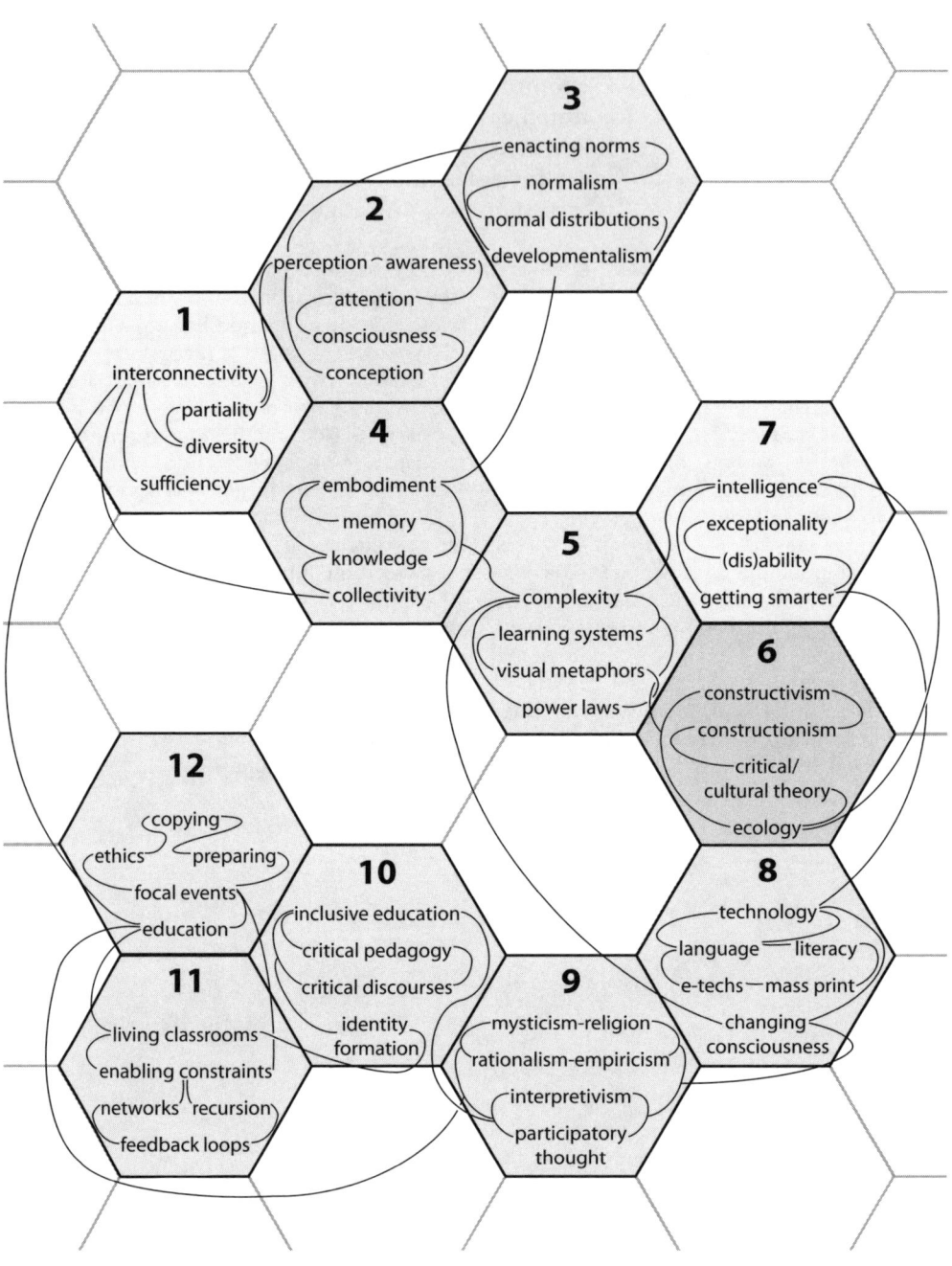

6   **Learning Positions**

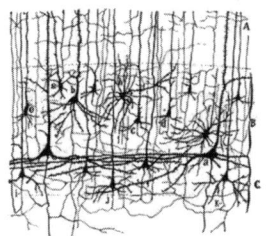

*

It was my first year of teaching and I was assigned a course outside my areas of expertise: Grade 8 Science. As I paged through the curriculum guide, I realized that what I knew of the topics barely went beyond what I had learned when I was in 8th grade, some 10 years earlier.

But I wasn't worried. I'd been armed with a curriculum manual that parsed the concepts into bite-sized lessons and a teacher's guide that provided supplementary information and sample tests. Just a matter of sequential presentation of facts, some relevant assignments, and regular quizzes. Couldn't be easier.

After all, the courses I had taken on theories of learning laid everything out for me. What really mattered, I'd heard, were clearly stated "behavioral learning objectives," which comprised intended outcomes, structured activities, and performance criteria to let me know whether students had learned what they were supposed to learn. Simple. Mechanical.

Even so, things quickly fell to pieces. The first unit of study was astronomy, the first topic was the solar system, and the first objective had to

do with explaining day and night in terms of planetary dynamics. I prepared an impeccable plan and presented a flawless lecture. Students responded appropriately. They were attentive, asked questions, copied notes. But when it came time to determine if the learning objectives had been met, something strange happened. It began with my asking, "What's wrong with the statement, 'The sun rises in the morning'?"

"Nothing. That's when it rises," one student offered.

Another disagreed: "Not always. Sometimes it rises at night."

"In some places it doesn't rise at all," still another elaborated.

It went on. Far from objecting to my statement's underlying premise that the sun is revolving around a stationary earth, the students didn't even seem aware there was an issue. In spite of my watertight explanation, completed only moments earlier, it was easier for everyone to interpret daybreak in terms of a sun that rises than in terms of an earth that spins us out of its own shadow.

* More than a century old, this representation of neurons in the cerebral cortex was drawn by Santiago Ramón y Cajal. Commonly identified as the "father of neuroscience," Cajal broke with scientific consensus to argue that the brain is not a continuous web, but made up of billions of interconnected tree-like neurons.

6.1 Correspondence Theories

As developed in chapter 5, until quite recently, most discussions of how humans learn were developed around two key, but problematical assumptions. First, processes of learning were seen in terms of mechanical, cause–effect dynamics that were understood as predictable and easily manipulated. Second, the words *individual* and *learner* were treated as synonymous and interchangeable. It was taken for granted that all learning happens in the heads of individuals.

These two assumptions actually underpin two theories of learning that seem radically different—namely *behaviorisms* and *mentalisms*. The former is focused on measurable physical actions, the latter on unseeable mental representations.

On the surface, these emphases might seem contradictory. However, as will be developed, there are some deep similarities. In particular, in both perspectives, it is assumed that the measure of learning is the fidelity of the match or *correspondence* between subjective (internal) models and objective (external) reality. For this reason, both behaviorisms and mentalisms are known as *correspondence theories*.

Behaviorisms. Through most of the 20th century, the most influential theory of learning within education was behaviorist psychology. Its orienting assumption was that, to be scientific, researchers and teachers should focus on what is observable and measurable. With regard to learning, that meant paying attention to overt behaviors and, by implication, avoiding the temptation to hypothesize about what might be going on in someone's head. What matters in this frame is what someone is doing (which is observable), not what someone is thinking (which isn't).

To be clear, behaviorists didn't dispute the importance of what's going on in the head. They simply regarded mental events as subjective, idiosyncratic, and inaccessible. In contrast, physical behaviors are objectively measurable. More importantly, one can observe the impact of specific interventions (e.g., rewards and punishments) on behavior, which means that one can begin to conduct some carefully controlled

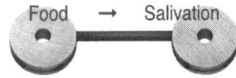

CLASSICAL CONDITIONING

1: Natural Association

Food → Salivation

2: Conditioning Process

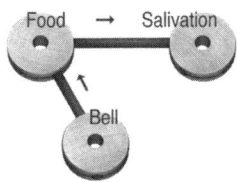

Food → Salivation

Bell

3: Conditioned Association

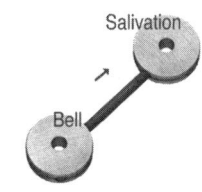

Salivation

Bell

Behaviorism refers to those theories of learning that are concerned with associations between discernible stimuli and particular *observable* behaviors.

Two mechanisms for forming such associations are illustrated. On the left is a case of "classical conditioning." A neutral stimulus (a bell) comes to elicit the same involuntary response (salivation) as a non-neutral stimulus (food). On the right, an instance of "operant

OPERANT CONDITIONING

1: Desired Association

Command: "SPEAK!" → Barking

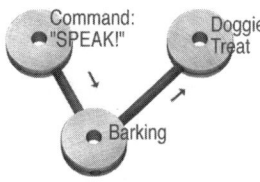

2: Conditioning Process

Command: "SPEAK!"   Doggie Treat

Barking

3: Conditioned Association

Command "SPEAK!"

Barking

conditioning" is illustrated. A reward (doggie treat) is used to increase the probability that a stimulus (the command "Speak") will elicit a particular voluntary response (barking).

Such learning mechanisms can be used to create long and complicated chains of behavior. This theory of learning underpins teaching practices that focus on mastery of isolated skills which have been linearly sequenced.

* The most famous and frequently cited of such claims can be found on page 104 of John B. Watson, *Behaviorism* (New York: Transaction, 1924/1988).

experiments. Of course, for controlled experimentation to make sense, one must also assume that behavior is rule-bound and the laws that govern activity can be determined.

The behaviorist research agenda was thus developed around efforts to train agents to make certain, desired associations through the careful administration of rewards, promises of reward, punishments, and threats of punishment. In other words, it was assumed that there was a logical and manipulable correspondence between internal associations and external events (see the sidebars). Not surprisingly, behaviorism tends to frame recommendations for training in terms of feedback mechanisms, well-sequenced and incremental conditioning structures, and clearly articulated goals—in short, complete control of the learning situation. Given such control, the early authors of the theory were known to assert that any *normal* learner could be trained to fulfill virtually any role.* This sort of claim is telling as it reveals an assumption that learners are interchangeable. The implicit suggestion was that the only thing that matters is experience.

Behaviorist research met with some impressive early successes. For example, it was demonstrated that humans and non-humans could be trained to perform feats that surpassed typical capacities: rats could master mazes, birds could make distinctions between images, cats could develop fear of mice, chimpanzees could make use of symbols, baboons could organize objects by abstract categories, humans could overcome irrational phobias, almost any creature could be trained to associate normally unrelated events (like ringing bells and lunchtime). In the process, behaviorists soundly demonstrated some important and enduring principles of learning, including that context is always critical and that conscious awareness is not always necessary for learning to happen.

Despite its successes and insights, behaviorism alone proved to be an inadequate basis for schooling. Among its shortcomings are the following:

• the contexts of schooling are simply too diverse and fluid to permit the sorts of rigid controls and monitoring required for effective administration of training regimes;

- most behaviorists did not distinguish between non-declarative and declarative memory systems (see chap. 4, esp. images on pp. 55 & 60), thus failing to recognize that different parts of the brain and widely varied dynamics were at work;
- the recent realization that human imaginings can be as powerful as actual actions (recall the discussion of mirror neurons in chap. 4) would suggest that a strict focus on overt behaviors is inadequate;
- the human tendency toward novel activities and interpretations (e.g., by combining elements in ways that have never been combined before) would frustrate the desire to train specific associations;
- behaviorism tends to ignore biological predispositions, working from the premise that such base tendencies can be overcome by conditioning (which turns out to be true over the short term, but often fails over longer periods as natural inclinations re-emerge);
- the framework rests on the premise that the relationship between experience and learning is linear and predictable whereas the evidence suggests a more nonlinear and emergent relationship.

The message of these points is not that behaviorism is "wrong." As already noted, its principles have been applied with great success in many situations involving humans. These include suppression of debilitating phobias, inhibitions, and other obstructions to social engagement. If the target behavior can be isolated and the training regime carefully controlled, the outcomes can be impressive. However, once again, such isolation and control are simply not appropriate to contemporary contexts of schooling.

Despite thorough critiques, many elements of behaviorism continue to be represented in schooling practices. In particular, two places where behaviorist sensibilities continue to be prominent are lesson planning and classroom management. For example, the practice of organizing mandated curricula around "learning outcomes" and "performance indicators"

When it comes to formal education, the major issue with behaviorist theories of learning is not that they are *inaccurate*, it's that they're *inadequate*.

In fact, these accounts of learning offer some important and effective-principles: Be focused, be strategically repetitive, be consistent, limit the amount of information, realize that associations are being made on implicit levels. On these counts, advertisers tend to do a much better job at exploiting behaviorist insights than educators, especially in their efforts to prompt consumers to make implicit associations among their products and success, normality, popularity, vibrancy, freedom, sexiness, and so on.

But these aims of advertising also highlight some of the limitations of behaviorism for teaching where the goal isn't mindless consumption or programmed action, but the development of capacities to gather, interpret, and weigh information.

(or similar phrases) is actually rooted in the earlier "behavioral objectives" emphasis that was prevalent in the 1970s. The explicit mechanisms of teaching are different, but the implicit associations are very much the same, including the mechanistic assumption that teaching *causes* learning.

The same mindset underpins discussions of classroom management, a topic that is often addressed in terms of controlling student behavior through regimes of reward and punishment. Indeed, "behavioral modification" programs are typically presented as fair-minded, even-handed, and ideologically neutral, but their implicit biases are evident in words such as *management*, *order*, and *control*. An assumed cause–effect logic infuses the belief that teachers can (and must) *regulate* everything that happens in the classroom.

These emphases might be contrasted with contemporary discussions of collectivity, in which notions of linearity and causality are rejected along with the implicit us/them separation that positions the teacher as the controller and students as the things controlled. By contrast, mutual respect and shared responsibility are foregrounded. As well, "good teaching" is recast not in terms of the separate tasks of managing behavior and managing learning, but in terms of structuring experiences that engage, stimulate, and challenge—in brief, that promote individual and group self-regulation.

Mentalisms. Behaviorism's predominance in the 20th century within the field of education is something of an historical anomaly. Most discussions of learning—prior to and since behaviorism's reign—have been concerned with trying to understand how the mind works. Among these discussions, by far the most prominent perspective is that learning is a matter of assembling an inner representation (or mental model) of an external world. In brief, it is assumed that the head contains a map, image, or other sort of facsimile that *corresponds* to the real world.

There is a range of theories that begin with this premise (i.e., that learning is about building mental models), and they tend to differ on their core metaphors. Historically, for example, the imagined process of assembling inner representations was understood in terms of sculpting, painting, writing, telegraphing, photographing, or filming an outer reality and, typically, the choice of imagery was reflective of the most current technology. More recently, the most common metaphor across mentalist theories is the computer. In this frame, internal representations are cast in terms of digital encodings in neurological networks rather than internal images or text. This particular perspective on learning serves as the commonsensical backdrop for most current discussions of schooling. It is manifest in such common phrases as *internalizing* or *inputting* information, *storing* and *processing* knowledge, expanding one's *database*, and *outputting* ideas.

Although the core metaphors might differ across mentalist theories, their common assumptions are revealed in phrases such as *taking things in* and *acquiring understandings*. To most hearers, such phrasings would sound unproblematic—in spite of the obvious fact that no-thing actually moves from the outside to the inside in moments of learning. Nothing is *taken in*, *gotten*, *picked up*, or *acquired*.

Even though the notion of taking things in is completely untenable, it continues to prevail. For example, at the moment, one of the most popular theories of learning revolves around discussions of learning/learner "types," "styles," or "modalities." Such constructs as *visual versus auditory learners,* or *concrete versus abstract thinkers* rely on the assumption that learning is a matter of filtering knowledge from the outside to the inside in order to build internal models. It follows that theories of learning styles aren't theories of learning at all; rather, they are extensions of mentalist assumptions. Although it is almost certainly the case that different learners make varied uses of the sensory modalities—and that different people think in different ways—such discussions often reduce the complexities of learning to simple prescriptions for teaching (which, of course, might be their appeal).

The major critique of mentalist theories is not focused on the assumed mechanisms or modes of learning but on the core notion of internal representations. When you peer inside someone's head, you are not going to

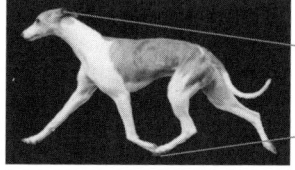

Mentalism refers to a broad range of theories that rely on the premise that learning is a matter of building an internal model or representation of an external reality.

Historically, these theories have drawn on prevailing technologies as sources of descriptive analogies. Early in the 20th century, for example, movie-making was used: eyes were seen as cameras, memory as recorded images, imagination and thought as projection, and so on. (Note that for this interpretation to make sense,

find any models of the outside world. Just as learning is not a matter of taking things in, understanding is not a matter of assembling raw materials into a sensible edifice of knowledge. The actual situation is clearly something much more complex than that.

Common Ground. Behaviorist and mentalist theories might appear to be opposites, given their radical disagreement on what should serve as the focus of attention in discussions of learning. However, in terms of underlying premises, they are very much alike.

In particular, both rely on a series of dichotomies, including internal/external, self/other, individual/collective, and knower/knowledge. Most significantly, these theories assume that the mental is distinct from the physical—an ancient belief that was already well established in the writings of the ancient Greeks, among others. The difference between focusing on external behaviors and internal representations, then, is more a matter of emphasis than of mindset. Ultimately, both are concerned with *correspondences* between mental constructs and physical worlds. Hence, although they are usually presented as opposites, they're better thought of as flip sides of the same coin. The simple fact is that both lines of thought seem to co-exist comfortably in most textbooks, curriculum guides, and classrooms. In fact, a more recent school of thought known as *neobehaviorism* concerns itself with both stimulus–response events (the domain of behaviorisms) and brain-based associations that arise through such events (the domain of mentalisms).

With regard to classroom practices, both frames tend to cast schooling as a linear process, one that seeks to control inner representations by minimizing ambiguity. Good teaching thus tends to be perceived in terms of highly structured curriculum sequences and instructional procedures. It is highly technical work, involving abilities to isolate factors, monitor circumstances, manipulate causes, and evaluate the correspondence between mental construct and physical reality.

As with the underlying theory of learning, this correspondence conception of teaching (and learning to teach) is merely a complicated, but not a complex one.

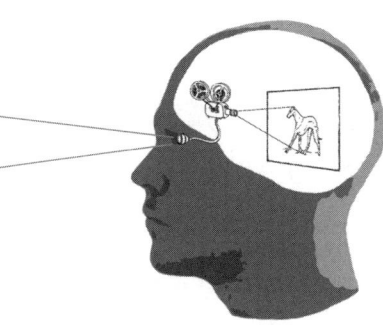

there has to be an observer inside the observer—and, presumably, an observer inside the observer inside the observer. This issue is often referred to as *cascading homunculi*, meaning "endless sequence of little men.")

More recently, electronic technologies have been taken up, leading to a different (but similarly troublesome) set of metaphors for cognition.

There is an appreciation of the difficulty of the task, but this difficulty tends to be interpreted in terms of classical mechanics. So conceived, the teachers' principal worries are with order, planning, prediction of outcomes, management of behavior, evaluation, and so on.

To put it bluntly, this desire to predetermine the outcomes of learning is untenable. Correspondence theories such as behaviorisms and mentalisms might seem reasonable and compelling, but in fact they ignore the complexities of human cognition and, in the process, oversimplify the complexities of teaching.

"Any suggestions?" I asked, after reporting on my failed lesson to colleagues in the staffroom.

I have since learned that posing such a question among a group of teachers is, in essence, an invitation for more advice than I might want.

Another science teacher began: "Explanations don't work for kids this age. You should probably do a demo—flashlight, volleyball, simple. You could also do phases of the moon with the same tools."

"You'd still be doing most of the explaining," another teacher countered. "You should put the problem to them. See what kind of theories and demonstrations they come up with when they put their heads together."

The vice principal interrupted: "So what's the point of teaching the concept in the first place? It obviously doesn't make much difference to their lives if they think one way or the other. The important thing to be teaching is the scientific method. How does science deal with these kinds of questions. The real issue isn't whether they know that the sun doesn't go around the earth. It's that they're supposed to have a sense of where these ideas come from and how to prove them."

"Still missing the point, if you ask me," another teacher countered. "The real issue here is how western science butts up against other ways of thinking."

It went on. By the time the lunch hour conversation turned to a different topic, I was even more at sea than when it began. And it didn't help when I sat down with the curriculum guide that evening to think through what I'd do the next day. As I reviewed suggestions for demonstrations and discussions around the topic of the earth's movement about the sun, it seemed that *all* of my colleagues were correct. Experiential, social, cultural and other elements were clearly represented. Teaching 8th grade science wasn't quite as simple as I had anticipated.

6.2 Coherence Theories

Over the past forty years, a number of alternatives to correspondence theories have risen to prominence in the educational literature. Dubbed *coherence theories*, these perspectives on human learning begin by rejecting the assumption that there are radical divisions between bodies and minds, selves and others, individuals and collectives, knowers and knowledge, and humans and non-humans.

There is a range of coherence theories, depending on the specific interest of the theorist. Among the foci are individual understanding, social collectivity, cultural knowledge, and environmental integrity. Despite this diversity of interest, the theories have some deep compatibilities, including the following:

• they all highlight the *vibrancy* of their particular interests, usually by invoking bodily and/or ecosystemic metaphors (e.g., body of knowledge, student body, body politic);

• descriptions of systemic dynamics tend to be phrased in terms of adaptation and evolution (i.e., notions rooted in biology) rather than cause-and-effect (i.e., notions drawn from physics);

• they focus on *fit* (coherence) rather than *match* (correspondence) in their accounts of how agents or ideas arise and persist, arguing that the criterion for survival is not *optimality/efficiency* but *adequacy/sufficiency* (if something works, it will probably endure).

More generally, these theories are focused on the manner in which "agents" in a system must cohere in order for the grander system to remain viable. The nature of the agents depends on the system under examination and might be a set of ideas (as in the case of an individual's understandings), customs and laws (for a society), species (for an ecosystem), and so on. The major point of departure of these *coherence theories* from earlier theories of learning is that they are organized around the assumption that what really matters is internal coherence. For a system to be viable, its parts must be compatible with one another—and it really doesn't matter if they match, reflect, represent, model, or otherwise correspond to a realm beyond the system.

This point might seem opaque. We proceed here with brief introductions to some of the more prominent coherence theories, illustrated with the example of the earth's movement.

Constructivisms. Constructivist theories tend to be concerned with the sense that individuals make of the world. For the most part, current discussions of constructivism within education are rooted in the work

MIND *versus* BODY?

What matters is the match between outer reality and inner models of reality. Hence we must focus on the **mental**.	Only overt physical activities can be observed and measured. Hence we must deal strictly with **behavior**.

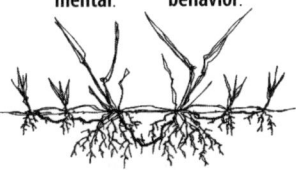

COMMON ROOTS: Commonly, mental is assumed to be separate from physical. Hence, learners are thought to be isolated and insulated from one another; learning is seen as a matter of internalizing a pregiven, external reality.

of French biopsychologist, Jean Piaget—a point that is somewhat ironical. Piaget never referred to himself as a constructivist in his written work (although he did mention it once during a public debate).

Constructivism can be difficult to understand because the central metaphor of construction tends to be associated with building, erecting, and assembling. In other words, the word *construct* itself seems to be pointing toward a correspondence theory of learning (in which it is assumed there is an inner model that corresponds to an outer reality) rather than a coherence theory.

The issue here is actually one of translation. Piaget used the French word *construire*, which can also be translated as "to construe." For most English-speakers, this translation is more easily fitted to what Piaget had in mind, so we use it here.

Piaget's project might be described as an effort to construe personal learning through the metaphor of emergent biological forms. He suggested the development of understandings was analogous to the growth of living systems, and so his theory is developed around principles of contingency, adequacy, adaptation, and fitness. In brief, Piaget argued that learning is a continuous process of updating one's sense of the world as prompted by new experiences. The learner is constantly construing and reconstruing in an effort to maintain a coherent system of interpretation.

There is an important shift from correspondence theories here. Piaget suggested that what really matters is coherence among personal interpretations, *not* correspondence between internal constructs and external realities. Such a shift is profoundly useful for making sense of how individuals who have very similar experiences to one another can interpret them so differently. One's entire history of experience and interpretation contributes to the manner in which a new event is understood.

Another way to say this is that, for constructivists, the biological body is not a structure through which one learns, but a structure that learns. Individual learning is not a brain-based phenomenon, but an ongoing process of embodying one's history. For this

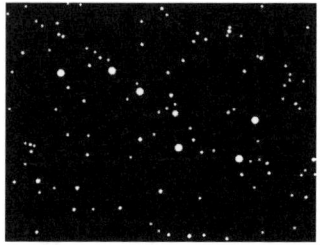

Constructivist theories are focused on individual sense-making.

In addition to the core images and metaphors mentioned on the previous page (i.e., living bodies, adaptive dynamics, and fitness-seeking), these theories invoke the notion of *construal*.

To elaborate, when faced with a strew of experiences, artifacts, or interpretive possibilities, humans tend to construe some manner of coherence. The process is not unlike what happens when images are discerned among the stars where there are no distinct forms in any objective sense. Such construals will be stable until the knower encounters incompatible experiences that force some sort of reconstrual.

reason, bodily action is not seen as a demonstration of internalized understandings; rather bodily action *is* understanding.

There are many practical implications. One of them is that constructivists do not regard children as "incomplete" beings. Rather, all knowers are seen as having adequate or sufficient understandings for their immediate circumstances. The aim of education, then, is not to guide learners toward completion, but to provide them with experiences that challenge and enlarge their understandings.

Another consequence is that the notion of *errors* has to be reconsidered. Within correspondence theories, errors are understood as mismatches between internal and external worlds and so, as this line of thought goes, when one arises, the teacher needs to correct the student's mistake. Constructivists reject that idea. For them, all actions are rooted in a coherent interpretive system and so, what is taken as an error on the social level is not an error on the individual level. That changes the teacher's responsibility. It is not about "fixing" a student's error, but about trying to make sense of the web of associations that render the interpretation a sensible one. Working from an appreciation that the student's action was part of a coherent worldview, the teacher would attempt to involve the learner in new sets of experiences that might support the construal of more appropriate interpretations.

Of course, to expect a teacher to keep track of the sense that 30 individuals are making seems a bit unreasonable. For this reason, although it might provide some provocative insights into how people learn, constructivism really should not be construed as a theory of teaching. In fact, far from serving as a theory of education, constructivism offers more advice on what teachers *can't* do than what they *can* do. Specifically, teachers cannot cause students to learn what they want students to learn, which would seem to undermine the project of formal education. At best, teaching is cast as a cycle of construals: the teacher tries to construe the student's construals so that a new set of experiences might be organized in order to prompt a new round of construals.

This point is an important one. Most of the original theoretical work on constructivist theories was done in French and organized around the word *construire*—which can be translated as either *construct* or *construe*, words with quite different meanings.

Close readings of source documents* reveal that the intended meaning is more toward *construe*, with its senses of flexibility and contingency (versus the more deliberate and preplanned associations that typically go along with the English word *construct*). This meaning is much closer to the word's Latin root, *struere*, "to spread" (which is also the root of *strew*, *destroy*, and *industry*).

* See, e.g., Jean Piaget, *La construction réel chez l'enfant* (Paris: Delachaux & Niestle, 1952/1990).

What might a constructivist deem important when teaching about the concepts of night and day?

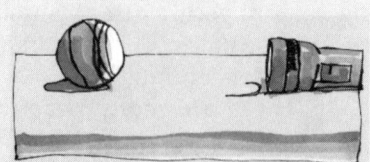

Working from the premise that personal knowledge is anchored to one's experiences in the world, the teacher whose practice is informed by constructivism might begin by examining the reasons someone might hold a geocentric ("earth-centered") rather than heliocentric ("sun-centered") conception of the earth-sun system.

In this case the major reason is obvious. It feels as though we're standing on solid and unmoving ground, and so it looks more like the sun is moving across the sky than the earth is spinning. As such, it's unlikely that a straightforward presentation of a heliocentric model—no matter how impeccably described—will do much to interrupt well-established habits of thinking. A more appropriate emphasis might be a series of activities designed to highlight the relationships among the movements of the earth, sun, and other bodies.

For example, the connection between earth's rotation and sunrise might be explored with a ball and a flashlight. This activity might in turn be elaborated for subsequent topics, such as seasons (by tipping the globe appropriately) and lunar phases (by introducing a smaller ball as the moon). The intention here is to involve learners in a coherent set of experiences that not only support certain, desired interpretations, but that can be extended and linked to other interpretations.

In each case, students would be asked to express their observations and to offer possible explanations for what is noticed. Such articulations enable sense-making and, at the same time, allow the teacher some insight into students' construals so that subsequent teaching events can be appropriately structured.

Constructionisms. Also known as "social constructivisms," constructionist theories are concerned more with interpersonal dynamics and collective activity than with personal construals. These theories focus on the sorts of phenomena that constructivists tend to set aside as context or circumstance, including language, social status, cultural background, and disciplinary knowledge.

The major point of departure from constructivist theories is an extension of the notion of a "cognitive unity." Constructionists do not regard the individual as the locus of learning but as a learning system within a grander learning system. For the constructionist, human cognition is diffuse, distributed, and collective. In this frame, "mind" is understood not as an individual possession but as a product of shared human interest that arises in an environment that is both social and physical.

Generally speaking, constructionist theories are concerned with the coherences within small groups (such as pairs of students or classroom groupings) as shared understandings are developed. Much less preoccupied with individual sense-making than constructivist theories, constructionist theories focus on conversation patterns, relational dynamics, social habits, and other collective phenomena. In this frame, cognition is always collective: embedded in, enabled by, and constrained by the social phenomenon of language; caught up in layers of history and tradition; confined by well-established boundaries of acceptability; defined by joint interests, shared assumptions, and common sense.

One of the major strands of constructionist thinking is known as "situated learning." Informed mainly by the work of Russian sociopsychologist Lev Vygotsky, this theory focuses on the processes by which individuals enter into established communities of practice. The theory's central metaphor is one of apprenticeship, through which learning is understood in collective terms of co-participation within and reproduction of the collective. As far as schooling goes, the theory's authors are clear on the point that the theory of situated learning is strictly descriptive and explicative—that is, suited only to the question of how children learn and perpetuate the social role of students.* This delimitation has been ignored by many educational researchers including, for example, some who frame school science or language arts in terms of children apprenticing to be research scientists or professional writers.

Other strands of constructionist thinking are more concerned with the emergence of bodies of knowledge, as opposed to the communities in which these bodies of knowledge arise (for instance, the discipline of *mathematics*, as opposed to community of *mathematicians*). Rather than focusing on social processes, the emphases here include criteria of validation, interpretive scope, and other conceptual issues. As well, these theories tend to address how emphases, methods, and insights in various domains are shaped by language, artifacts and tools, and belief systems and, of course, how knowledge domains come to affect language, artifacts and tools, and belief systems. Applied to classrooms, this strand of discussion has contributed to calls to be explicit about how claims come to be seen as facts

In addition to the core images and metaphors mentioned on page 99 (i.e., living bodies, adaptive dynamics, and fitness-orientation), constructionist theories tend to invoke the notion of *shared labor*, highlighting the manner in which complex knowing is distributed across a web of individuals.

This metaphor was proposed by Lev S. Vygotsky,** whose research was conducted in the Soviet Union in the first half of the 20th century when notions of co-laboring had a certain ideological prominence.

* See, e.g., Jean Lave & Etienne Wenger, *Situated learning: Legitimate peripheral participation* (Cambridge, UK: Cambridge University Press, 1991). They comment that their theory "is not itself an educational form, much less a pedagogical strategy or teaching technique. It is an analytical viewpoint on learning, a way of understanding learning" (p. 40).
** See, e.g., Lev S. Vygotsky, *Thought and language, revised edition* (ed. Alex Kozulin; Cambridge, MA: The MIT Press, 1986).

and truths. For example, a topic that might have once sparked controversy such as negative numbers, interracial marriage, or heliocentrism might be studied both as a category of established knowledge and as an occasion to investigate how knowledge comes to be established.

What might a constructionist highlight in a lesson about night and day?

A possible emphasis is the way that this particular topic might be used to frame the question, "What is science?" For example, through an examination of the shift from geocentric to heliocentric theories, questions might be raised about the way scientific theories are developed, presented, defended, accepted, and rejected. After all, when first proposed, heliocentric theories were scorned by the scientific and non-scientific establishments alike. It might be interesting to contrast this history with that of other once-controversial theories, such as Continental Drift, Evolution, the Gaia Hypothesis, and Complexity Theory—all of which were met with tremendous skepticism, yet all of which have since become part of the scientific mainstream. More broadly, a teacher might want to take on the question, "What does science do?" That is, how does scientific inquiry differ from other modes of thought and research? What are the roles of imagination, discussions, debate, and experiment in science? How might in-class activities reflect the work of scientists, and in what ways do formal educational structures militate against such efforts? How has science exploited and contributed to the development of different tools?

Of course, not all of these topics have to be addressed at once. In fact, they shouldn't be. The important point is that such topics should be a major part of science classes since understandings of these issues are used to separate scientific from non-scientific theories. If a teacher doesn't foreground such topics of discussion and debate, there is a risk of reducing science to a collection of facts to be mastered rather than appreciating it as a specific orientation toward inquiry.

Cultural and Critical Theories of Learning. One of the major shifts in discussions of education over the past several decades has been a "broadening of the conversation."

Through most of the 20th century, the bulk of educational research was focused on individual learning and social contexts and was oriented by theories drawn mainly from psychology and sociology. This shouldn't be terribly surprising. Up until about fifty years ago, most of the professors in colleges and faculties of education were drawn from departments of psychology and sociology. However, through the 1960s and 1970s, as researchers with backgrounds in anthropology and philosophy entered the field in larger numbers, increased attention began to be given to issues such as cultural context and the social implications of schooling.

One might say that the conversation was broadened to include issues of the body politic. And while this part of the conversation is not often associated with constructivist and constructionist theories, it shares the tendency to invoke body-based metaphors and to describe events in terms of evolutionary dynamics. A major difference, however, is that cultural and critical theories tend to delve into issues of morality and ethics—seeking, for example, to uncover the ways that schooling contributes to (or, more hopefully, might interrupt) social stratification, gender roles, and other cultural habits of differentiation. In other words, cultural and critical theories are principally concerned with deeply entrenched habits of interpretation and implicit associations that support social constructions of gender, race, class, sexuality, ability, disability, opportunity, and so on. A parallel focus has to do with the manners in which certain domains, such as mathematics and science, have been given privileged voices in the contemporary academic world. One might say that cultural and critical discourses attempt to shift the topic of conversation from the individual's efforts to shape an understanding of the world to the manners in which the cultural world shapes the understandings of the individual.

For the most part, educational recommendations emerging from these frames tend toward what Brazilian commentator Paulo Freire called *conscientização*—the effort to render explicit the cultural conditions that delimit possible worlds and acceptable identities.* In this project, it is recognized that one cannot draw tidy distinctions among individuals, social groupings, and cultures. Rather, these are understood to be three nested, self-similar levels of one phenomenon and, as such, all three must be addressed simultaneously to effect change. In other words, educationally speaking, it is not enough to offer critique of a specific cultural phenomenon. Rather, following Freire, one must work with individuals and social collectives to consider and embody alternatives. (See chap. 10 for an extended discussion of this topic.)

An issue that emerges as one delves into theories of learning—particularly coherence theories—is that they can't really be separated from one another into tidy and discrete categories.

Rather, strands of thought get wound up in one another and, in the process, are mutually transformative. In terms of an organic image, something more like the tangled and fused limbs of a wisteria is a more fitting image than that of a typical tree.

* Paulo Freire, *Pedagogy of the oppressed* (New York: Seaview, 1971), p. 54.

What might cultural and critical theories have to say about theories of night and day?

Historically, the transition from a geocentric to a heliocentric model of the solar system marked a dramatic transition in western sensibilities. It occurred at the dawn of the scientific era and was accompanied by rapid spreads of capitalism, industrialization, urbanization, and European imperialism.

Cultural and critical theorists might thus be interested in the social and cultural movements that contributed to and that emerged from these sorts of historical convulsions. One might, for example, investigate the impact of a male-dominated, Euro-centric science on global politics and cultural genocides.

Alternatively, one might attend to the contribution of emergent heliocentric models to the growing schism between religion and science. Why couldn't the religious establishment tolerate the theories of Copernicus and Galileo? What was at stake? How is a world structured by religious faith different from one structured by scientific doubt? Or how are these the same?

More pointedly, how has the success of modern science been woven into prevailing worldviews? How are these worldviews enacted or how might they support cultural imperialism, gender inequity, and other social injustices?

In brief, what is being taken for granted in science and in science education, and why should we be wary of these assumptions?

Ecological Theories. Although most commonly used to refer to environmental issues, the word *ecology* actually has a much broader meaning. Derived from the Greek word for household, *oikos*, ecology was coined to refer to the study of relationships.

Within the educational literature, then, ecologically oriented studies of classroom dynamics, community contexts, and other topics that foreground relational issues are quite common. Typically these sorts of studies are readily aligned with one of the theories mentioned above. In particular, body-based metaphors, evolutionary dynamics, and coherence-oriented themes tend to figure prominently. That is, in one sense or another, constructivist, constructionist, and cultural and critical theories can be considered ecological.

Unlike these theories, however, ecological thought also extends into the more-than-human world,* taking into consideration interspecies relationships and planetary dynamics. It is this broader interest that makes it of particular interest to educators. In particular, over the past 50 years, ecological studies have helped to highlight that many—and perhaps most—of the problems and crises that humans now face are rooted in untenable conceptions of the relationship of humans to the more-than-human world. More cogently,

* The phrase is borrowed from David Abram, *The spell of the sensuous: Perception and language in a more-than-human world* (New York: Pantheon, 1996).

ecological theories tend to regard humanity as one species among many in a grand web of relations—that is, as part of a grander body whose cognitive processes are seen by humans as ongoing co-evolutions of species and habitats.

Consider some examples: the ways that energy use and farming practices are contributing to global warming; the growing paranoia over global pandemics involving drug-resistant contagions that can spread at the speed of jet travel; the proliferation of ailments and disabilities (including autism, asthma, and hyperactivity) that appear to be at least in part triggered by environmental contaminants, just to name a few. All of these phenomena are linked to a habit of thinking of the planet in terms of a context to be exploited rather than in terms of a relational web that includes humans.

Given the apparent acceleration of these and other problems, it would seem reasonable to argue that formal education must begin to think in ecological terms. It is thus that ecological theories offer a much-enlarged conception of cognition: rather than being cast as a locatable process or phenomenon, cognition is reinterpreted as a joint participation or mutual effect as agents act together to open up new possibilities. Again, the core theme is one of coherence. To pull together a few themes from this and earlier chapters, *learning* refers to a system's ongoing adaptations that enable it to maintain both its internal coherence and its external coherence. That is, an agent's learning is simultaneously about the its *memory* (i.e., internal co-activities of subagents) and its *knowing* (i.e., the ways its actions are entangled with others' actions in grander systems).

In this sense, a bacterium is a thinking system as is a species and a rainforest. And, insofar as these thinking systems influence one another, humanity participates in their cogitations as they participate in ours. That is, our habits of thought/action are entwined with and implicated in the evolving structures of many other systems. We are, simultaneously, cognitive unities, assemblages of cognitive unities, and agents in grander cognitive unities.

An upshot is that we are caught up in even broader sorts of memory systems than are described in

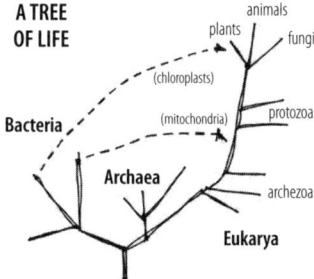

A TREE OF LIFE

animals
plants
fungi
(chloroplasts)
Bacteria
(mitochondria)
protozoa
Archaea
archezoa
Eukarya

Coherence theories of learning all assume an evolutionary dynamic. A mapping of the history and the horizons of a learning system would resemble an evolutionary tree (a partial image of which is shown above) or a phase space (see p. 84). A more complete image would be more fractal, similar to the parsley images on pages 26–27.

chapter 4. Our species' memories, for instance, are largely encoded in DNA, reflecting learning that has occurred over eons. We don't learn how to breathe or to digest in our lifetimes; these are things we are born knowing because they were learned (i.e., they evolved) on the species level. Even more broadly, one might say that humanity is part of the planetary memory.

To reiterate, then, ecological theories make use of the same sorts of logics, metaphors, and images as other coherence theories. Applied specifically to issues of human interest, ecological theories help to explain why it *seems* like our knowledge *corresponds* to an external reality. Our knowledge fits with the world for the same reason that our lungs match the earth's atmosphere: They evolved and are evolving together.

Common Ground. The vital point put forward within coherence theories is that we shouldn't mistake *coherences* for *correspondences*. As is developed in greater detail in Part C, specific assumptions about knowing and learning underpin specific teaching practices, and so a compelling but untenable assumption (like the belief that we're carrying around internal models of an external world) can contribute to ineffective and inappropriate teaching approaches and emphases.

Part C provides a more detailed discussion of the pragmatic implications of coherence theories. In the meantime, there is one consistent theme when it comes to the topic of prompting change. Across coherence theories—whether focused on conscious understandings, unconscious habits, social norms, cultural traditions, worldviews, species, or other complex events—it is argued that a phenomenon will persist until the effort required for the agent to maintain it exceeds the effort required to revise it. And, given that change may entail reworking an extensive web of relations, the effort required may be substantial regardless of how seemingly untenable or unfit an idea or other phenomenon may seem.

Pedagogically, an immediate implication is that events intended to prompt learning must reach a certain "critical mass" in order, first, to interrupt entrenched patterns and, second, to present viable

Ant movements offer a useful analogy for processes of learning.

When searching for food, ants' paths appear aimless and erratic. When food is found, an ant traces its own chemical scent back to the hill, cutting corners as it goes. Other ants join in, and the trail gradually smooths into an almost-straight route.

Human learning on individual and collective levels resembles this process, starting with seemingly random joint explorations and gradually discarding unnecessary "movements" to create efficient routines.

The ants-finding-food analogy can also frame an answer to the question: "Who/what is the learner?"

The knowledge of the food is not in the individual ants. Rather, it exists in their situated and distributed activity. That is, the learner is the collective.

alternatives to existing habits. Effectively, then, prompting change or learning is a matter of disequilibrium, not definitive argument, weight of evidence, or force of will. As an agent of psychological, social, epistemological, and cultural change, the teacher is always looking for an experience, a strategy, or an event that might tip the balance.

What might an ecological theorist highlight in a study of night and day?

One might begin with the question, "What happened to beliefs about humanity's place in the universe when the earth lost its status as the center of creation, demoted to the status of a minor planet around an average star on the edge of a typical galaxy?

Historically, a heliocentric conception of the solar system rose to prominence at the same time as a dramatic reconfiguration of humanity's relationship to the non-human. In particular, there was a change in worldview that contributed to a redefinition of humankind's role in the universe—less as participants in an unfolding creation, and more as detached observers of a believed-to-be stable reality. Planets and clusters

You are here

of stars ceased to be personified and deified as they were reduced to inert lumps and balls of gas whose dynamics are determined by simple physical laws, not deep mysteries. More than a change in objective knowledge is represented here. There is a transformation in the star gazer's personal relationship to the universe.

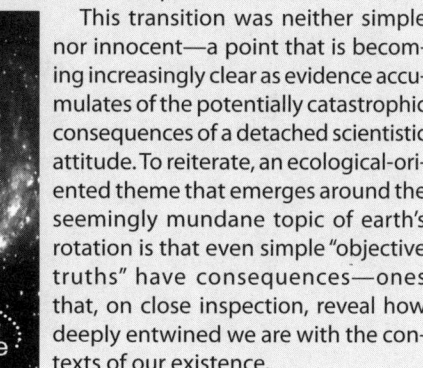

This transition was neither simple nor innocent—a point that is becoming increasingly clear as evidence accumulates of the potentially catastrophic consequences of a detached scientistic attitude. To reiterate, an ecological-oriented theme that emerges around the seemingly mundane topic of earth's rotation is that even simple "objective truths" have consequences—ones that, on close inspection, reveal how deeply entwined we are with the contexts of our existence.

6.3 Complexity Theories

To recap the previous sections, correspondence theories of learning (i.e., behaviorisms and mentalisms) have been subject to extensive critiques over the past several decades, prompted by insights from many domains of inquiry. For example, there is no neurological evidence for the sorts of internal connections, representations, or models that these theories assume. Psychologically speaking, these theories cannot explain how imagination and creativity arise, nor why individuals differ so radically, especially when subjected to the same sorts of training regimes. Sociologically, they don't even begin to account for collective phenomena, including competencies like language and tendencies like altruism.

By contrast, coherence theories (such as constructivisms, constructionisms, cultural and critical theories, and ecological theories) offer insights into these sorts of phenomena. A major contribution of this family of theories is the rejection of assumed separations between mental and physical, self and other, individual and collective, and knower and knowledge. Whether or not such phenomena are *perceived* as distinct, it is suggested, depends on the level of observation. For instance, if one is interested in personal achievement, clearly the focus must be individual performance and so matters of social context and cultural milieu would be minimized or ignored. Alternatively, if one is interested in cultural dynamics, the individual is assumed to be part of the collective.

This attention to multi-level dynamics—*all* of which are relevant in discussions of the purposes and pragmatics of education—marks a dramatic shift in educational thought and practice. Such is the purview of complexity thinking, which in the context of education might be taken as a recommendation to simultaneously consider an array of coherence theories.

To reiterate a point made in chapter 5, complexity thinking is more an umbrella notion than a specific theory. On this count, all of the frames identified in this chapter as "coherence theories" might also be described as specific examples of complexity thinking. What complexity thinking adds, however, is an insistence that these theories and their foci should be addressed at the same time. That is, education is a *transphenomenon* and, as such, requires a *transdisciplinary* attitude. Phrased somewhat differently, education simultaneously affects and is affected by many overlapping, intertwining, and nested learning systems. In addition, with its interest in knowledge-producing systems, complexity prompts attentions toward the possibility that other, unanticipated levels of complex coherence might arise.

In fact, complexity thinking prompts attentions to other levels of evolving coherence that are not typically addressed within discussions of education including, for example, thinking of a class of students as a collective learner rather than merely a collection of learners,

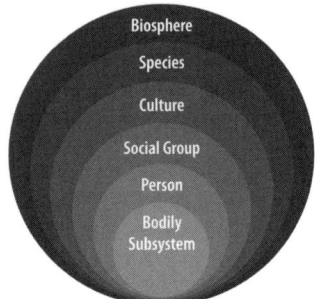

TRANSPHENOMENALITY

To emphasize an important point, complexity thinking is not a *meta-theory*—that is, an explanatory system that exceeds or subsumes all others.

Rather, complexity thinking is an *inter-theory*—that is, a notion that arises when other frames are brought into conversation with one another.* It not only points to the overlapping,

* For an extended discussion of this point, see Brent Davis & Dennis Sumara, *Complexity and education: Inquiries into learning, teaching, and research* (Mahwah, NJ: Lawrence Erlbaum, 2006).

or considering human subsystems as coherent learners in and of themselves. For example, recent research into the immune system reveals it to be capable of selecting, remembering, forgetting, recognizing, erring, and re-covering—knowing and learning—in a complex dance with other (bodily and non-bodily) systems. Neither fully autonomous nor a mere mechanical component of a larger whole, it seems that one's immune system is related to oneself in the same way that the individual is related to the collective. Even more provocative, and turning to the matter of educational relevance, the well-being of one's immune system is inextricably tied to attention span, conscious awareness, and ability to remember—not to mention capacities to interact with others and maintain social relations.

The discussion could be taken to many other levels of complex dynamics from the subcellular through the planetary. Significantly, the point here is *not* that all educators must be consciously aware of or attuned to these learning systems, but that they should be more cognizant of the sorts of qualities that distinguish a complex learning system from a mechanical system. For centuries, educational theory and practice have overlooked or ignored the distinction, opting to cast individuals and other learners as manageable, control-lable entities. For this reason, perhaps more than any other, educators should be attentive to theories and the ways that those theories position them as teachers.

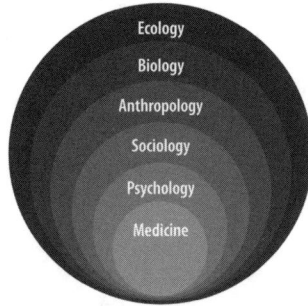

TRANSDISCIPLINARITY

Ecology
Biology
Anthropology
Sociology
Psychology
Medicine

intersecting, and nested aspects of certain dynamic phenomena (facing page), it also highlights how different discourses and disciplines might be understood as profoundly comple-mentary (above image).

Stated more concisely, complexity thinking prompts educators to think in *transphenomenal* terms, requiring a *transdisciplinary* research attitude.

As did the first year, my second year of teaching began with the topic of the earth's orbit around the sun and how an understanding of this mo-tion enables one to make sense of night and day, the seasons, and a range of astronomical observations.

Keen to avoid the "telling" mistake I had com-mitted at the beginning of the previous year, I decided to open the topic by asking the Grade 8 students to account for night and day.

As might be expected, the first answers were anchored to an assumption that the sun was go-ing around the earth. A few students also offered a theory based on earth's rotation.

"How would you go about proving that?" I asked advocates of both opinions. What followed was a discussion for which I wasn't entirely prepared. In particular, it turned out that it is no small feat to demonstrate that the earth is spinning like a top and this detail that I'd treated as a matter of common sense the year before took us into, among other explorations, experiments with Foucault's pendulum and discussions of Occam's razor. In the process, we touched on issues such as the nature of scientific truth, what constitutes "proof," the impact of new insights, the dangers of taking too much for granted, and the paces of change.

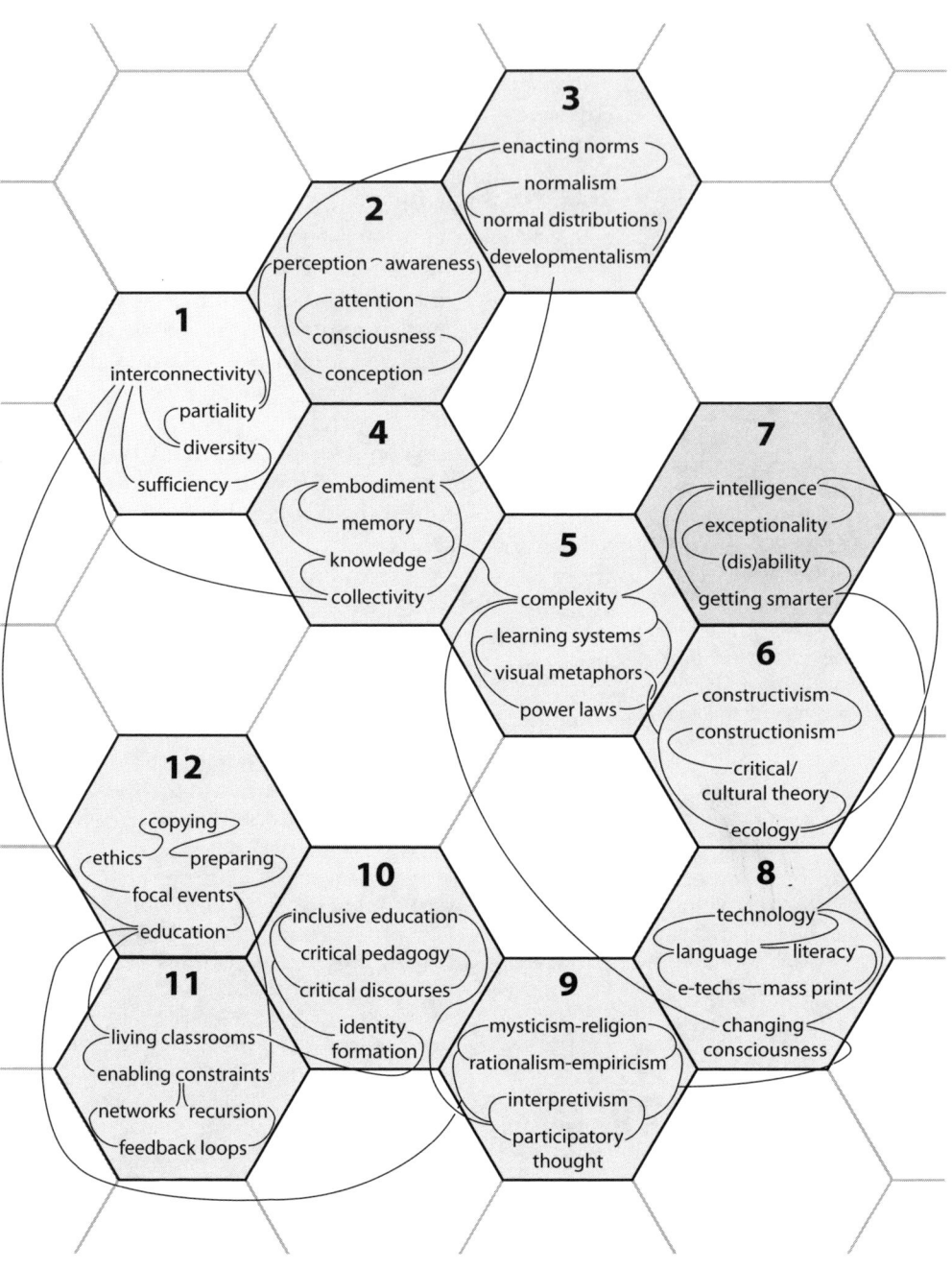

7 Learning Minds

I first met Krista in the autumn of 2001. An outgoing 14-year-old with an easy laugh and a quick wit, she had been referred by a colleague who knew of my interest in mathematics learning.

To say that Krista had been having trouble in math class would be a serious understatement. She had just started the 9th grade and, according to a battery of standardized inventories, appeared to be functioning at a second grade level. She had also been identified as a "behavior problem" by her teacher, especially at quiz and exam times when she would "go ballistic." These issues were neither new nor had they been previously ignored. Since her early elementary school years, her schools had provided her with special assistance, her teachers had made arrangements for extra time during tests, her parents had hired a series of tutors, and she had sought out friends who she hoped might help to shed a little light on this obscure subject matter.

Having almost no other information, I began with an informal assessment of Krista's understandings. I started with some grade-appropriate questions involving algebra and different number systems, but she appeared to have no idea what I was asking. Quickly I worked my way downward through grade levels, asking more and more basic questions, and soon found myself asking, "What's 6 plus 7?"

Krista paused and looked down. I watched her as she stared at her barely twitching fingers, realizing that she was trying to conceal how she was dealing with the question. After a few seconds she glanced up and, in a tone that betrayed her uncertainty, responded with a question: "Is it 12?"

7.1 Intelligence

Educators are frequently confronted with these sorts of situations, and they are usually expected to offer some sort of effective intervention. However, a teacher usually has very little information to work with, often no more than is provided in this chapter's introductory anecdote. What are the issues here? What actions might be undertaken? Can a useful diagnosis be made? Such are the sorts of topics addressed in this chapter, the broader themes of which are intelligence and ability/disability.

"Intelligence" is a contentious topic among educators, mostly because there is no broad agreement on exactly what the word means.

There is one point of general agreement. Intelligence is what is called on when an agent doesn't already know what to do.* As such, it is something about being able to discern what really matters in a situation—a notion that hearkens back to the word's original meaning (from the Latin *inter-legere,* to choose between). Apart from that point, different commentators argue that a fulsome definition must (or must not) include memory, adaptation, wit, judgment, logical reasoning, analogical reasoning, problem solving, and/or understanding.

The list actually goes on, as suggestions for elements of intelligence get more contentious. Some commentators have argued that versatility and the capacity to juggle several ideas at once are vital; others have proposed almost the opposite, that the ability to sustain concentration on a single focus is the hallmark of intelligent behavior. Some have argued that intelligence is mostly about interpreting the past, and some that intelligence is mostly about appropriate action in the present, some that intelligence is mostly about prediction of the future. Some have included creativity, wisdom, and morality; others have argued that *capacities* like intelligence shouldn't be conflated with *virtues* like goodness. Some have argued that intelligence depends mostly on a broad knowledge base; others have countered that intelligence is more about "processing power" than "storage capacity." Extending the

NATURE *versus* NURTURE?

Personal traits and capacities are innate; development and brain power are controlled by genetics. That is, it's all about **nature**.	Abilities and traits are acquired, and so context and experience are responsible for shaping who we are. That is, it's all about **nurture**.

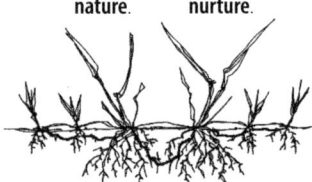

COMMON ROOTS: The persistent nature-nurture debate is rooted in the belief that we are born with pre-established potentials, but the context must provide adequate conditions to realize these potentials (nurture supports nature).

---

* This suggestion was developed by Jean Piaget in *The origins of intelligence in children* (New York: W.W. Norton, 1936/1963).

computer metaphor, some have suggested that hardware (i.e., biological constitution) is the basis of intelligence, while others have argued that it's all about software (i.e., what we know). Clearly, whatever intelligence is, it cannot be captured by a single definition.

Krista's situation helps to illustrate some of the issues here. Based on her performance in most of her classes and in everyday life, she could certainly be described as intelligent—although, perhaps, underachieving in some areas—but it would be a stretch to use that term in reference to her mathematics. Cases like hers have prompted some theorists to propose different sorts of intelligence (e.g., verbal, logical, social, musical, etc.),* learning styles or modalities (e.g., visual, auditory, etc.), and thinking styles (e.g., random, sequential, abstract, concrete, etc.).** Unfortunately, it is difficult to sort through the varied literatures around these topics. Furthermore, despite their popularity, there is very little evidence to support these perspectives.

For example, theories of varied intelligences are often based on some neurological research that shows different competencies are associated with different regions of the brain. However, it turns out that chimpanzee, gorilla, and other primate brains have all the same modules as human brains,*** and so efforts to map human competencies onto brain regions is inadequate for a robust theory. Another troublesome pillar in these theories is the popular belief that persons who are challenged in one domain will likely be outstanding in another. This principle of fairness might have some emotional appeal, but apart from rare cases of region-specific brain damage (discussed in the next section), it is not often manifested in humans. People who score low on tests in one category usually do poorly on tests in other categories, and people with high scores in specific areas tend to do well across the board.

Somewhat ironically, it's easier to make sense of these sorts of theories by looking into the social realm than by looking at individuals. Clearly, one is never simply intelligent, one is intelligent *about something*. Displays of cognitive ability are always in relation to some sort of culturally relevant activity such as doing math, playing the piano, or hunting boar. Otherwise

A century ago, the consensus was that training for athletic events was tantamount to cheating. It was considered an unfair way to enhance performance, thereby obscuring *natural* (from the Latin *naturalis*, "by birth") ability.

Discussions about intelligence have tended to share a similar attitude about innate ability. As discussed in this chapter, evidence is mounting that suggests this opinion is almost entirely unfounded.

* The most prominent proponent of "multiple intelligences" is Howard Gardner. See, e.g., his book, *Frames of mind: The theory of multiple intelligences* (New York: Basic, 1993).
** There is an extensive list of writers and researchers who have discussed learning/thinking/cognitive/mind styles. See the wikipedia entry on the topic for a cursory overview (http://en.wikipedia.org/wiki/Learning_styles).
*** See Donald, *A mind so rare.*

abilities won't be noticed, or if they are noticed, they might be seen as pathological. This point was demonstrated in the late 1990s when a few new "intelligences"—ones dealing with ecological sensitivity and spirituality—were added to some lists. Persons demonstrating exceptionality in one or the other of these categories might have been seen as fanatical or deluded only a few decades earlier. (In fact, the American Psychiatric Association listed "strong religious belief" as a mental disorder until 1994.)

On the positive side, discussions of different intelligences and learning modalities have prompted educators to vary presentation styles and to structure more active engagements with topics, among other emphases. Similarly, theories of multiple intelligences have been taken up to argue for more varied curricula and opportunities for specialization. This is an important shift in institutional contexts, which are most often characterized in terms of generalized methods and generic goals.

There are downsides, however. For example, in Krista's case, how helpful is it to suggest that she is a more random (vs. sequential) thinker, or that she lacks logico-mathematical intelligence? At best, these are merely descriptions with little advice to educators; they might point to symptoms, but they provide no sense of cause and no recommendations for intervention. At worst, they might be used to justify decisions to ignore particular aspects of her education. After all, if she lacks mathematical intelligence, why would we inflict the subject matter on her day after day?

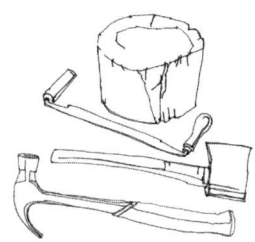

Which of the four items pictured above (i.e., hammer, saw, ax, or block of wood) does not belong?

The answer actually depends on the mode of reasoning you use.

If this were a formal IQ exam, in which logical reasoning is tested, you'd want to answer "log." All the other items can be collected in the abstract category "tool."

However, if you were thinking narratively—that is, according to day-to-day experiences—you might select either the saw or the ax, reasoning that one could stand in for the other if necessary. While critical for daily life, this manner of thinking can be a detriment in formal testing settings and has contributed to lower test scores for persons with particular socioeconomic, cultural, and educational backgrounds.

I must confess that by the end of that first meeting, I held out little hope for Krista's mathematics learning. In fact, having done a little reading around disabilities that are associated with neurological trauma, I was almost certain that she must have suffered some brain damage at some point.

Working on that suspicion, I agreed to a series of tutorial sessions. My selfish intention had very little to do with helping her learn mathematics; rather, I was more interested in how other capacities might be affected by her difficulties with math. I wondered, for example, if Krista might have a general difficulty with logical inference, which might also prove troublesome when she interprets linear narratives. Or perhaps her difficulties with numbers would contribute to problems in social studies or science classes when statistics and other quantitative data were presented.

Somewhat to my surprise, these suspicions proved to be completely off track. Krista was doing well in her other classes and was well above average in some of them.

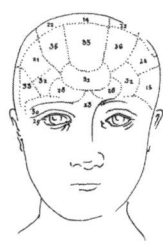

Different human capacities tend to be associated with highly localized parts of the brain—a discovery that has been used by some researchers to argue for an array of different sorts of intelligences.

More recent research has shown that, regardless of the specific task it is working on, all of the brain is active. And so, even though it is clear that particular regions do specialize, it is just as clear that the brain is not modularized. This more complex understanding of brain activity helps to explain why, for example, art-based and physical activity can enhance abilities in other domains.

In brief, the notion of discrete intelligences seems to be an oversimplification of a more complex phenomenon.

7.2 Exceptionality

Giftedness is almost as slippery a term as *intelligence*, but there does seem to be more general agreement on how to operationalize the notion within educational contexts. In many jurisdictions, for example, it is agreed that from 2 to 5% of students deviate sufficiently from the norm in some category of performance to be labeled as gifted.

There are as many categories of giftedness as there are domains of human activity, and so cultural bias plays into identifications. For example, in modern western societies, one will find gifted computer programmers, gifted mechanics, gifted translators, and gifted dog breeders—this is an easy list to extend—most of which wouldn't be found in other places and other eras. In terms of schooling activities, an overwhelming majority of young prodigies in the western world have exceptional abilities in memory, calculation, or the fine arts—that is, categories in which performance supercedes interpretation. By contrast, in other settings and at other times, individuals are or were more often singled out for exceptional social skills, wisdom, compassion, empathy, story telling, and insight where interpretation rather than performance is the vital quality.

Where does giftedness come from? The most common assumption seems to be that extraordinary talents are simply inborn, and this belief is reflected in popular books and movies in which disadvantaged protagonists with exceptional assumed-to-be-innate abilities manage to overcome daunting barriers. This belief is actually suggested by the term *gifted*—something handed over, unearned, fully formed upon bestowal.

In fact, there are no validated accounts whatsoever of exceptional giftedness erupting full-blown without years of concentrated study and focused practice. Simply put, there is a strange lack of hard evidence to substantiate the belief in the importance of innate talent. By contrast, the preponderance of evidence suggests that exceptional abilities are not *gifts* at all; they are not *given*, they are *earned*. Experts aren't born, they're made. Across domains—writing, chess, music, athletics, and so on—the top performers tend to share three qualities:

- they began early in life;
- they engage in intense (usually) solitary practice consisting mostly of repetitive drill work, direct copying, and/or focused examination of others' work for more than 20 hours each week extending over at least a decade; and
- they engage in *effortful study*, which involves taking on challenges that are just beyond their competence.*

The last point is of particular importance. It helps to explain why, even though many people might continue to practice, only a few tend to excel—explaining, for example, why in a nation of car drivers, so few are exceptional. A critical quality is that practice must test the limits of one's current abilities. "Effortful study" points to a sort of work/play that is undertaken not because it is easy, but because it is hard.

Does it make sense to compare the intelligence of humans to that of dogs, cats, dolphins, or monkeys?

On some levels, such comparisons do make sense: other species seem to be able to adapt, to abstract, to reason,

Some cogent evidence of this point is a contemporary proliferation of chess prodigies, which is believed to reflect the availability of chess programs that make it possible for children to study more already-played games and engage in more practice against competent opponents (i.e., effortful practice). Along similar lines, studies of professional athletes suggest that their success has to do more with training than with talent.** In a nutshell, the evidence indicates that exceptionality is much more about dedicated and sustained effort (even obsession) than it is about inborn ability—which is not to say that genetics don't matter. Of course they do, as do childhood experiences, dates of birth,*** social opportunities, precocity, and so on. The point is that exceptionality is tightly linked to hard work. To invoke a popular joke:

Q: How do you get to Carnegie Hall?

A: Practice, practice, practice.

One of the things that this practice does is provide the individual with the capacity to deal with huge chunks of information all at once. For example, a chess

* See Ross, "The expert mind."
** See Janet L. Starkes & K. Anders Ericsson (editors), *Expert performance in sports: Advances in research on sport expertise* (Champaign: IL: Human Kinetics, 2003).
*** Ibid. For example, among professional athletes, there is a disproportionate representation of those whose birthdays fall in the first few months after league cut-off dates. These individuals would be slightly older and, on average, slightly larger and more experienced than their teammates and, by consequence, would tend to enjoy slight advantages that would contribute to more playing time and greater success. A positive feedback loop emerges that can exaggerate a slight head start into a major advantage.

master can see the entire board rather than having to focus on each piece, or a concert pianist sees a score rather than individual notes. In turn, this capacity to chunk enables the master or virtuoso to consider much broader ranges of possibility than the non-expert can keep in mind. As well, it appears to contribute to the ability to memorize domain-specific information—games, musical scores, mathematical proofs—accurately and rapidly. However, outside their particular realm of mastery, geniuses do no better than others on general tests of memory.

In fact, exceptionality is so tightly linked to repetitive practice that many cases of genius have been associated with clinical obsession, compulsion, paranoia, bi-polar disorder, and/or manic depression. The frequency of these phenomena is about 10 times greater among those identified as geniuses than in the "non-genius" population. Obsession-related predispositions can contribute to exceptionality (and, of course, can prevent it).

In quite a different vein, a small portion of instances of genius are associated with location-specific brain injuries. In some instances, localized traumas can lead to diminished capacities in specific domains and enhanced capacities in others. The latter seem to be linked to sudden releases of resources in the brain. As one region no longer requires such resources, a nearby region might be able to exploit them.* But, once again, the specific capacities require sustained exercise. Instances of genius related to brain injuries are actually quite rare. This dicussion oriented attention back to the case of Krista. Did she perhaps fall into this category?

As it turns out, she didn't, and that should have been obvious from her efforts to respond to "6 + 7." In most cases where mathematical abilities are impaired by neurological trauma, individuals not only have great difficulties knowing *how* to perform specific operations, they are typically unable to understand *when* or *why* those operations are used. Krista clearly knew what to do when asked to add and the sorts of situations that called for the operation of addition. She just could not do it well.

to plan, and to communicate. Moreover, interspecies comparisons have highlighted that "intelligent" animals use play to expand their repertoires of experience and possible response.

However, superficial interspecies comparisons (based on brain size, trainability, etc.) miss the essential point that human intelligence derives in large part from the way our brains are linked into a single cognitive system through language. Nonhuman minds are not dulled or lesser versions of human minds. They are qualitatively different.

* Among the most compelling accounts of this phenomenon are the many accounts presented by Oliver Sacks. See, for example, his books *Seeing voices* and *An anthropologist on Mars*.

Oriented by my interest in the broader implications of Krista's apparent disability, I requested some information on her history. It turned out that she had been formally diagnosed as having a mathematics learning disability in the third grade. This diagnosis had since been reaffirmed every year. (This label was required by the school district for access to the special needs classroom.)

We arranged for weekly 90-minute meetings. These were complemented with daily exercises of 15 to 20 minutes that were supervised by her parents. For our first month, we focused on the topics of addition and subtraction using counters, Base-10 blocks, grid paper, an abacus, and other tools that are prominently represented in the literature.* Her homework was organized mostly around flash cards: for a total of a few hours each week, her parents worked with her on sums and differences of numbers up to 30.

By the end of the month she had developed considerable confidence with addition and subtraction, including with paper-and-pencil calculations involving multi-digit numbers. The improvement was actually startling, and I commented to Krista that I was very impressed at how she had learned to add so quickly.

Her response was a somewhat indignant, "I've always known how to add. I just wasn't very good at it."

It was at that moment I realized that, in fact, Krista wasn't suffering from a learning disorder—at least not one of the extreme sorts associated with neurological trauma. She understood the process. She knew what it was, how to do it, and when to do it. It wasn't a matter of cognitive impairment.

So, then, what was it?

7.3 (Dis)Ability

In terms of currently recognized learning challenges, Krista's mathematical competence was indicative of a learning disability (LD). The most important qualities for an LD diagnosis are, first, a significant performance deficit in one domain relative to others and, second, an at least average intelligence in most areas. On this count, LDs might be considered the flip side of the "multiple intelligences" coin, with the former referring to domain-specific deficits and the latter to domain-specific strengths. Both have had the positive effect of prompting school districts and other agencies to provide resources, either to ameliorate difficulties or to nurture abilities.

Learning disabilities are only a recently recognized phenomenon, with the first diagnoses dating back to the 1960s. The most commonly identified sorts of LDs are dyslexia (difficulties with reading), dysgraphia (difficulties with writing), and dyscalculia (difficulties with mathematics), but a performance deficit in any domain is a candidate for the status of a learning disability. Dyslexia, the most common, may affect up to 4% of people and has been associated with atypical brain activity. Dyslexics can, however, become

* For an introduction to some of these topics and tools, see John A. Van de Walle, *Elementary and middle school mathematics: Teaching developmentally*, 6th edition (Boston: Allyn & Bacon, 2006).

competent, even outstanding readers, but they often require specialized strategies and different sorts of practice than is typically provided in school, indicating that at least some LDs are more matters of *difference* than *disability*. Schools have historically been organized around the assumption that all brains are structured in very much the same way whereas neurological studies of some learning-disabled individuals reveal that in fact there are some rather significant differences in how some people learn.*

Like multiple intelligences, LDs are descriptions not explanations. They provide little insight into underlying causes; rather, they are symptoms of some deeper issue. And therein lies one of the major criticisms of a learning disabilities diagnosis: naming a problem and dealing with it are two very different matters. For example, knowing that Krista had dyscalculia (which had actually been diagnosed every year between Grades 3 and 9) had obviously provided her teachers, special educators, tutors, and parents with no useful information at all for addressing the problem. Other criticisms include the fact that the vast majority of LD diagnoses involve children from middle or upper class families, most often Caucasian. Given that an LD label usually brings access to specialized educational resources, it has thus been argued that the phenomenon of learning disabilities has been deployed as a mechanism to widen gaps that already exist between the educational opportunities of different groups.**

Similar sorts of criticisms have been leveled against a number of classification schemes and diagnoses within educational institutions. Rather than attempt to review the current ranges of labels and classifications, the strategy in this chapter is to focus on just one, very prominent disorder—namely, hyperactivity—and use it as a case study for the practices of defining differences, assigning labels, and structuring interventions.

Hyperactivity (and a cluster of associated diagnoses, including Attention Deficit Disorder, ADD, and Attention Deficit Hyperactive Disorder, ADHD) is seen by many as an epidemic of sorts. Production of the drug most often prescribed for hyperactivity, Ritalin, increased by 500% through the first half of the 1990s in

While recognized dysfunctions are far too numerous and diverse to survey, a sense of their range can be gleaned from a glimpse at the *Diagnostic and Statistical Manual of Mental Disorders*, published by the American Psychiatric Association. More than 800 pages long, this regularly revised document lists the thousands of labels that are currently in use, along with the established diagnoses as determined through majority votes of the Association, and so pathologies change as evidence is presented, cultural opinions evolve, and so on.

* For an elaborated discussion of learning disabilities and the issues that surround their diagnosis, see Robert G. Sternberg & Elenor L. Grigorenko, *Our labeled children: What every parent and teacher needs to know about learning disabilities* (New York: Perseus, 2000).
** Ibid.

the United States, and still continues to rise. By 2000, from 3 to 5% of school-aged children in North America (and more than 10% of boys in elementary school) took Ritalin or other drugs to help manage their behavior. In some jurisdictions, the rate was as high as 20%.*

Those statistics don't actually give the complete picture, since drug therapies aren't the only response to hyperactivity. Dietary regimes (e.g., limiting sugar, protein, or certain fats) and behavior modification programs (i.e., rigid structures of reward and punishment) are also widely employed. Less common strategies include neuro-feedback, psychoanalysis, small group learning structures, and direct parent involvement in classrooms. In every case, success is varied.

One might be tempted to think, given these well-defined responses, that there is broad agreement on what hyperactivity is and what causes it. In fact, its symptoms are rather vaguely defined, covering such qualities as distractibility, restlessness, inattention, poor concentration, fidgetiness, impatience, noisiness, inconsideration, and excitability. One reason that has been proposed for the apparent lack of precision in these symptoms is that hyperactive behavior may itself be just a symptom. In other words, drug therapies and other strategies might only be masking undiagnosed problems.

There is hardly consensus on this topic. One prominent theory on hyperactivity suggests that some cases are caused by a certain neurotransmitter in the brain's pre-frontal lobes—the brain region most associated with logical analysis and self-control—contributing to a certain loss of inhibitions. It is believed that Ritalin and other drug therapies substitute for or improve the efficacy of these neurotransmitters. In such instances, the basis of the disorder would indeed be treated.

Given the effectiveness of drug regimes, it would be tempting to believe that this scenario is generally the case. However, a troubling situation arises every summer: as soon as school is let out, the use of behavior-controlling drugs falls precipitously. That must mean that either hyperactivity is context-specific, or that many schools cannot tolerate levels of activity that vary too much from the norm. The latter seems more likely. In fact, changes in opinion on what constitutes "normal

Indicators of HYPERACTIVITY

- poorly sustained attention in most situations;
- low task-persistence when no immediate consequences;
- impulsive, can't delay gratification;
- difficulty regulating or inhibiting behavior in social contexts;
- more active and more restless than most children;
- difficulty adhering to rules.

A quick comparison of some of the most often mentioned "symptoms" of hyperactivity and "qualities" of giftedness should give educators some pause. (See footnote on page 124.)

* These data are drawn from Sydney Walker III, *The hyperactivity hoax* (New York: St. Martin's Press, 1998).

behavior" are usually cited as the most likely reason for the rise in Ritalin sales. An inadequately explored option to drug interventions, it is further argued, is a broadened conception of acceptable behavior, preferably coupled to diversified and active learning contexts.

Whether or not that is the case, the fact is that difficult and disruptive behavior is a growing problem. A number of researchers have been attempting to identify factors that contribute to such behaviors, and the current list includes both biopsychological triggers and sociological influences.* Among the array of possible biopsychological causes are

- low-grade poisoning (e.g., lead, mercury, manganese, carbon dioxide)**;
- malnutrition and nutrient deficiencies, prompted in large part by modern diets that are very different from the diets that prevailed through most of the evolution of the species***;
- skipping meals****;
- eating foods with high glycemic indices (i.e., ones that contribute to rapid changes in blood sugar levels);
- chemical dependencies (e.g., alcohol, nicotine, solvents, recreational drugs);
- pollutants (e.g., pesticides, molds, disinfectants, air fresheners, furniture polish, smoke, insect repellent);
- medical conditions that might restrict oxygen or other vital constituents in the brain (e.g., brain tumor, head injuries, diabetes, allergies, fetal alcohol syndrome, petit mal seizures, organ deformities).

Sociologically speaking, problems might stem from

- difficulties at home;
- difficulties with/among peers;
- difficulties with classroom tasks or efforts to divert attention away from low academic achievement;
- limited academic challenge or meaningful engagement;
- excessive information or stimulation—particularly in the form of background noise;
- lack of exercise;
- changes in expectation.

Indicators of GIFTEDNESS

- poor attention, boredom, daydreaming in specific situations;
- low tolerance or persistence on tasks that seem irrelevant;
- judgment lags behind intellectual development;
- tendency toward power struggles with authorities;
- high activity, may need less sleep;
- questions rules and traditions.

---

* For extended discussions of these possible influences, see Walker, *The hyperactivity hoax.*

** See, e.g., Christopher Williams, *Terminus brain: The environmental threats to human intelligence* (London: Cassell, 1997).

*** See Jean Carper, *Your miracle brain* (New York: Quill, 2000).

**** See Michael J. Murphy, "The relationship of school breakfast to psychosocial and academic functioning," in *Pediatric Adolescent Medicine*, vol. 152 (1998): 899–907.

Against this backdrop, it would seem reasonable to argue that the quick-fix solution strategy of drug intervention might be helping to compound the problem.

Finally, just to underscore how little is known about the underlying causes of hyperactive behavior, consider the disturbing similarities among criteria for ADHD and the criteria for giftedness as illustrated in the margin note on the previous page.*

And so, what conclusions can be drawn? Perhaps only that the situation is almost certainly more complex than can be captured with any sort of taxonomy of gifts or deficits.

Krista and I rarely missed a meeting. Our first six months were spent almost entirely on addition, subtraction, multiplication, and division.

When I realized that the issue was more complex than first imagined, I began to think of my work with her in terms of "educating her intuition"—a phrase I used to refer to the development of embodied senses of quantities and operations. For instance, we spent a total of about six hours (a month's work together) figuring out different ways to estimate the number of grains of rice in a bowl and, by the end, Krista was able to offer rapid and reasonable estimates for the numbers of bricks in a wall, leaves on a tree, and so on. We spent considerable time on paper-based activities such as folding, cutting, assembling, and dismantling—after which she had a surprising facility with fraction concepts.

As mentioned earlier, I insisted on practice at home. It began as simple drills on facts but was elaborated into writing out explanations of why things work, spending time on non-routine problems, and so on. In fact, these activities created a bit of a problem: Krista's parents—both well-educated professionals—often found them too difficult, and so were unable to assist.

At about the six-month point, the psychometrician who had worked with her for three years was surprised to note that her score on the mathematics portion of the test had soared from Grade 2.3 (at the end of Grade 8) to Grade 10.8 (in the last half of Grade 9). I mention this statistic with caution. I didn't see the actual test, so I have no idea what was being evaluated. And I'm deeply suspicious of such one-shot, summative assessments. But it nonetheless indicated that something important had happened. Clearly, Krista could no longer be formally diagnosed as learning disabled nor as lacking mathematical intelligence.

7.4 Getting Smarter

There is a range of issues associated with current habits of labeling (of both strengths and weaknesses). Three that are flagged in this chapter are, first, that most labels are premised on the idea that intelligence is an internal, brain-based phenomena; second, there appears to be an assumption that ability is more-or-less fixed and measurable and, hence, subject to stable labels; and third, discussions of difference tend to be

* This comparison was first assembled by James T. Webb & Diane Latimer, "ADHD and children who are gifted," in *ERIC Digest*, vol. 522 (1993, ED358673).

The following are among the many persons who as children are reputed to have been identified as "inattentive," "uncreative," "developmentally delayed," "autistic," or even "stupid": Ludwig von Beethoven, Richard Branson, Cher, Winston Churchill, Tom Cruise, Charles Darwin, Thomas Edison, Bill Gates, Whoopi Goldberg, Florence Nightingale, Carl Jung, Louis Pasteur, Isaac Newton, Auguste Rodin, Vincent van Gogh, James Whistler, Virginia Woolf.

organized around silent assumptions about the way things "are supposed to be." As developed in chapter 3, abnormality (whether giftedness or disability) makes no sense if some sort of normality isn't taken for granted.

Consider these issues in relation to Krista's case. How can we make sense of her rapid development after so many years of poor performance in mathematics? Did she suddenly realize a mathematical intelligence that had been previously suppressed? If so, at what point could that intelligence be said to have appeared? Is it now fully realized? How can we know? Is she the exception or the rule around overcoming a perceived disorder?

We could continue for some time with these sorts of questions. The bottom line is that cases like Krista's represent a profound challenge to some deeply entrenched assumptions about intelligence. In this section, we move through some critiques of these assumptions.

The measurability of intelligence. Over the past century, discussions of intelligence have been greatly influenced—and at times totally dominated—by the construct of Intelligence Quotient (IQ).

By definition, IQ is a ratio of mental age to chronological age. Given that chronological age is empirically measurable, this definition reveals an assumption that mental age must have a similar status—a point that is, to say the least, contentious. There is no broad consensus around this idea at all.

For the most part, IQ tests are structured around knowledge- and logic-based performance tasks. Some include items that deal with vocabulary, comprehension of narratives, and/or memory. In every case, tasks are selected and refined in order to generate normal distributions when administered to large enough groups of people. (In fact, test-makers have not yet achieved this goal.)

From the beginning, there have been challenges to the idea that IQ is a valid construct. The fact that designers have never managed to generate a test that produces a truly normal distribution is a prominent criticism. Other critiques focus on the assumed definition of intelligence, arguing that it is a more fluid, complex, and contextually sensitive phenomenon than can be measured by one-size-fits-all tests. Still other critiques focus on cultural and ageist biases. Consider the following contrived question, for example:

> For the group consisting of Barney Rubble, Betty Boop, Bugs Bunny, and Burt Bacharach, identify one quality that distinguishes each character from the others.

Clearly, middle-aged North Americans would have a distinct advantage here, so it's not clear if one is testing mental ability or exposure to popular culture.

Historically, the cultural biases woven into IQ tests have had some troubling consequences. Two prominent examples from the early 20th century arose in the screening of immigrants and the identification of "officer material" from among army recruits. In both cases, based on test results, priority was given to upper middle class, English-speaking Caucasians over people from other social classes, nationalities, and races.

Of course, it could be argued that the tests were being misapplied. But another historical event supports the assertion that IQ tests do little more than measure the imposed assumptions of their designers. Until the mid-1930s, the average IQ score was a few points higher for men than for women. At a meeting of designers, it was agreed that the test should be analyzed for those items that contributed to this difference. Those items were eliminated and, as a result, women and men have since had similar average scores. However, the same sorts of efforts to isolate and remove items that contribute to measured differences among racial, cultural, and other social groups have not been undertaken even though it would not be difficult to do so.

An even more dramatic demonstration of the statistical manipulation of IQs unfolded in 1973 when in a single day, with a simple shift in definition, 8 million US citizens were suddenly no longer "mentally retarded." Simply by shifting the definition of "borderline" mental retardation by one standard deviation, the official prevalence rate was made to fall from 3% to 1%.

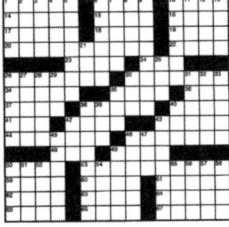

Does intellect decline with age?
A few long-term studies* have shown that abilities can be maintained if people keep their brains busy. Eighty-year-olds who have made a habit of such activities as playing bridge, doing crosswords, and building jigsaw puzzles tend to score as well as they ever did on tests of mental acuity. Those who never made a habit of activities that demand mental effort are more prone to significant declines. They also appear to be more susceptible to degenerative brain diseases.

* See Carper, *Your miracle brain*.

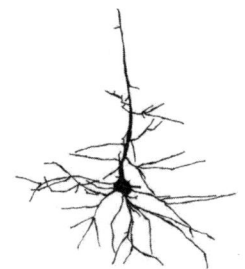

A human brain has about 50 billion neurons, and each neuron has between 1,000 and 10,000 synapses to connect with other neurons. In other words, there's an astronomical number of possible links and associations.

Neurons and their interconnections are constantly changing, as new synapses grow and other synapses are lost. Two popular adages serve as important reminders of the roles of neurons in personal memory: *Use it or lose it*, and *neurons that fire together, wire together*.***

* Carper, *Your miracle brain.*.
** This research was conducted by Michael Norden, a psychiatrist at the University of Washington. The story was released in the popular media, and varying accounts can be found by googling key words, *Frisbee*, *Norden*, and *SATs*.
*** * The adage was coined by neurologist Donald Hebb. See Donald O. Hebb, *The organization of behavior* (New York: Wiley, 1949).

Other problems with the assumption of measurable intelligence are that a person's IQ score can vary considerably with modest environmental change or through instruction in how to write IQ tests. Further, IQ varies dramatically through the day, depending on levels of fatigue, hunger, thirst, and motivation. (Try solving a sudoku puzzle when you're tired.) Even when conditions are reasonably stable, the margin of error in IQ testing is typically about 15 points, meaning that an IQ measurement of 95 could mean anything between 80 and 110. Age is also a big issue as it contributes to different strategies for intelligent action. Young people tend to have a more "fluid" intelligence (able to adapt quickly to novel situations) whereas older people tend to rely more on "crystallized" intelligence (extensive memories, well-honed verbal abilities, considered judgments).

Finally, several decades of research have demonstrated that the principal justification for the original IQ tests—to predict academic success—has never been realized. At best, it appears that IQ scores can account for about 10–25% of the variation among students' school grades and roughly 5–10% of people's performances later in life. (A compounding problem here is that education itself has been demonstrated to increase IQ scores, at least in part because the demands of academic work make for a more lively and resilient brain that is better able to resist deterioration and disease.*) Other measures, including socio-economic standing of families, careers of parents, and course grades assigned by teachers have proven to be much more reliable predictors.

More recent efforts to identify and measure different capacities, including emotional intelligence and scholastic aptitude, have not had much more predictive success. Two brief examples illustrate the point. First, in a study of the different predictors of academic excellence involving all private national universities in the United States, it turned out that a school's ranking in Ultimate Frisbee is a much better indicator than are grades and Scholastic Aptitude Test (SAT) scores.** Second, in a very different sort of study, researchers investigated some of the implicit associations (see chap. 2) of race and academic achievement that might affect test scores. They had two groups of black college students complete a selection of questions from the Graduate Record Examination (GRE), a widely used tool to screen applicants for graduate schools. The sets of questions were identical, but there was a minor difference in how the test was administered. Members of one group were asked to identify their race on a pretest questionnaire. That simple act was enough to cut the average score in that group by half.* It's not clear what the test was measuring, but it is fair to say that it was neither intelligence nor intellectual potential.

In brief, whatever intelligence is, it does not appear to lend itself to measurement.**

The nature of intelligence. Perhaps the most common reason given for the immeasurability of intelligence is the likelihood that it's simply not a unified phenomenon.

Some of the strongest support for this insight comes from a surprising domain: research into artificial intelligence (AI). Since its beginnings, AI has tended toward overly optimistic forecasts. Originating in the 1950s with the development of reliable electronic computers, the field began with confident predictions that electronic minds would soon surpass flesh-based intellects. The reasons behind the relatively slow achievement of this goal are instructive.

The principal reason had to do with what tends to be seen as intelligent behavior in humans—namely extraordinary performance on logic-based tasks that one finds in IQ tests and mathematics texts. Very early on, AI researchers had tremendous success in programming computers to outperform humans on such tasks, prompting many to predict that computers would soon outperform humans on "simple" tasks such as recognizing faces and words. However, the consensus was that it would take much longer to make computers smart enough to beat chess masters or to prove mathematical theorems (i.e., activities that programmers found difficult). The opposite turned out to be the case. Specialized computers can defeat the best chess players and have created novel logical

Want to think more clearly? Then ...

EAT: The brain requires ten times more glucose and oxygen for its size than any other organ, which means that proper nourishment is vital to its function. The best "smart drugs" are to be found in a healthy diet.

DRINK: The brain must be well hydrated. Even modest reductions in fluid levels can prompt fatigue, distractibility, and irritability.

* Claude Steele & Joshua Aronson, "Stereotype threat and intellectual test performance of African Americans," in *Journal of Personality and Social Psychology*, vol. 74, no. 4 (1995): 797–811.
** For a much more detailed discussion of issues around efforts to measure intelligence, see Stephen Jay Gould, *The mismeasure of man* (New York: W.W. Norton, 1996).

proofs. As for recognizing faces and words, computers lag behind not just young children, but also the young of many other species.

And so, somewhat ironically, AI has demonstrated that the critical indicator of generalized intelligence is not facility with advanced logical tasks, but what most children learn before arriving at the school's door. Researchers are only beginning to create machines that can perform such everyday competencies as using language flexibly, distinguishing among objects, predicting outcomes, interpreting indirect references, and wending through crowded rooms. Significantly, it appears that computers cannot simply be directly programmed to do these sorts of things. They have to *learn* them. That is, machines have to be constructed that are capable of experiencing the world and adapting accordingly.*

In this regard, an area of AI research that is showing considerable promise—arguably the most promise—is a branch of robotics that does not rely on powerful central processors or preprogrammed pools of data. Instead, robots are equipped with several independent control systems that must learn to "work together" to achieve goals like moving around a room or manipulating objects. This strategy of imitating the organization of complex forms (i.e., of smaller systems coming together into grander unities) is having some surprising successes in contrast to the strategies of the previous 50 years of AI research. Machine intelligence is progressing toward human-like intelligence at a relatively rapid and accelerating pace—so rapid, in fact, that some predict collective intelligence will evolve to be trillions of times greater over the next century.**

In and of itself, the claim that humanity will grow ever smarter is a challenge to common assumptions. As suggested by the phrase "not working to her potential" and as embodied in formal intelligence tests, there is a popular belief that ability is predetermined and its limits are fixed. But can we become more intelligent?

The location of intelligence. More than a century ago, psychoanalysts posited that human minds are not unified phenomena. Rather, identities, actions, and

---

BE MERRY: The neurochemicals that prompt emotional arousal also prompt the brain to make lasting memories, so we remember better when there is an emotional impact.***

VARY ACTIVITIES: Regular, sustained, and strenuous exercise is vital to mental and physical health, prompting the brain to release endorphins ("feel good" chemicals), improving the functioning of all organs, boosting oxygen levels and blood flow, and speeding the removal of toxins—making people happier, less anxious, less depressed, and more intelligent. The distraction provided by exercise can also be productive. History is rife with tales of many great insights that happened when minds are otherwise occupied—while getting on buses, dreaming, chatting with friends, and so on.

---

* See Rodney A. Brooks, *Flesh and machines: How robots will change us* (New York: Pantheon, 2002), for an introductory discussion of the current emphasis on embodied experiences within AI research.
** Ibid. See also Ray Kurzweil, *The singularity is near: When humans transcend biology* (New York: Viking, 2005).
*** See Steven Johnson, *Mind wide open: Your brain and the neuroscience of everyday life* (New York: Scribner, 2004).

abilities arise in the often-conflicted interactions of different motivations, possibilities, and brain regions.

Neuroscientific research of the past 100 years has confirmed this suspicion. In fact, it has demonstrated that Freud and his contemporaries underestimated the diverse and conflicted nature of the human psyche. Freud suggested that the conscious *ego* was torn between two masters, the subconscious *id* and the embodied cultural norms of the *superego*. Contemporary brain research indicates that individuals are subject to vastly more "drives," each vying for attention.*

This current research has rejected mechanical metaphors of the brain (e.g., as steam engine, telephone switchboard, or computer) and taken up something more toward "brain as society" or "brain as ecosystem." That is, it appears that the brain operates like a complex social or ecological collective. Thought and behavior arise in the simultaneous co-activity of many influences—significantly, in absence of a centralized controller dictating what must and must not be done.

That doesn't begin to tell the whole story because, of course, internal influences are affected by contexts and experiences. The picture that is emerging is that intelligence arises in the complex interplay of dynamically changing brain structures within an active body within varied social-and-natural environments. Intelligence in this frame is not located *inside* a person, much less inside a brain. Rather, intelligence is all about being able to initiate the next move in real-world situations. It is located in the space of activity, where the agent meets the world.

This expansion of the notion of intelligence has some surprising implications. For instance, it suggests that other complex processes might be appropriately described as "intelligent." The evolution of a species or the emergence of a new virus, among many other examples, might be seen as intelligent responses to particular circumstances. (Of course, these examples prompt the question of *what*, exactly, it means to be intelligent.)

Another implication is that the idea of *limits* on intelligence is inherently problematic. It opens the

> language-
> effected
> thought

Imagine a dog, surrounded by cans of beans, winking at you.

This is an easy mental task.

Despite its simplicity, though, only humans are capable of such imaginings, thanks to our languaging abilities.

And it's not just that language makes it possible to think odd thoughts. Everything that has passed through your mind while reading this book is simply unavailable to non-language users. Language is the house of our intelligence (see chap. 8).

* See Johnson, *Mind wide open.*

door to the provocative possibility that we can become smarter.

The limits of intelligence. Something curious has been happening over the past century and especially over the past several decades. Scores on standardized tests of intelligence have been rising at a pace that simply cannot be explained by genetics, improved nutrition, or other organic influences.*

You don't actually have to look to the results of IQ tests to realize this point. Every one of us can readily understand ideas that were beyond the grasp of all but the best minds of past generations. Ninth grade students, for example, are routinely expected to perform calculations that no one could do a few thousand years ago. And high school students deal with topics that were accessible to only geniuses a few centuries ago.

So what's going on here?

At least two issues need to be raised to address this question, both related to technology. The first is the influence of and participation in popular culture; the second is the ongoing evolution of and access to cultural tools.

On the former, the evidence suggests that video games, popular television (including reality TV), graphic novels, the internet, and other often-maligned forms of "diversion" seem to be contributing to capacities to gather and sift through information, to generate diverse interpretations, to identify and solve problems, and to make critical and rapid discernments. That is, these products of popular culture aren't "dumbing" people down. The exact opposite appears to be the case, as these forms present participants with more complex environments and make greater intellectual demands on cognition—such as attending for prolonged periods, juggling details, making logical leaps, following multiple threads, making decisions that are nested in other decisions, probing, choosing, prioritizing, and so on. These demands might be described as "collateral learning," because the critical aspect is not *what* you are thinking about (i.e., what's occupying your attention), but *how* you are thinking. And that "how" registers on intelligence tests as more flexible, more imaginative, further reaching ability.

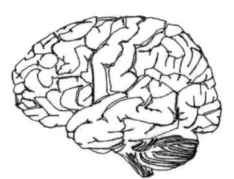

What makes some brains smarter than others?

There have been two prominent hypotheses: One is that the smart brain "runs hot"; that is, it has a good deal of energy to burn when faced with a mental task. The other is the opposite: the smart brain is cooly efficient.

It appears that each view is partly correct. The smart brain starts out by devoting considerable resources to a problem. Once the discernments needed to understand the situation have been made, the smart brain quickly routinizes the task, slipping into unthinking routine and freeing up concentration for new problems.

* See Steven Johnson, *Everything bad is good for you: How popular culture is actually making us smarter* (New York: Riverhead, 2005).

Of course, as already argued, intelligence tests fall short of offering nuanced and informative profiles of personal abilities. So the point here is not that it's "all good"; it's that popular culture has presented educators with some important new insights into the learning process. In particular, it has highlighted that people don't avoid activities simply because they're challenging or there's a threat of failure. Quite the contrary, the major appeal of most video games is that they are exceedingly demanding. A sure way to destroy a game's appeal is to reduce it to a sequence of "steps to success."

Clearly, there is much more to augmented intelligence than engagement in popular culture. The question still remains of why most people can understand ideas that, in past generations, were beyond the grasp of all but the most remarkable minds. The answer may be found in an examination of the role that cultural tools—that is, technologies—play in shaping intelligence.

Anthropologists have been looking at the issue for some time, and some have provocatively suggested that the artifacts and tools created within a culture are not simply *products*, but *bestowers* of intelligence. Certain technologies, such as language and writing, help to orient attentions, enable one to offload cognitive demands, and thus allow even novice learners to focus on new details. Consider, for instance, the impact of the calculator on mathematics learning. Relieved of the burden of tedious calculations, young learners are now able to focus their attentions on a much broader range of less contrived mathematical situations. (See chap. 8 for an elaborated discussion.)

Such artifacts have a snowball effect as simple external props and practices empower thought, giving rise to more complex forms. In effect, a powerful feedback loop is set up that can allow for exponential increases in ability. This sort of situation, supported by the exponential increases in processing power currently experienced, has prompted some futurists to argue that there may be no limits on what we know as "mind." Or, if there are limits, they may vastly exceed those currently experienced.*

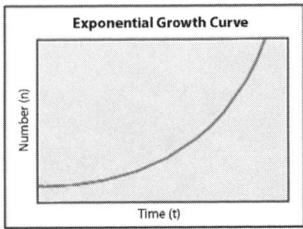

Two basic models of growth for complex unities, *exponential* and *logistic*, are illustrated here.

If the rate of reproduction is constant, growth will be exponential (above image). However, rapid growth might deplete the resources needed to survive—and so, over long periods, growth might level off to match the carrying capacity of the context. This situation is depicted by a logistic curve (below).

At present, it appears that both human population and human intelligence are experiencing exponential growth, although there are signs that population might be starting to level off. The opposite trend is observed with collective intelligence, which continues to accelerate.

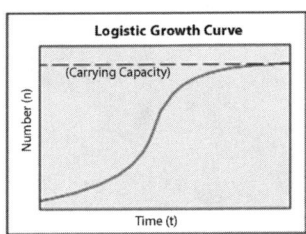

* See Kurzweil, *The singularity is near.*

Krista sailed through high school mathematics courses, with averages in the 80% range. Her grades in other courses were up as well.

We continued to work together through the tenth and eleventh grades, by the end of which I realized I didn't have much more to teach. In particular, many of the topics in her mathematics courses were developed around the use of graphing calculators, and she simply was far more adept at using this technology than I was. And so, more often than not, she would offer solutions and explanations for problems as fast as I could pose the problems.

Sometime in the middle of her Grade 11 math experience, I asked her how her test writing was going—a question that was prompted by a recollection of earlier exam anxieties.

"Oh, fine," she responded. And when I asked about why, in her opinion, tests were no longer the sources of such angst, she explained that a few years earlier, her "brain would just go haywire in math tests." She couldn't focus, she couldn't remember. But by Grade 11, she had reached a place where her "brain just goes calm" when she looked over the questions and realized she could do most if not all of them.

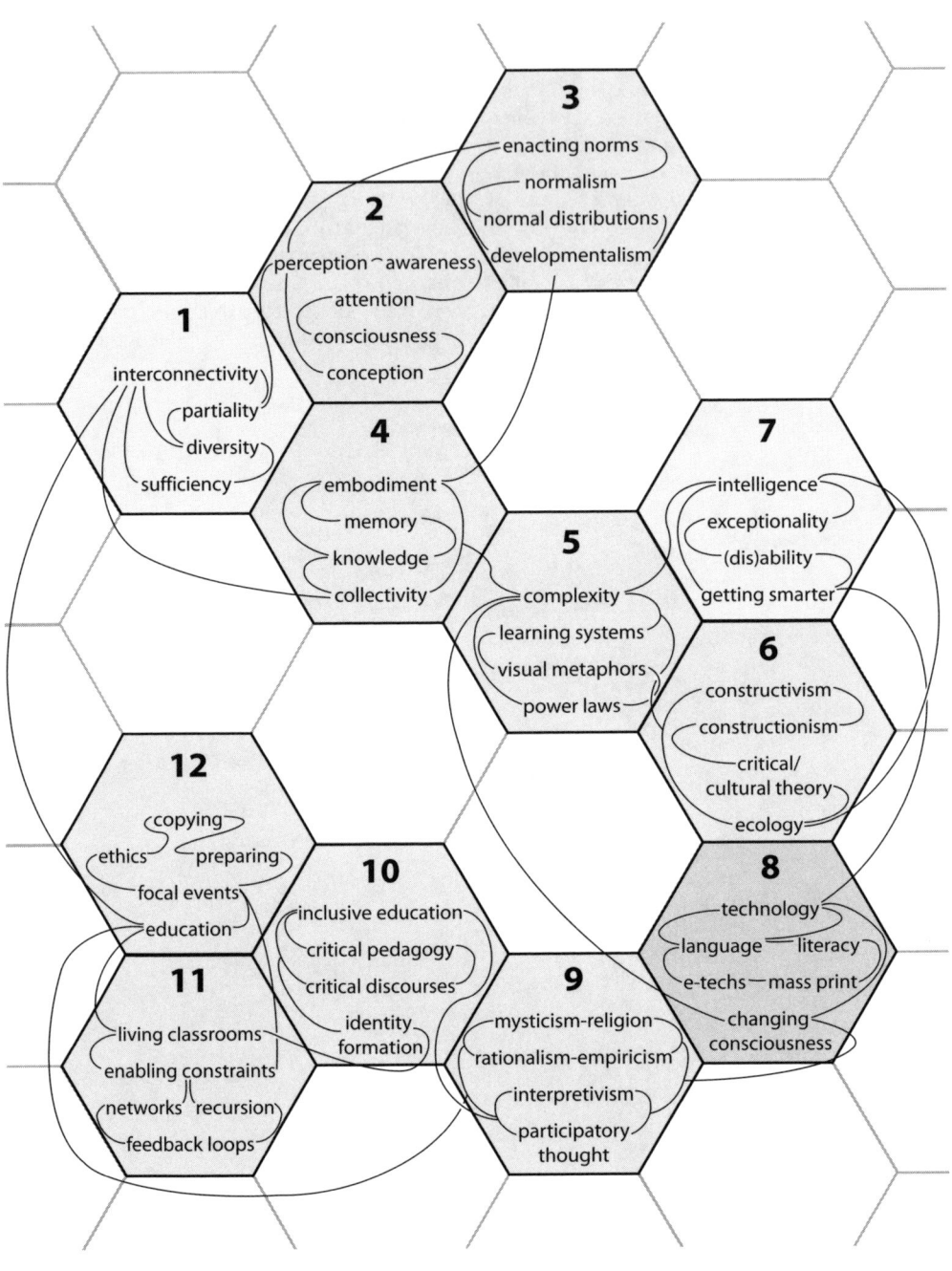

8   Learning Forms

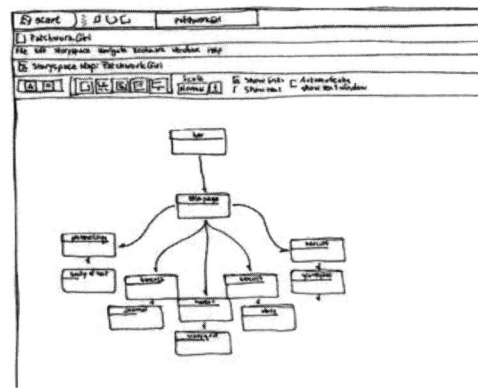

Shelley Jackson's *Patchwork Girl: A Modern Monster** is a satirical writing about the experiences of Frankenstein's female monster. The image of the stitched-together monster greets one at the entrance of the e-literature and ultimately becomes a symbol of a patched story where a reader will find herself at times immersed in the consciousness of a monster pieced together from multiple characters. Other times, she will hear the monster's creator, Mary Shelley, and at still others, the text itself discussing its creation. The hypertext, like the monster, is stitched together, its ruptures plainly visible as it explores how identity is multifaceted.

Over the past year, I have invited adolescents to read this hypertext and create their own e-literature using the software program, *Storyspace*. I focused on how they engaged with a digital genre—one that draws on and departs from literary traditions. One of the participants—a 16-year-old girl named Stevie—responded to the project with enthusiasm. Reading *Patchwork Girl* and writing e-literature, she thoughtfully explored different aspects of identity.

---

* Shelley Jackson's *Patchwork Girl*, other examples of e-literature, and the Storyspace software, are available at http://www.eastgate.com.
** An extended account of this event is provided in Rebecca Luce-Kapler, Teresa Dobson, Dennis Sumara, Tammy Iftody, & Brent Davis, "E-Literature and the digital engagement of concsiousness," in *55th Yearbook of the National Reading Conference* (eds. James Hoffman, Diane Schallert, Colleen Fairbanks, Jo Worthy, & Beth Maloch; Oak Creek, WI: National Reading Conference, 2006): 171–181.

8.1 Technology

Usually the word *technology* calls to mind the latest mechanical and electronic gadgets. This is certainly the case in discussions of incorporating technologies into the classroom where the word pulls attentions toward computers, the internet, hypertexts, and so on.

The term actually has a much broader meaning, however. Derived from the Greek *tekhne*, "art" or "skill," technology refers not just to artifacts and tools, but also to the array of methods, theories, and practices that define a culture. To borrow from one analysis,* this more generous definition encompasses branches of technology that include physical, chemical, biological, biosocial, social, behavioral, epistemic and philosophical interests, artifacts, and competencies.

Across such a breadth, perhaps the most pervasive and powerful technology is language. In language, human brains have been equipped with habits, methods, associations, and information—in effect, mind-tools—that draw from the experiences of billions of other lives and that have been honed over thousands of generations. This technology underpins the human ability to come together in grander cognitive systems, ones with capacities that vastly surpass the abilities of individuals.

This sort of claim may seem a little exaggerated. But consider how novelists and poets have demonstrated that, thanks to the incredible flexibility of linguistic technologies, there is no limit to the characters and events that can be created and experienced. Or, as is demonstrated in every high school course, teachers can expect students to deal with problems and paradoxes that mystified the human race for generations.

A language is more than a system of words. It is a network of associations that extends across time and space, a reservoir of variation, a sea of possibilities. A language might be characterized as an evolving form that constantly modifies and reorganizes itself through the continuing interactions of humans as they negotiate the world. On this count, human language has the remarkable capacity to be turned onto itself: language can be used to examine and elaborate

The word *grammar* refers to the organizing structures of language, and it tends to be interpreted in terms of mechanical rules.

Its earlier uses, however, suggest somewhat richer notions. The Middle English *grammarye* had to do with the occult and magical lore. (The word *glamour*, with its sense of alluring charm, is from the same root.) *Spell* has a similar history.

These terms suggest an awareness of the transformative power of language and, in particular, of the written word. The use of relatively stable symbols to represent transient experience was understood to affect those experiences.

* From Mario Bunge, "Ethics and praxiology as technologies," in *Techne*, vol. 4, no. 4 (1999): 1–3. For a discussion of the educational import of this sort of classification scheme, see Stephen Petrina, *Advanced teaching methods for the technology classroom* (Hershey, PA: Information Science Publishing, 2006).

What is the meaning of this symbol?

Of course, the only sensible answer is, "It depends." The symbol might be an "I," an "L," a "1," a "/," or any number of other things, and each of these interpretations unfolds into another web of possibilities. That is, the meaning is not in the symbol, but in the webs of association that the symbol triggers when it is used in a particular context. Such is the power of letters, words, icons, and so on: they collect together and trigger an immensity of associations.

As such, symbols are a powerful technology for thinking. With them, we can chunk together ideas and "smuggle" more into consciousness than would otherwise be possible. Without them, consciousness would be something entirely different.

language, creating a recursive loop that has set the stage for philosophy, science, and other technologies.

With its capacity to adapt, language fulfills many functions. For example, it serves as a sort of dynamic repository of collective knowledge. A variety of linguistic devices, including metaphor, metonymy, and analogy, help to preserve associations among categories of experience. In the process, these strategies greatly reduce the demands on our conscious brains while they amplify interpretive reach. As well, the extraordinary technology of language enables increasingly complex modes of thought by allowing us to ignore, defer, or offload cognitive tasks. An instruction like "Run to the store and pick up a carton of milk" may sound simple, but only because it collects and compresses so much knowledge. (Try to imagine what you would have to do to program a robot to follow the instruction.)

Perhaps the most useful aspect of the technology of language is the way it allows us to experiment with possibilities without committing to them, potentially saving not only time and effort but also lives. Most other species can only learn the consequences of a sequence of actions by actually engaging in those actions, but humans can think through probable outcomes. Language enables forethought, anticipation, planning, and strategizing. In other words, language frees us from the confines of the immediate present.

Of course, it's not all good. As with any technology, language succeeds by culling possibilities and channeling thought. In doing so, language renders some interpretations automatic and others impossible. Language helps to shape realities. It's not hard to imagine the webs of linguistic association that supported the 19th-century "discovery" that slaves suffered from *drapetomania* and *dysaethesia aethiopica*, or an irrepressible desire to escape servitude and a tendency to disobey … or the early-20th-century demonstration that blacks are cognitively inferior to whites … or the mid-20th-century designation of homosexuality as a disease. One can only imagine what the next generation will think about some of the bizarre things that we hold to be self-evident, thanks to the way they are suspended in a web of linguistic associations.

The irony of a technology such as language is the manner in which it conceals its tremendous complexity. We don't see language as a technology because we embody it. By contrast, cutting-edge tools impose themselves on our consciousnesses, demanding focused attention to understand and manipulate. On this count, the educator has two major responsibilities when it comes to technology: opening up new vistas of possibility by attending to emergent technologies, and preventing the shutdown of other possibilities by technologies that have become invisible to their users.

As she began to read *Patchwork Girl*, Stevie noticed that she'd have to take a different approach. She described how she used many of the visual elements of the text to get a sense of the different characters present and how she checked the story chart to see the underlying relationships. From that view of the hypertext, she could "look at all the big parts" to organize her reading, by using the colors of boxes and noting the names of sections and links. For instance, she focused first on the red-colored boxes because she believed they had a certain importance regarding character and plot. She also recognized that the font shifted in size according to which character was speaking. She offered this theory:

I guess that way you could easily tell who is talking. I mean, sometimes there are books written and they'll be in first person, but here there are three characters in first person and so the font is different.

Stevie also pointed out how the author used links to include what she identified as "after-thoughts." In literary work, writers usually omit such details or relegate them to a back page as they balance the demands of story with the minds of characters. With e-literature, as Stevie noted, the author is able to signal that these ideas are part of the character's consciousness, but they're not necessarily critical to the storyline.

She explained:

In Patchwork Girl there was one word, "Dream," and then you clicked on it and the whole thing was in brackets like one long continuing extension. So you can have the same experience reading it as the writer had writing it. It makes you feel closer to the story.

Stevie recognized that the writer wanted to develop the character's dream or stream-of-consciousness. The writer was able to do so by employing a visual cue from the print tradition (parentheses), and also by creating a separate textbox for the character's musings—one that functioned as an aside.

8.2 Writing

It might be tempting to think that the issue of how to incorporate new technologies into formal education—or, more fundamentally, *whether* they should be introduced at all—is a new one.

In fact, it's an ancient worry—at least as old as the technology of writing. For example, in *Phaedrus*, Plato wondered if the written word might damage thought.

Writing eased the demands on memory, he reasoned, perhaps dulling abilities to juggle thoughts and recall important details.

He was probably at least partially correct on this count. However, while writing reduces the need to exercise working memory, it also frees up consciousness so that we can deal with issues in more focused and prolonged ways. Something is lost, but more seems to be gained. Through writing, we no longer have to rely on intermediaries. We can draw directly on other's insights even when separated by seas and centuries.

The technology of writing did more than affect how much could be known, how it might be preserved, and how it can be accessed. It also presented a new metaphoric frame for knowing. In oral cultures, it makes little sense to think about knowledge as though it has an existence independent of a knower. To preserve knowledge, it must be rehearsed; to access knowledge, you have to seek out someone who knows. In such contexts, knowledge plainly exists in, consists of, and persists through action and interaction. So understood, language is never neutral. It has the power to *invoke*, to *evoke*, to *provoke* (all from the Latin *vox*, "voice"). Voice ties the discussion to mystical-religious conceptions of teaching (see chap. 9) and to current interests in spirituality (from the Latin *spirare*, "to breathe"—see the margin notes on pp. 66–67).

The written word changes things as it provides a means to detach knowledge from its author and its audience, giving knowledge a sort of permanence and rigor (literally, "stiffness"). Notions of objectivity and subjectivity arise as describer is separated from description, knower from known, and self from other. These tendencies were amplified as representational systems evolved from pictographs to alphabets that retained little or no trace of their grounded, experiential origins.

On the matter of subjectivity, careful examinations of cultural groups that are relatively uninfluenced by the literate world have shown that citizens of oral societies tend to describe themselves in terms of their relationships to others and their responsibilities in the

The word *read* derives from the Latin *rede*, "stomach of the cow." While perhaps not the most appealing image, it brings to mind such associations as digesting ideas, chewing over suggestions, ruminating, and regurgitation. In the process, this historical root highlights an early insight: like all aspects of language use, reading and other literacies involve far more than decoding symbols. They are acts of reconstitution and profound transformation.

collective. That is, self-descriptions are situated and distributed as people identify themselves in terms of their roles and relations. Members of literate societies tend to be more self-referencing and inward looking, describing themselves in terms of personality traits and personal interests. The implication is that members of literate cultures are much more prone to think of themselves as autonomous, individual, self-contained, and self-sufficient. They frame their identities more in terms of the personal than the interpersonal and the independent than the interdependent.*

Senses of independence are also projected onto words themselves in literate settings. With no access to the writer, the reader has no opportunity to query meanings, which supports a tendency to treat words as stand-alone objects with stable definitions. By contrast, there is much less concern for standardized definitions in oral settings where intended meanings are negotiated in face-to-face interactions. An upshot is that languages that aren't associated with written representations are much more fluid than those accompanied by systems of writing. Oral languages evolve and bifurcate into dialects (and, eventually, new tongues) much more rapidly than written languages.

With this emergent sense of word-objects, it's perhaps not surprising that the technology of writing is associated with logical modes of reasoning. The word *logic* is derived from the Greek *logos*, "word." Writing compels an orderly, linear presentation of ideas. Analyses of some of the earliest written texts reveal that linear argumentation was not the preferred mode of reasoning at the historical moment in which some cultures made the transition from orality to literacy. Such works as Herodotus's *The Histories* (c. 450 BCE) consist of what to us might seem a strange mix of conjecture, myth, gossip, opinion, and fact. These early texts are often very difficult to "follow"—difficult, at least, to those who have come to expect a coherent strand of thought to be carried from the start to the end. Part of the reason is that such writings likely consist in large part of transcriptions of actual face-to-face accounts in which the central concern is not unambiguous explication, but a compelling narrative.

Assumptions about the "thing-ness" of knowledge are prominent in literate societies. The notion is supported by metaphors of words-as-meaning-containing-objects, as heard in phrases such as "put ideas into words" and "empty words."

By implication, communication is understood as a matter of exchanging containers and extracting meanings.

These habits of thought are knitted through language, and are so pervasive that a person raised in a literate society would almost certainly hold a very different world view from a member of an oral culture—whether or not he or she has learned to read.

* See David R. Olson, *The world on paper: The conceptual and cognitive implications of writing and reading* (Cambridge, UK: Cambridge University Press, 1996).

Of course, rigor and logic are arguably the most important aspects of writing technologies. They powerfully support the development and proliferation of knowledge, especially when coupled to the means offered by the written word for off-loading demands on memory by, for example, keeping notes, making lists, assembling reference books, and organizing information alphabetically. Through the relatively modest investment of cognitive resources associated with learning to read, we gain access to accumulated human knowledge.

This manner of discussion begs the question, "How might emergent technologies be contributing to transformations in how we think about ourselves, our knowing, and what it means to learn?" Certainly technologies such as chat lines, text messaging, blogs, and online gaming—none of which were even imagined even a few decades ago—are challenging entrenched assumptions on such fundamental matters as the natures of literacy and individuality. They're also enabling different sorts of narratives. As publications such as *Patchwork Girl* demonstrate, the rigid form and logical sequencing of the print text is giving way to more fluid and participatory forms that engage readers in different ways.

Throughout our conversation about her reading, Stevie searched to find language to describe the opportunities to experience the characters' consciousnesses through e-literature. Much of what she drew from were standard literary terms, but it became clear that she was finding them not entirely adequate to describe her experience with hypertext. This became apparent when she talked about the use of point of view. Stevie commented that when reading first person, the reader thinks of that "I" being almost like oneself, but with *Patchwork Girl*, there is an ever-shifting cast of first person opportunities that at times can be confusing. When she finally gave an overall assessment of the story, however, she was able to point directly to the notion of how one experiences consciousness through literary engagement. "I think it works," she said, "because the whole story is thoughts basically. I know that my thoughts bounce from one thing to another, so I think it's almost a stream-of-consciousness. It's like a written portrait of the human mind almost."

Shifting between the thoughts of three or more minds in the story, Stevie never became immersed in the reading because the text demanded she attend to who was speaking and to be aware of the mind she was experiencing. She had to be more conscious of her response to the text and how those thoughts were represented as dreams, asides, and storytelling. As in a conversation with her friends, Stevie had to remain alert to what was unfolding with a level of attentiveness that was different from the sort of awareness associated with reading novels. This attention meant that she also continued to monitor how the text related to her experience and her shifting sense of self-identity.

8.3 Reading

How does the technology of writing influence us? In what ways might the ability to scribe contribute to transformations of who we are and what we know?

Whether the writer is composing a private letter, personal narrative, historical account, technical exposition, or literary fiction, in every case she or he must engage in some act of imagination. The act of writing is not simply a mopping up process; that is, it's more than a matter of transcribing thoughts that have already occurred. Writing is an act of thought and reformulation; it is a recursively elaborative process that affects interpretations of experiences.

The imaginative dimensions of writing extend even further. To write is to invent webs of relations: the writer formulates images to represent thinking; the writer structures narratives to account for these images; and the writer imagines a reader who will interpret and respond to these representations. In other words, writing and reading are always acts of fictionalizing.

The suggestion here is not that linguistic representations are fabrications or misrepresentations. Rather, the notion of "fictionalizing acts" is intended as a reminder that all reportings reflect writers' partialities—conscious and nonconscious. They are as much statements about the perceiver (including the personal and social conditions of perception) as they are about the phenomenon perceived.

This statement applies to both deliberate fictions (e.g., short stories, novels, and movies) and to accounts that are presented as accurate or factual depictions of experience (e.g., diaries, scientific reports, political ads, news stories, curriculum guides, and books about education). As with all written records, these texts are rife with context- and era-specific assumptions and concerns. As powerfully evidenced by textbooks and encyclopedias from a century ago—and, we (the authors) might add, by editions of books on knowing, learning, and teaching from less than a decade ago—all efforts at representation are (or eventually come to be seen as) fictionalizing acts.

SKILL *versus* UNDERSTANDING?

To read is to decode. It relies on mastery of the rules of grammar, spelling, and so on. Teaching should thus focus on **skills**.	To be able to read is to be able to extract appropriate meaning from a text. Teaching should thus be global and focus on **comprehension**.

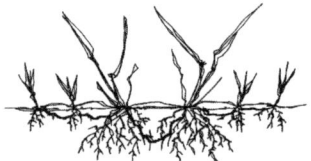

COMMON ROOTS: Perhaps the most heavily debated topic in reading education, the skills/understanding dichotomy tends to be anchored to the assumption that reading is a matter of gleaning meaning through some process of translating print into oral language. (Similar debates are prominent in other disciplines, especially mathematics.)

Such claims, of course, raise important questions about the distinction between "truth" and "fiction." If all narratives are understood as fictionalizing acts, does that mean that we should approach poetry and novels in the same way that we approach memoirs and scientific reports (or vice versa)? This issue is further complicated by publications in which writers have invented characters to narrate events from their own lives. Should such writings be considered factual or fictional? Or, conversely, what of the case of a writer who decides to invent events but to present them as autobiographical? What if an anthropologist visits a foreign culture and writes about it from her or his own ethnocentric perspective?

Literary theorists have long been dealing with such issues. Among theorists, there is a general agreement that what is at stake is not whether something is fact or fiction, but how the text is presented to the reader. Particular formatting strategies and expressive devices have been developed that, in effect, announce to the reader how to engage with the genre. For example, the way that the lines of a poem are organized on a page, or the unusual juxtapositions of images within a play, or the tempo of a short story, or the manner in which a character is introduced in a novel, all suggest to the experienced reader that the text should be engaged as a literary work. And that manner of engagement is not the same as the way one would approach, say, a history text.

What's the difference between these two genres? In brief, the historical (or scientific, or mathematical, or journalistic, etc.) text asks the reader to believe that what is being stated is an accurate account of some event or insight. The literary text, however, only asks the reader to *pretend* to believe what is being presented. The pretense creates very different interpretive conditions for the reader.

Why do these structural and experiential distinctions matter?

As discussed in chapter 2, we are consciously aware of only a tiny fraction of the stimuli that impinge on our senses at any given moment. Moreover, our habits of perception are largely conditioned by social

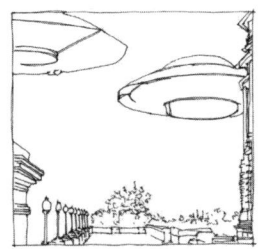

In 1938, Orson Welles' *War of the Worlds*, a story about a Martian invasion of Earth, was broadcast on radio stations across the United States.

It was presented in the style of a live news cast—that is, it had all the markers of non-fiction. This detail was announced at the start of the broadcast. Unfortunately, many listeners who missed the first few minutes took the program literally. Some even committed suicide rather than waiting helplessly for Martian domination.

Fortunately, most literary forms use explicit devices to announce to readers that they should not believe, but *pretend to believe*, what is written.

and cultural contexts. In other words, experience is always larger than attempts to interpret and represent it. There can never be a "full account," an "objective rendering," or a "literal representation" of an event or phenomenon. This limitation is a problem for texts that claim to be factual. These sorts of writings are subject to critical questions about their partialities: "Who is speaking?" "Whose truths are being represented?" "Which details are omitted?" "Whose interests are being served?"

The case for the literary text is quite different. Although still limited by the writers' and the readers' culturally conditioned habits of perception, the literary fiction aims more at presenting occasions for alternative interpretive possibilities than at presenting already-interpreted accounts. The literary text is one that uses language playfully as it points to different ways that events can be experienced and understood. To enlarge the interpretive possibilities of the reader, authors interrupt habits of perception and interpretation through such literary devices as metaphor and irony.*

Once again, a key quality of the literary fiction is that it does not ask readers to believe but *to pretend to believe*. Whereas the factual account is principally aimed at providing information, the literary work is more about providing access to experiences that are not otherwise possible. (Recall, as discussed in chap. 4, the same clusters of neurons are activated whether imagining an activity or actually engaging in that activity.) In effect, through one's participation in fictional events—that is, through these deliberate engagements of the imagination—one's sphere of experience can be expanded. And with widened experience, the doors are opened to new and different perceptual and interpretive possibilities. Writing does have the potential to take us "out" (or, perhaps more descriptively, "beyond") our imagined selves.

This may be part of the reason that religious texts, folk tales, mythologies, and other cultural narratives figure so prominently in all societies. These accounts are much more than tales. They are collecting places for wisdom, moral direction, and knowledge gleaned

The word *literate* derives from the Latin *litteratus*, "learned" or, more precisely, "acquainted with *littera*, the letters of the alphabet."

That original meaning is quite telling. It highlights an early realization that the written word was a powerful technology. A simple knowledge of the alphabet was enough to separate the learned from the unlearned.

The term has, of course, come to imply far more since it was first used, now referring more broadly to any discipline or body of knowledge that relies on formal symbol systems.

* See Dennis Sumara, *Why reading literature in school still matters: Imagination, interpretation, insight* (Mahwah, NJ: Lawrence Erlbaum, 2002).

over the generations. These texts demonstrate that certain writings needn't be taken literally to be taken seriously. They are powerful because they make it possible for hearers or readers to imagine themselves in the narrative, allowing the narratives to become collected within the totality of the reader's remembered experiences. Fact-based accounts, which make it difficult to invoke the powers of the imagination, rarely have the same effect.

Once again, however, this situation may be changing as new genres of writing are developed. As illustrated in the example of wiki spaces—and wikipedia.org in particular—electronic technologies have enabled more democratic, collective, and participatory writing spaces in which such issues as power dynamics, authorial voice, distributed knowing, and networked intelligence are dramatically transformed, as are possibilities for writing spaces that are organized around specialized interests, cross-fertilization of ideas, and creation of virtual communities.*

To elaborate, in the era of paper-based texts, communication was mainly unidirectional and unidimensional, but emergent technologies in which the screen takes the place of the page open up multidirectional and multidimensional spaces. Emails, chatrooms, and text-messaging are three obvious illustrations at the moment and likely only just a hint of what's on the horizon. Not only do they enable instantaneous responses, but they also make it possible to complexify authorship by altering the texts received.

Further, electronic messages are more image-oriented than the paper-based notes that they are replacing. As authorship is distributed and diffused and as the linearity of written text is interrupted, authority of the written word is diminished, reshaping concerns about power and privilege.** Our world changes with the tools used to represent it—and this realization should prompt us to wonder about how emerging technologies might enable and constrain interpretive possibilities.

Writing technologies aren't innocent. What worlds do they open up, and what worlds do they close down?

The pprusoe of tihs mriagn ntoe is to povdire a qicuk dmeo of the cailm taht randeig cnonat be rdceued to spimle donicdeg.

It tnrus out taht, so lnog as the frsit and lsat ltetres of ecah wrod are crocert, msot raedres can mkae out the ientnedd mennaig.

Tihs is pabolbry a hpapy tinhg, gvein smoe polpee's tinpyg adn splinleg sklils.

* See Colin Lankshear & Michele Knobel, *New literacies: Changing knowledge and classroom learning* (Berkshire, UK: Open University Press, 2006).
** See Gunther Kress, *Literacy in the new media age* (London: Routledge, 2003).

Stevie's reading of the identity themes in *Patchwork Girl* became more obvious as she wrote her e-story in Storyspace. This program opens textboxes for the creator to insert text, image, or sound and then link them together in whatever pattern the author chooses. Also available to the writer—and, if she wishes, her reader—are various underlying views of the overall text, including a chart, outline, and map view as is the case with *Patchwork Girl*.

Stevie's e-literature jumps across time and it features a narrator who has no name and a shifting gender similar to Virginia Woolf's *Orlando*. As Stevie explained,

It sort of jumps ahead, maybe several hundred years. It's the same character, but it could be a reincarnation of him or something. I was thinking about whether or not to make this in first person,

because I didn't even know if I wanted it to be a man or woman.

In one section, which Stevie identified as being from the female perspective, a reader is introduced to the character and her friend Keziah, who are clearly being considered as slaves for purchase. The character described herself as meek, serene, and silent—and, indeed, the descriptions have a certain softness about them, even though the character is afraid. The section "Sold" begins:

We are led into a long house with high walls and a beautiful garden. The men who guard us carry whips and warn us to smile and be serene. Keziah, beside me, grabs my hand and squeezes it before a whip lashes and barely misses licking her skin. She drops my hand and stares resolutely forward."

8.4 Mass Printing

The technology of spoken language greatly enabled the coupling of minds and, with that, the elaboration of ideas. The technology of the written word greatly amplified the abilities to preserve and distribute insights.

The invention of the movable type by Johannes Gutenberg in 1447 proved to be another profoundly important technological innovation. The printing press permitted the mass production of books, which in turn had two major cultural impacts. First, on the individual level, the general populace became more literate with better access to affordable texts on a range of topics. Second, it prompted a sudden proliferation of specialized knowledge.

On the first point, the invention of print technologies made it possible for almost anyone to buy or borrow books, making them naturalized parts of the modern citizen's life. The pervasiveness of the printed word prompted a transformation in the nature of reading from a mainly public event to a mainly private one. (Prior to mass printing, one was usually read *to* or lectured *at* in churches, universities, and other gathering places. The terms *reader* and *lecturer* are still used as synonyms to *teacher* in some contexts.) The new technology of private and silent readings soon became one of the expected "basic skills" of a modern citizen. And it transformed teaching.

Along with silent reading came the possibility for (and expectation of) rapid reading. Prior to mass production of books, there tended to be little attention to such details as uniformity of font, evenness of spacing, standardization of spelling, and consistency of punctuation in handwritten manuscripts. Such issues were not of major concern since public readings were typically slow and context-specific. However, formatting of texts intended for a mass market had to be more standardized, which in turn made it possible to decode texts more quickly. So strong was this emphasis on *decoding* that it is sometimes equated with *reading*, which, as developed in the preceding section, is troublesome. As mentioned, reading is a participation in a literate culture and entails many and varied interpretive skills.

Even though scarcely a few centuries old, rapid silent reading has become so important in our society that children who aren't able to master the competency are often identified as challenged in some learning domain. (As discussed in chap. 7, most learning disabilities are associated with reading.) Such diagnoses, in turn, often support a remedial emphasis on decoding. This consequence has supported teaching practices that sometimes give short shrift to vital stages in learning to read, including an emphasis on interpreting texts, recognizing genres, and being exposed to oral models.

As for the second major influence of the printing press, artisans and craftpersons began to use this technology to publish details of their production methods, providing general access to knowledge that had previously been confined to guilds and other closed communities. Once accessible, this information provided scientists with the technical knowledge they needed to conduct more sophisticated experiments (which, when published, prompted even more sophisticated experiments). As well, it enabled industrialists to capitalize, pulling together different categories of expertise. In

One of the foremost goals of conventional reading instruction is the mastery of silent reading—a practice that has been argued to have contributed to the modern belief in the separability of mental and physical events.

In fact, there is considerable bodily activity during acts of silent reading, including persistent subvocalizations—that is, one's silent readings are always accompanied by a sort of silent speaking—as well as neurological activity that is virtually indistinguishable from what goes on when engaging in the physical actions that one is reading about.

In other words, the internalness or mentalness of silent reading is an illusion. Like all acts of knowing, silent reading is a bodily engagement.

brief, the printing press appears to have been a critical spark in the European Renaissance, the rise of modern science, and the emergence of an industrialized Europe. An alliance of science and technology enabled increased productivity and improved armaments, which in turn prompted needs for more raw materials and the means to acquire them. European imperialism and western capitalism soon extended their reach around the planet.

Educationally, the modern school was one of the major products of the era. There was a sudden demand for a moderately literate workforce and, at the same time, a need to keep children of the lower classes out of the labor market. This highly regimented public institution was largely organized around the contexts where its students would eventually find themselves: the factory.

Unlike educational institutions that preceded it, which were mainly intended for members of the upper and ruling classes, the modern school was focused on technical competence with an emphasis on "basics" for all. Even though it is impossible to argue that the bits of knowledge that were basic to factory workers of the 16th century are basic to citizens of the 21st century, contemporary curricula are strikingly similar. The lack of change is suprising, given the recent emergence of tools that transform the nature of information and access to it in ways that are at least as dramatic as the invention of the printing press.*

Educationally speaking, a difficulty with symbol-based technologies (like alphabets and numerals) is the way their roots in the physical world tend to become obscured as they evolve.

Having lost obvious ties to the ground of experience, symbols are often treated as arbitrary and abstract operators that disconnect, rather than contextual and concrete artifacts that link self to other, past to present, and individual to collective.

* See Madeleine Grumet, "The curriculum: What are the basics and are we teaching them?" in *Thirteen questions: Reframing education's conversation* (eds. Joe L. Kincheloe & Shirley R. Steinberg; New York: Peter Lang, 1993).

In another section of the hypertext, Stevie wrote about an earlier time in history. In contrast to the account of the meek, serene, and silent girl awaiting sale, this time the character is clearly male, as becomes evident in a description found in the textbox entitled "My Body":

I stand above the small stream running through cracks in the earth. It is almost dry now, and soon we'll have to move on. But there is enough water to see my blurred reflection. Dark skin, hair, and eyes glare back at me from the depths. The creature in the reflection has thick skin, a wide jaw, solemn lips. This is me, I think, and I *am suddenly struck with a powerful awareness of my existence.*

Stevie was clear about how *Patchwork Girl* focused on each character's consciousness, rather than being concerned about the plot. Furthermore, as she "read" across minds, her sense of the story as an exploration of identity emerged. When she came to write her own e-literature, she chose to create one narrator, but reflected the concept of shifting identity by traveling across time and creating a character who at some moments was female and at others male.

8.5 Electronic Technologies

If one thing can be said about human technologies, it is that the pace of their development is constantly accelerating. The growth is exponential. This insight is one that has only recently become commonsensical, prompted by the fact that change is now so rapid that it occurs on a similar time scale to individual learning. (Just a century ago, the rate was so slow that development was seen as a steadily paced but not an accelerating phenomenon.)

By consequence, we find ourselves in a proliferation of previously unimaginable possibilities. Those with privileged access to information technologies can locate facts, acquire texts, distribute insights—in brief, exchange vast amounts of information—in a manner that wasn't conceivable even a few decades ago.

The new technologies also enable new, immensely interactive and participatory "mass collaborations."* Whereas print technology is principally one-way, current information technologies allow for multidirectional conversations that can involve hundreds of thousands of people. Websites such as wikipedia.org and answers.com are powerful illustrations of this point. As well, they allow for "critical masses" of people to assemble around ideas and interests that previously might never have been popular enough to attract a community.

As mentioned in previous chapters, the conditions for ever-faster-paced expansion of human possibility are in place—which, as noted in chapter 7, has prompted some commentators to suggest that human intelligence might be trillions and trillions of times greater by the end of this century.** Even if humanity falls far short of such projections, it's clear that enhanced knowing and learning will almost certainly prompt dramatic changes to conceptions and enactments of schooling.

It is impossible to address such matters in any deep way, but there are some issues that can be highlighted. For instance, the accelerating pace of technological development appears to be contributing to an amplifi-

The term *technology* is usually used in reference to mechanical devices, especially the most recent of inventions. The word originally referred to any means of enhancing capabilities. In this sense, and as developed in the first half of this chapter, perhaps our most important technology is language.

Technologies have a way of fading into the backdrops of our lives, folded  into our beings so seamlessly that we are oblivious to the fact that we're all, quite literally, cyborgs.

* See Don Tapscott & Anthony D. Williams, *Wikinomics: How mass collaboration changes everything* (New York: Portfolio, 2006).

** See Kurzweil, *The singularity is near*.

cation of the differences between haves and have-nots on many levels, including access to resources, technologies, and information. In a different vein, humanity has reached the point that it can use cultural knowledge to transform biological forms, although insights into the consequences of such interventions seem to be much slower in coming. Also, as with previous waves of technology-prompted cultural change, the texture of the work world is clearly going to be different. A century ago, 30–40% of the North American workforce was employed on farms. Now the corresponding figure is in the range of 3–4%. Similar trends have been noted for factory labor, and there are signs of spillage into other career domains.

On the more immediate and pragmatic level, emergent technologies have transformed the nature of reading. Being a fluent reader of a standard, paper-based text usually means being able to read every word. Nearly the opposite is true on the internet, where reading fluency means being able to skip words in order to locate relevant information. Knowing what *not* to attend to is as important as knowing what to attend to.

Perhaps the most important issue for educators is the manner in which individual and collective identities are affected by current and upcoming innovations. As noted earlier, the inventions of language, writing, and mass printing had massive impacts on human identifications; there's every reason to anticipate that digital technologies will trigger similarly dramatic shifts.

The modern school is largely organized around print technology. Clearly, whatever formal education is, it's going to have to change.

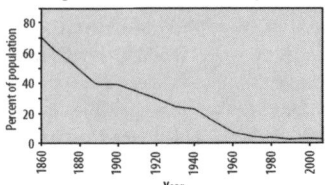

Percentage of North Americans Working on Farms

Over the past 150 years, the population of North America has shifted from predominantly rural to overwhelmingly urban. This decline is commonly linked to different innovations, some of which required abundant labor, while others improved farm productivity. Hence, there's a popular sense that technological advance *caused* urbanization.

In fact, the reverse can also be argued—that is, the explosion of innovation over past centuries was enabled by the concentration of thoughts and desires into compact urban spaces. The modern megacity enabled progress.

It's likely that neither causality nor linearity are useful notions here.

Stevie's reading of *Patchwork Girl*, with its metonymies, interruptions, and connections, reminded her of the sense of self-identity that each of us experiences. She compared the story to the way the mind works, suggesting that it is like a "stream-of-consciousness," where connected ideas unfold in a type of loose narrative. Unlike our actual experience of consciousness, however, e-literature provides the enabling constraint of a planned structure. When engaging with e-literature, readers must actively construct meaning by choosing and clicking on a matrix of links that connect numerous media—such as text, image, and sound. Because of this array of alternatives, writers must anticipate and include possibilities that may have been discarded in the past, broadening the story possibilities as more fragments are kept in play.

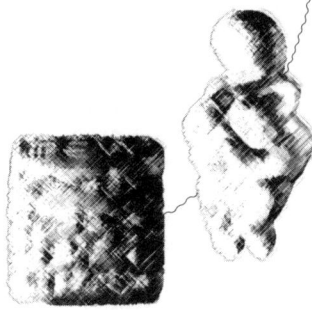

It has been argued that conscious experience is hinged to the sorts of tools that are available. These images represent four different eras of technology, and they might be indicative of four distinct ways of "being"—namely episodic, mimetic, mythic, and theoretical modes of consciousness.

* The account provided here is based on Merlin Donald, *Origins of the modern mind: Three stages in the evolution of culture and cognition* (Cambridge, MA: Harvard University Press, 1991). Other accounts include Terrance Deacon, *The symbolic species: The co-evolution of language and the brain* (New York: W.W. Norton, 1997); Daniel C. Dennett, *Kinds of minds: Towards an understanding of consciousness* (New York: Basic, 1997); Julian Jaynes, *The origin of consciousness and the breakdown of the bicameral mind* (New York: Penguin, 1979); Steven Mithen, *The prehistory of the mind: The cognitive origins of art, religion and science* (London: Thames and Hudson, 1996).

8.6 Changing Consciousness

For the most part, "technology" has been understood in terms of physical tools and machines. Sometimes language, mathematics, and other areas of human competence are included. But it's unusual to encounter discussions of how these artifacts and capabilities are incorporated into human existence. The principal interest has been how we shape our technologies, with less concern for how we embody our technologies.

It has become increasingly clear that technologies do more than affect what can be known or done. Our choices for and manners of representation contribute to self-identities, owing in large part to the ways that they affect what we notice, know, and do. (Try to represent who you are without mentioning who and what you identify with.) Identities arise from interactions. They are not pre-given, self-contained phenomena.

Stated somewhat differently, technologies participate in the transformation of minds—that is, experiences of consciousness—by shaping how experiences are represented. There is an abundance of evidence for this claim in the archeological record, in which there are indications of clear and rather abrupt advances in technologies that correspond with different social structures, different intellectual demands, and different preoccupations. These shifts might also be described as sudden lurches in intelligence as humans expanded their repertoires of possibility at a pace that simply cannot be explained through biological evolution.

Different commentators organize eras and developments in different ways. For the sake of brevity, only one frame is presented here—one developed by psychologist Merlin Donald. (Other accounts are cited in a footnote.*)

Donald argues that the complexity of technology can be taken as an indication of the level of consciousness. For instance, it appears that until about two million years ago, the prevailing technologies were tools that were found rather than made, such as sticks and broken rocks. These items were for immediate use by individuals. They are the sorts of things that call on only short-term memory, and so are discarded and perhaps forgotten once the task is complete. Donald suggests such technologies are indicative of an *episodic consciousness*—an awareness of the here and now, but of little more.

According to current interpretations of the archeological record, a new category of technology appeared about two million years ago, one that was associated with the deliberate manufacturing of tools. Such tools required long-term memories that made it possible to select from past experience and contemplate future needs. Using the phrase *mimetic consciousness*, Donald suggests such a mode of awareness was more social and highly reliant on imitation (mimesis).

According to Donald, as these technologies proliferated and were improved, there arose a need for more flexible technologies to collect and organize ideas. Donald associates this transition with the emergence of sophisticated languaging technologies that made it possible to distribute memory across communities and to extend capacities to interpret the past and project into the future. This *mythic consciousness*, he suggests, emerged a few hundred thousand years ago.

Much more recently, in the order of 5,000–10,000 years ago, capacities to think abstractly were greatly enhanced. This sort of *theoretical consciousness*, as developed in previous sections, has been associated with the technology of writing, which makes it possible to deal with information in a more detached way and to stabilize insights by offloading memory onto physical artifacts.

Donald ends his analysis there, but it seems reasonable to argue that we are witnessing a further evolution of consciousness. In fact, using the markers suggested by Donald—that is, enhanced technologies, improved abilities to mass-link minds, increased intellectual capacities that can't be explained by biological evolution, emergence of new memory systems to store and access information, and shifts in social and cultural organization—it would seem likely that we are on the cusp of a new mode of consciousness. In fact, projects are underway to digitally chronicle every aspect of a person's life,* enabled by advances in video and data storage technologies. Clearly such enhanced memories

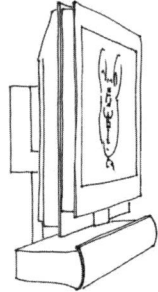

When motion pictures were first invented, many educators saw them as having the potential to streamline instruction and to even out inequities in schooling experience. The hope was that important details and concepts could be presented uniformly and unambiguously, thus avoiding such educational "noise" as teacher error and social circumstance. Similar (and even more grandiose) claims have been made of television and, more recently, of computers. But none of these hopes or expectations has been realized.

Why not?

One reason seems to be that such media operate at a low information

* See Gordon Bell & Jim Gemmell, "A digital life," in *Scientific American*, vol. 296, no. 3 (March 2007): 58–65.

present the possibility of dramatically transforming experience—and, hence, consciousness.

It's probably premature to try to specify the nature of a new form of consciousness that might be triggered and enabled by new technologies. However, an emergent mode of being will likely embody growing awarenesses of the complexity of learning phenomena and the participatory nature of knowing.

Why should we care?

It is clear that education is wholly complicit in the emergence of new possibilities. As educators, we are participating in the evolutions that we're witnessing. An interesting question at this point would be what sorts of educational processes might be associated with the different modes of consciousness mentioned above. For example, as illustrated by this chapter's interspersed narrative, it is apparent that "literacy education" is about far more than decoding and encoding. Rather, while engaging with *Patchwork Girl*, such skills were embedded in a more expansive pedagogy in which Stevie and others collaboratively developed a critical consciousness of their textual engagements through recursively elaborative processes of reflection and action.

Such events reveal that narratives and artifacts that might appear to be produced by an individual are more appropriately understood in terms of collective production. They involve many minds and mediating technologies and, in turn, they affect not only personal imaginations, motivations, and consciousnesses, but also cultural senses of truth, rationality, and justification. Against this backdrop, it is perhaps ironic that much of schooling practice still seems to be organized around the linearity of print-based texts, the singular authority of a mandated curriculum, and an ideal of individualism (embodied in evaluation schemes, classroom arrangements, and teaching strategies). The irony increases when one considers that the massive successes of video-gaming and related technologies are at least partly due to the ways their creators have deliberately exploited principles of learning related to collectivity, sociocultural contexts, shifting identities, embodiment, implicit associations, effortful study, nonlinear path-

level—one that has been deliberately adjusted to suit what consciousness is able to accommodate. And so, while these technologies can give access to immense stores of data, they operate at a very low level of stimulation.

Human sense organs, however, function at a capacity that is about one million times greater than conscious perception. As such, abundant use of the so-called "information technologies" may actually result in a starvation of the senses, an information poverty.

ways, and other notions presented in this text in ways that have been largely ignored by schools.*

The issues here could be phrased in terms of the way that "teaching" emerged and evolved alongside human consciousness. For instance, with the here- and now-ness of Donald's episodic consciousness, teaching would be largely accidental and nondeliberate, as novices copy the actions of experts. With the development of mimetic consciousness, as humans created task-specific tools, teaching had to become more intentional, taking on dimensions of showing and correcting.

With the emergence of abstract language and sophisticated narratives of a mythic consciousness, teaching would have had to become elaborated once again as the needs to rehearse and interpret were added to established instructional practices of showing, correcting, and modeling. Correspondingly, the emergence of a theoretical consciousness prompted an explosion of possible roles, presenting a need for a mode of teaching that is as much about anticipation of the future as maintenance of established knowledge.

It is becoming more obvious that teaching is nearing a new crossroads as it faces another shift in emphasis, away from *individuals* who *pass on* established *knowledge* and toward *collectives* who *elaborate* emergent *knowings*. As is explored in Part C, teaching is taking on a more participatory emphasis, and what it might become will have everything to do with the forms that are created for and by learning.

LEVELS OF CONSCIOUSNESS

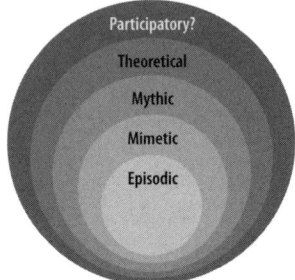

As with developmental stages (chap. 3) and nested learning systems (chap. 5), emergent modes of human consciousnss don't replace prior modes. Rather, all seem to be available, presenting needs for more nuanced, more complex forms of teaching.

* See James Paul Gee, *What video games have to teach us about learning and literacy* (New York: Palgrave Macmillan, 2003).
** See N. Katherine Hayles, *My mother was a computer: Digital subjects and literary texts* (Chicago: University of Chicago Press, 2005).

Stevie's experience highlights the necessity of planned engagements with digital technologies. We learn how to read e-literature by acknowledging that each example will teach us its rules of engagement. As these rules become clear, we then re-read with greater awareness. Further, as with all literary forms, we learn by creating our own examples. Stevie's understanding of *Patchwork Girl* was considerably deepened after she wrote her tale in Storyspace.

As her responses suggest, she was aware of how her body was engaging with e-literature, and she noted that the immersion she experienced with print novels was not possible with the digital text. This complex relationship between bodies, texts, and different forms of media is a manifestation of intermediation.** In reading or creating e-literature, we draw upon the narrative and poetic structures to which we are accustomed. E-literature, while certainly depending on elements of those literary structures that have come before it, incorporates new ways of organizing story and text. For instance, it also borrows from computer gaming, film, and visual arts, among other media. While literature has been an embodied art form, the presence of digital technology broadens the interaction of text and body to text, body, and computer.

PART C · teaching

Etymology

The word teach is derived from the Old English *tæcan*, which meant something like "sign" or "point," and by which any object or event could potentially serve as a teacher. To teach was to affect perceptions of the world. The act of teaching, that is, was understood more in terms of its effects on the learner than in terms of any deliberate effort to affect a learner.

Synonyms

advise, alter, ameliorate, better, brainwash, break in, brief, care, catechize, coach, communicate, condition, convert, convince, cram, cultivate, culture, demonstrate, develop, direct, discipline, drill, draw in, draw out, edify, educate, enable, encourage, enculturate, enlighten, exercise, explain, expound, facilitate, feed, form, forward, foster, further, give lessons, grill, ground, guide, hone, illustrate, imbue, impart, implant, improve, inculcate, indoctrinate, induct, influence, inform, initiate, instill, instruct, interpret, lead, lecture, mediate, mentor, model, nourish, nurture, occasion, open eyes, persuade, point out, pound into, prepare, profess, proselytize, ready, rear, refine, reform, remediate, school, sharpen, show, support, tell, train, tutor

Antonyms

abandon, answer, harm, ignore, learn, listen, neglect

Cognates

diction, token

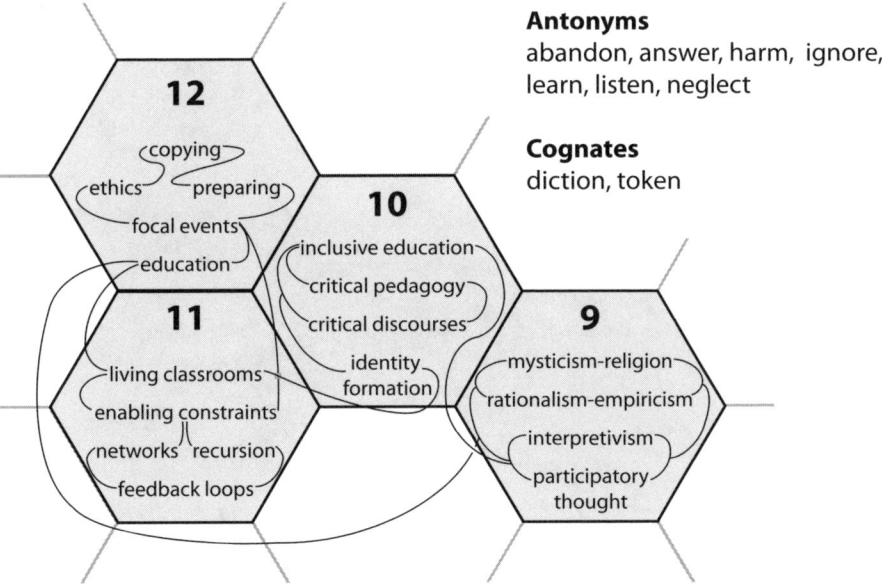

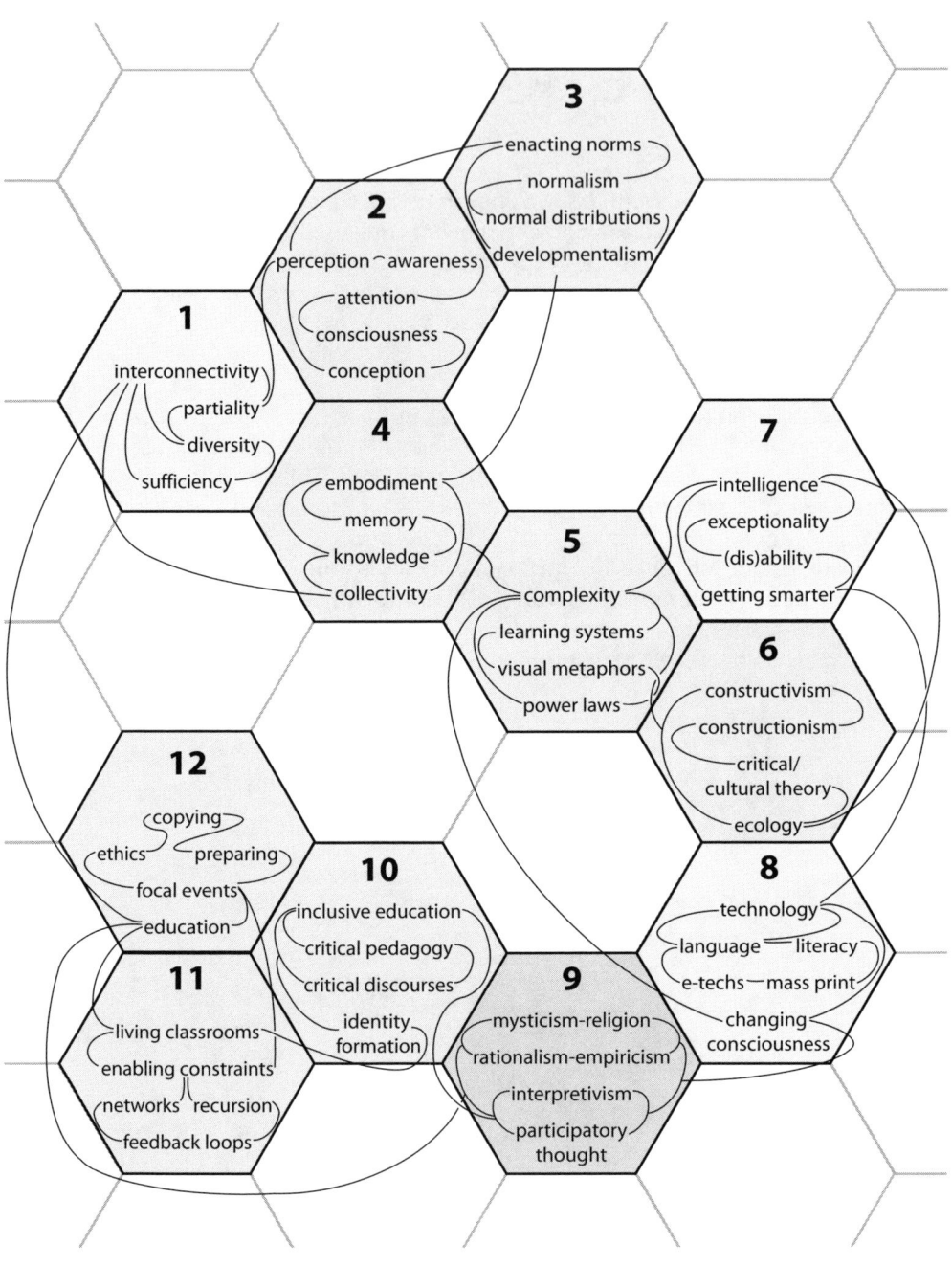

Teaching Frames

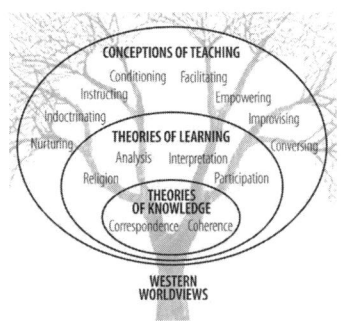

CONCEPTIONS OF TEACHING
Conditioning   Facilitating
Instructing
Indoctrinating   Empowering
Nurturing   Improvising
THEORIES OF LEARNING
Analysis   Interpretation
Religion   Conversing
Participation
THEORIES
OF KNOWLEDGE
Correspondence   Coherence

WESTERN
WORLDVIEWS   *

"They know that I'm afraid of them!" Jamie thinks as she waits for the Grade 7s to settle into their seats for the first class of the morning. Although she has carefully prepared for this moment—attending university seminars on curriculum and pedagogy, spending many hours on lesson and unit planning, buying new "teacher clothes," and adopting a well-rehearsed "firm but friendly" demeanor—Jamie doesn't feel like a teacher. She feels out of place, out of sorts, disoriented, worried. Her breath catches in her throat, her heart pounds, her face is flushed. She sees that the students are not settling as they should.

"Okay, I have to tell them what I want them to do."

As Jamie opens her mouth to speak, however, only a croak emerges. She tries again. Another croak, this time louder. She feels her throat tighten—and then, suddenly, a surge of energy, a moment of memory, and a slightly shaky but very assertive, "Okay class, we're ready to begin. Take your seats, settle down, and open your books to Chapter 2. I'm going to start by asking you a few questions about last night's readings."

To Jamie's relief, the class responds. The roar of chatter falls to a hush, then to a hum, finally to the sound of students sitting and books opening. Within a moment almost all eyes are on her, the teacher.

Jamie's initial panic is replaced by a new sureness. Her voice seems to come from somewhere else, her movements as if owned by another body, her responses like those borrowed from ghosts of teachers past. And yet, although strange, Jamie's experience of teaching this class is familiar. This is deeply satisfying to her. "Now I feel like a teacher!" she thinks, but also puzzles, "When did I become this person who these students see as the teacher? And what will become of the person that I was before?"

* This image and the discussion of varied conceptions of teaching presented in this chapter are based on Brent Davis, *Inventions of teaching: A genealogy* (Mahwah, NJ: Lawrence Erlbaum, 2004).

9.1 Conceptions of Teaching

As mentioned on the title page for this final part of the book, the word *teach* originally had to do with "signs" or "pointing." These associations are helpful for making sense of phrases such as "That'll teach you," that are so often used in reference to unforeseen consequences of actions. So conceived, any event or experience that prompts learning can properly be called teaching. Teaching is not about what the teacher does, it is about what happens to the learner.

It is reasonable, therefore, to expect a large assortment of words that describe teaching in terms of the actions by which a learner is taught. For example, at a typical conference on educational research, you can expect to hear most of the following in reference to what different people imagine should (or, in some cases, should not) be happening in the classroom: *conditioning, disciplining, educating, empowering, enlightening, facilitating, guiding, indoctrinating, instructing, leading, lecturing, mentoring, modeling, nurturing,* and *training.* (Note that many of these terms don't show up in thesaurus entries, such as the ones used to compile the list on p. 155. This sort of absence is an indication that sensibilities continue to evolve.)

Often, several of these terms will be used in the same presentation with little or no awareness that many of them point to very different, even contradictory, sorts of associations. In fact, a closer inspection can reveal some troublesome tensions and inconsistencies. How, for example, can teaching simultaneously be about enlightening and indoctrinating, or disciplining and empowering?

This chapter represents an attempt to address this sort of question, and the strategy is to develop a genealogy of various conceptions of teaching in which synonyms and metaphors are linked to particular theories and worldviews. Building on a principle developed in previous chapters—that is, that words are not packets of information, but nodes in webs of significance—the aim here is to foreground some of the associations that lend meaning to the array of terms that are used to characterize teaching.

Where, if anywhere, are the boundaries of *self?* Is there a border or a membrane that separates *me* from *not-me?* Is there some sort of shell that circumscribes identity? On what bases do we make such distinctions as self/other, private/public, individual/collective, human/world?

We use these questions as organizers for several of the margin notes in this chapter, arguing that conceptions of teaching are inextricably entangled with conceptions of personal identity.

As a genealogy, this chapter is structured around different families of thought and is organized in a tree-like manner. The following image might be useful to keep track of where you are in the reading.

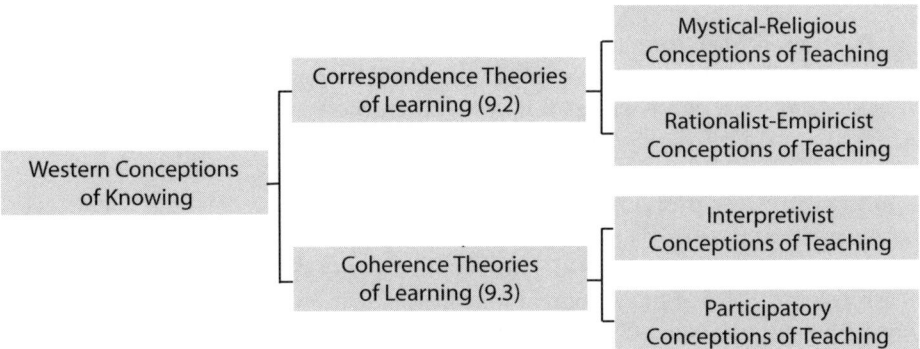

One important note: the following discussion should not be interpreted as a chronology, since concepts don't emerge and die off in the way that organisms give rise to and succeed one another. Critical moments in the evolutions of vocabularies can occur at any time, with new branches of thought growing out of old roots or dormant stumps. As well, multiple strands of thinking can be represented at the same time and even by the same person. The image above, then, is a frozen simplification of a more complex and evolving situation. Further, the intention in this chapter is not to argue what one should believe. It is, rather, to be attentive to what tends to be taken for granted in discussions of teaching. As is developed, the word *teaching* is anything but innocent or transparent …

… or simple. As one delves more deeply into the co-implicated questions, "What is it that we believe?" and "How did we come to think this way?" it becomes more and more obvious that we humans are capable of not only hanging onto many different strands of incompatible beliefs, but also combining them freely. To reiterate, then, the point of this chapter is not to tell readers how they should think about teaching. Rather, it is to raise awareness of how we are probably already thinking and, in the process, open the door to more complex possibilities.

What can we say about Jamie's initial terror—that is, her inability to feel part of this
situation. What about her eventual success?

How might different conceptions of teaching
be used to make sense of Jamie's and her students' actions?

9.2 Correspondence Theories and Teaching

As developed in chapter 6, most popular understandings of learning are rooted in an assumption of *correspondence*. That is, learning tends to be framed in
terms of assembling an internal model that mirrors,
represents, or otherwise maps onto the external world.
Among the many problems with this conception, two
prominent issues are (1) that nothing actually passes
from the outside to the inside during moments of
learning and (2) that neurological research has found
no evidence whatsoever of internal representations.
(See chap. 6 for more detail.)

The web of implicit associations that supports correspondence theories of learning is a very old one,
and it can be traced back at least to the writings of the
ancient Greeks. A central tenet in the philosophies of
Socrates, Plato, Aristotle, and their successors was that
pure knowledge existed on an ideal plane, beyond the
physical realm (hence the word *metaphysical*, "above
the physical"). Truth was assumed to be "out there"
and learning was understood as a matter of apprehend-
ing, recovering, or discovering it.

The assumption of ideal, eternal, and human-
independent knowledge was shared by many traditions and was articulated in different ways. In terms
of current influence on conceptions of teaching, the
two main traditions are mystical-religious thought
and rationalist-empiricist thought.

At the moment, these frames are often treated as
incompatible and even conflicting—a tension that
is frequently expressed in such terms as God versus
Newton, religion versus science, and the transcendent
versus the reductive. In earlier times, however, they
were both seen as essential and complementary. The
key to their comfortable coexistence was a tidy distinction that situated each in its own domain of expertise,
as preserved in the dyads *gnosis* and *episteme* (Greek)
and *mythos* and *logos* (Latin).

"Discovery learning" is a popular classroom approach that tends to be rooted
in correspondence theory assumptions
that knowledge is "out there" and that
learning is about dis/un/recovering
pre-existent truths.

Careful analyses of discovery-based
classrooms* have shown that, in fact,
teachers tend to impose rather rigid
and artificial boundaries on activities
to ensure that students arrive at desired insights. Discovery learning can
be just as contrived and directive as
more traditional teaching approaches.
Its various manifestations are often
just a disguised form of telling.

* See Derek Edwards & Neil Mercer, *Common
knowledge: The development of understanding in
the classroom* (London: Routledge, 1987).

In more ancient times, the mystical-religious realm (i.e., *gnosis* or *mythos*) dealt with issues of existence and meaning. As elaborated below, it was associated with the creation of forms and artifacts that were intended to sponsor creative interpretation. The rationalist-empirical realm (i.e., *episteme* or *logos*) was concerned with matters of how the world works. It was associated with how-to, practical knowledge. Understood to serve different and non-overlapping purposes, both mystical-religious knowledge and rationalist-empirical knowledge were regarded as necessary—and so, although they're presented as two categories here, they can (and should) be understood as complements.

Mystical-Religious Conceptions. Mystical-religious knowledge, with a focus on meaning of existence, tended toward more poetic genres and made use of such figurative devices as myth, parable, fable, allegory, personification, analogy, and metaphor. In contrast to the reductive certainty of formal logic or the demonstration-seeking attitude of experimental science, poetic figurative devices that pervade mystical-religious texts are generative. They are more aligned with the sensibility that some things exceed the human capacity to understand in explicit, direct, and totalized terms.

Figurative devices, such as myths and parables, aren't intended as factual, but they are anchored to a conviction that tales need not be taken literally in order to be taken seriously. Myths and parables tell us how to be human. Their powers lie in their use of metaphors and symbols to address matters of meaning that cannot be addressed by logical arguments and physical proofs. In the process of providing a map of the conceivable universe, myths serve ethical, pedagogical, sociological, and psychological purposes. They sketch out the contours of right and wrong, they teach people how to conform and advance in society, and they help to foster social cohesion and collective efficacy. In brief, mystical-religious knowledge has to do with the big questions that are addressed through narratives that provide context, ascribe purpose, and offer meaning.

You are here.······

In correspondence theory terms, *self* tends to be discussed as though it were a kernel of identity that springs forth, fully formed, at either the moment of conception or the moment of birth.

The pervasiveness of this conception of an encapsulated self is evident in the many novels and movies whose storylines involve the transplantation of an identity from one body into another (or into an animal, a machine, etc.). This sort of plot relies on the belief that identity is independent of body, brain, experience, knowledge, context, and so on.

Notably, formal educational systems in the western world were originally focused exclusively on this category of knowing. It was assumed that everyday know-how (i.e., the domain of rationalist-empirical knowledge) would take care of itself, as individuals moved through the world. However, it was also felt that people needed help in making sense of the deep truths of the universe. The result was a core emphasis on the "liberal arts" (literally: arts that are liberating), oriented by a sentiment that was concisely stated by Socrates: An unexamined life is not worth living.

A common thematic across western mystical-religious traditions is that humans were once part of a grand, unified whole, but have somehow become separated from that unity. Hence, the core issue in matters of learning and teaching is a recovery of a lost unity or wholeness. Teaching comes to be seen either as *drawing out* or *drawing in*, depending on whether the means for the recovery of wholeness is understood as coming from inside or outside the learner.

For example, the word *educate* is derived from the Latin *educare*, "to drag out or pull out." To educate was to draw out, by whatever means, what was assumed to be there already, woven into one's being from the beginning. The same sentiment is implicit in a cluster of terms that includes *nurturing* (from the Latin for "suckle"), *fostering* (from the Old English for "providing food"), and *tutoring* (from the Old French for "to protect"). All of these terms were incorporated into English to refer to teaching before the middle of the 15th century—prior to the Scientific and Industrial Revolutions, the rise of capitalism, the advent of European imperialism, and the emergence of the modern public school.

Perhaps the most familiar pedagogical strategy associated with teaching-as-educating is the Socratic method. Concerned with drawing out what is presumed to be already present in a learner, the Socratic method is a question-posing technique in which the teacher's queries are based on the learner's answers. The intention is to prompt learners to notice inconsistencies in their reasoning, thereby cutting away errors and revealing pure, unimpeachable, and innate knowledge.

This pair of images illustrates some dramatic changes in pedagogical approaches that occurred in the 17th century. In the image on the left (by Van Ostade, early 1600s), the pedagogue is positioned among the learners who are engaged in a range of activities. It is clear that the learning that is occurring is not under the control of anyone in particular. Rather, each person influences every other person's activities in some manner.

The institutional setting on the right (artist unknown, mid-1600s) is much more ordered, reflecting the regimentation of rationalist-empiricist thinking. The teacher is physically separated from the students, directing the activity from the edge of the classroom. Students are grouped according to age and are all focused on the same subject matter. Each individual faces the same direction, is working from his own textbook, and operates under the surveillance of the teacher.

However, some western mystical-religious traditions begin with the assumption that humans are either inherently evil or unavoidably prone to deception and, as such, teaching is conceived not in terms of drawing innate goodness out of the learner, but as drawing the learner into belief and social systems that are deemed to be good. The words *induction* and *indoctrination* are used to refer to the teacher's task within this sensibility.

Among the common synonyms for teaching derived from this stance are *rector* (having to do with setting *right*—see chap. 3), *master* (from the Latin for "direct"), *doctor* (linked to "doctrine," so the doctor's task was to indoctrinate), *professor* (from the Latin for "to declare openly"), and *lecturer*—all of which presume a pregiven truth that is external to the knower. From that, it follows that the teacher's task is to draw the learner into that truth (e.g., by righting, directing or indoctrinating) or to transmit that truth into the knower (e.g., by professing or lecturing). It is a very telling sense of teaching.

How might mystical-religious conceptions of teaching be used to interpret Jamie's experience?

In some ways, this question doesn't make sense. Events of schooling in ancient times were not organized in the ways that they are today. Contemporary schooling is structured around beliefs that might have been nonsensical in earlier contexts, including the assumptions that there are distinct subject areas and that the teacher is the one who is primarily responsible for creating the conditions to support learning. In contrast, disciplinary boundaries in earlier times, if and when they were drawn, were much more fluid and ambiguous. The mathematical was mixed with the mystical, science existed comfortably with theology, and so on.

Similarly, in mystical-religious interpretations, the task of teaching was generally considered more in terms of *accompanying the learner* on a journey than in terms of *directing the learning*. As such, teaching was considered a *vocation*—literally, a (divine or spiritual) calling, a mindful participation in the cosmos.

To become a teacher, then, was to heed the call. It is thus that teachers were often the priests, the mystics, the prophets, the shamans—those persons who, it was believed, had a special relationship with the more-than-human world. (Notably, *rabbi* and *doctor*, among a host of other titles, mean "teacher" in their original languages.) The teacher, from this perspective, is not merely a person who has learned a discipline or a set of pedagogical skills. Rather, the teacher is a person who lives where human culture meets the more-than-human world.

Becoming a teacher, then, is not principally a matter of personal decision. It is more a matter of being identified as someone who is able to assume the roles of cultural interpreter and spiritual mediator. Jamie's experience, then, would not be seen as a moment of personal triumph, but of attunement and fulfillment, a participation in a grander order. It is thus that, when Jamie stepped into the role that she had been fated to take on, there was a sudden harmony of action among teacher and students. She was doing what she was meant to do.

Rational-Empiricist Conceptions. The "Enlightenment" is generally seen to have begun in the early 1600s, as England and continental Europe turned a rather remarkable corner in the history of knowledge. Historically, this period is associated with such co-implicated cultural events as the emergence of mass communication through print media, the rise of capitalism, the Industrial Revolution, the Scientific Revolution, urbanization, democratization, and European imperialism. Philosophically, the period might be described as the triumph of scientific reasoning over mystical-religious knowledge as the reach and power of analytic science quickly exceeded its modest roots in everyday know-how (*episteme*) and pressed into the sorts of deep mysteries of the universe that were once in the exclusive domains of mystical-religious thought.

The two main philosophical frames associated with the rise of modern science are most popularly known as *rationalism* and *empiricism*, and they are often (mistakenly) presented as opposites.

Superficially they seem very different. Rationalism focuses on the products of mind. Following a model of truth that is based on the mathematical proof, rationalists were concerned with the production of unimpeachable claims that are, first, firmly grounded on self-evident propositions and, second, solidly constructed through impeccable logic. By contrast, empiricism is more anchored in experience. Empiricist researchers focused on demonstrations that could be replicated, arguing that claims to truth must be rooted in reliable observations and valid measurements. Empiricist truths are derived inductively as theories are proved or disproved on the basis of rigidly controlled experiments.

However, if you peer underneath these contrasting emphases, there are a number of shared assumptions. In particular, both are rooted in a correspondence theory of knowing, although the recommendations for arriving at truths are quite different (rationalism is based in logic; empiricism is anchored to experience). Both assume that mental is distinct from physical, the self is an insulated and isolated kernel of being, and cognition is purely an individual phenomenon

RATIONAL versus EMPIRICAL?

All claims to truth must be logically derived from self-evident, irrefutable premises. That is, to be valid, claims must be deductively **rational**.	All claims must be based on replicable experiments on worldly phenomena. That is, to be valid, claims have to be inductively **empirical**.

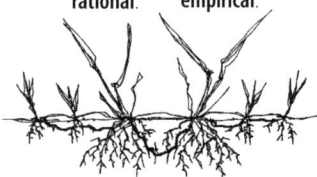

COMMON ROOTS: Often seen as opposing mindsets, rationalism and empiricism both assert that all phenomena are reducible to fundamental principles and particles. As these are discovered, we progress toward a complete understanding of the universe.

that happens inside the individual's head. Further, both assume a stable, unchanging reality that can be understood by reducing it to its most rudimentary parts—fundamental particles, universal laws, first principles ... that is, the basics.

In brief, then, the only way to construe rationalism and empiricism as opposites is to ignore their common underlying worldview. This point is amplified in the fact that few scientists seem to have any trouble aligning themselves with both traditions. For example, Isaac Newton is frequently identified *both* as one of the great rationalists (especially for his invention of calculus, which is just one of his many significant contributions to modern mathematics) *and* as one of the great empiricists (in particular, for his studies of light, gravity, and motion).

Even so, when it comes to recommendations for teaching, rationalist and empiricist recommendations can seem worlds apart. Rationalism, with its focus on logical mental constructs, underpins mentalist theories of learning (chap. 6). It supports a very tightly controlled curriculum that begins with fundamentals (i.e., the "basics") that are gradually elaborated into more sophisticated competencies. A rationalist curriculum is linear, incremental, carefully sequenced, and punctuated by frequent testing to ensure individuals are keeping pace and drawing appropriate conclusions. Synonyms for teaching in this frame include *explaining* (from the Latin for "to lay flat"), *telling* (from an Indo-European root for "count" and, by extension, "recount" or "convey"), *instructing* (i.e., indicating a focus on the *structure* of knowledge), and *directing* (from the Latin for "straight").

In contrast, with its focus on observable and measurable phenomenon, an empiricist attitude is more supportive of a behaviorist theory of learning. As detailed in chapter 6, teaching in this frame is more about *conditioning* individuals to respond in desired ways or *training* them to exhibit predetermined behaviors. It also places a heavy emphasis on testing as a sort of ongoing "quality control" to ensure that internal products match to—that is, *correspond* with—external realities.

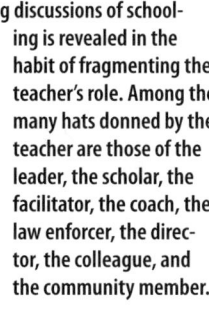

In a modernist conception, identity is seen as multi-faceted, but coherent, well bounded, and unchanging. In popular terms, the self is a "hat wearer." That is, as one moves from one setting to another, one selects the appropriate behaviors from one's repertoire of possibilities — but one's core identity remains constant regardless of the hat worn.

The prominence of this perspective among discussions of schooling is revealed in the habit of fragmenting the teacher's role. Among the many hats donned by the teacher are those of the leader, the scholar, the facilitator, the coach, the law enforcer, the director, the colleague, and the community member.

What might a rationalist-empiricist perspective suggest about Jamie's experiences of learning to teach?

First, it would be assumed that the project of becoming a teacher is a developmental one. One's full achievement in a role occurs through a process of learning, an aspect of which is the deliberate acquisition of skills and knowledge. Jamie's initial fear, from this perspective, would be seen to arise from inexperience—and from the fact that she is caught between the roles of student and teacher. So conceived, her eventual success with the students on that day might be taken as a triumph over this ambiguous positioning through the successful projection of a teacher identity. From this perspective, becoming an effective teacher is a matter of acquiring and deploying a set of technical competencies.

Modernist conceptions of self suggest that Jamie would be able to fully represent her experiences as a new teacher to herself and to others. Further, once represented, she would be able to critically interpret these personal narratives. Such abilities, although framed by her university courses and practicum experiences, would be seen as Jamie's personal achievement. Becoming an effective teacher, then, from a modernist perspective, is conditioned by social and cultural forms, but is, in the end, an example of how it is up to the individual to set and achieve personal goals.

9.3 Coherence Theories and Teaching

As developed in chapter 6, a defining distinction between correspondence theories of learning and coherence theories of learning is around contrasting beliefs on the nature of knowledge. Within the former, knowledge is assumed to be something that is already inscribed in the universe. From that belief it follows that learning is a matter of uncovering, discovering, recovering, or otherwise acquiring that pre-existent knowledge.

In contrast, coherence theories are organized around the assumption that knowing is a dynamic, evolving, and relational phenomenon that is manifest in and across all levels of organization. Knowledge cannot exist independently of a knower; rather, knowledge is understood in terms of established but mutable patterns of acting through which an agent maintains its fit within its dynamic context.

At the heart of this distinction is a difference of opinion on the nature and role of human perception. Across the worldviews that assume a correspondence model of learning—including most mystical, religious, rationalist, and empiricist attitudes—perception is regarded as an unreliable (oftentimes distortion-causing) information conduit that sits between the objective outer world and a subjective inner world. And so, even though the means to access truth vary across traditions—including most prominently, mystical divination, religious dictation, rational deduction, or empirical induction—the implicit goal is the same: somehow one must overcome the fallibility of perception.

As discussed in chapter 2, coherence theories begin with a very different perspective on perception. It is not seen as a problem-ridden conduit between outside and inside, but as a sort of interface or membrane. Far from a sort of barrier that stands between an agent and its context, a unity's perceptual system is the means by which it is coupled to or stays in tune with its surroundings. But to make sense of this suggestion, one must reject the idea that learning is about internalizing an external reality. Rather, learning has to be recast in terms of maintaining coherence at multiple levels of organization, including within the agent and between the agent and its context.

Clearly, this shift in thinking about learning compels some very different ways of thinking about teaching. Teaching cannot be about overcoming the fallibilities of perception. Rather it must have to do with attending to and seeking to affect the webs of implicit and explicit association that render our individual and collective worlds coherent.

Interpretivist Conceptions. Most contemporary coherence theories are focused on human phenomena—specifically, individual understanding (constructivisms), social collectivity (constructionisms or social constructivisms), and culture (cultural studies and critical theories). Another way of saying this is that they are concerned with interpretation.

The word *interpretation* is derived from the Latin *inter-* (meaning "between" or "among") and the Sanskrit *prath* (meaning "to spread abroad"). As originally intended, then, interpretation is understood to occur between disparate moments or happenings. To interpret is to create coherence, as one experience is read against another. In the context of human knowing, interpretation is about the continuous process of incorporating new experiences into the ecosystem of associations that has emerged from previous experiences. It is about an

---

Interpretivist thinkers have argued that the belief in a unified and fully knowable universe is untenable. We live instead in a world of partial knowledge, local narratives, situated truths, shifting selves.

This "postmodern world" is endlessly contemporary, a constantly emerging hyperreality of cyberspace, Disneyland, Barbie, MTV, and so on. Many of these forms originated in the rationalist-empiricist—that is, the *modernist*—project of making models that correspond to reality. However, the resulting models prompted the emergence of a strange new reality in which there are no universal truths and no grand unifying themes—apart, perhaps, from a rejection of modernist claims to reductive, totalizing truths.

ongoing process of recursive elaboration—not *building on* what has been learned, but *transforming* prior learnings to include new experiences.

Learning, then, is an uncontrollable phenomenon because it arises in physically experienced, socially situated, and culturally conditioned situations. An upshot is that teaching cannot be construed as "causing" or "compelling" learners to learn specific things in specific ways or at specific times. In brief, learning is not *determined* by teaching. However, learning is *conditioned by* and, hence, *dependent* on teaching. It matters what teachers do (or don't do).

As for specific conceptions of teaching, those depend on the level of evolving coherence—that is, the specific learning system—that's serving as the focus of attention. For example, if the focus is individual sense-making (i.e., the domain of constructivisms), teaching tends to be construed in terms of *facilitating* (from the Latin for "making easy"), *guiding* (in the sense of "prompting" or "orienting"), or *enabling*. The overriding message here is that teaching is not about telling, but about organizing experiences that orient learners' perceptions to particular details and prompt them to associate those details with other details. A familiar example is around the learning of number symbols. Relevant experiences to support the development of numeracy include acts of counting and exposure to symbols, and the teacher's task is to ensure that these experiences are juxtaposed in ways that encourage the child to associate the symbols with the chanting of the counting words.

Constructivisms actually offer very little direct advice to teachers. This point should not be surprising, since they are theories of how individuals learn, not theories of how people should be taught. Constructivists recommend that attention be paid to prior learning and that experiences should be both rich and focused. They characterize teaching in terms of chains of interpretation in which the teacher prompts the student toward one interpretation, then interprets the student's interpretation to decide on the next prompt, and so on.

By contrast, constructionisms have more pronounced interests in interpersonal processes, social

Let sleeping dogs lie!

There's a popular perception, generally found among persons who speak only one language, that translation is simply a matter of exchanging one set of words for a set of corresponding words in another language.

This belief betrays a lack of awareness of ways that word meanings occur in complex webs of relationship and association. As such, literal translations can often be highly problematic.

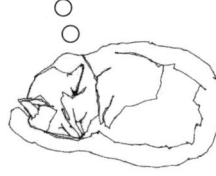

Ne réveillez pas le chat qui dort!

They might ignore the associations woven through one or both languages—an ignorance which could give rise to very different meanings.

Difficulties with translations foreground the role of interpretation in any event of language. They also illustrate the importance of thinking in terms of coherence rather than correspondence in discussions of knowing, learning, and teaching.

* See Lave & Wenger, *Situated learning.*

norms, and cultural tools (including language and physical artifacts). As such, they tend to focus more on how individuals become integral parts of collectives. The unit of analysis in this frame is not the individual sense-maker, but human interactivity. Such interactivity is seen as purposeful, driven by particular needs, embedded in an established community of practice, and often mediated by specific tools. From these emphases, it follows that teaching is a matter of *mediating* (from the Latin for "to be in the middle"), *mentoring, modeling, initiating,* and *enculturating.*

Once again, very little practical advice is offered to teachers. In fact, teaching in this frame is often portrayed as a largely incidental activity with few deliberate pedagogical interventions. As illustrated in this chapter's narrative of a newcomer's adjustment to the unfamiliar social role of teacher, most of what is going on is indirect, nonconscious, and even accidental. That said, constructionists do offer one explicit and deliberate recommendation, suggesting that neophytes should be meaningfully engaged in peripheral activities. That is, newcomers should contribute to the work of the community by working on legitimate tasks, but ones that are not pivotal to collective success. Only gradually should they work their way to more significant responsibilities. The thinking here is that a social role like teaching is so complex that beginners simply can't be expected to appreciate most of the generally unarticulated nuances.*

Somewhat in contrast, cultural and critical theorists tend to argue that educators have an ethical responsibility to be attentive to social structures, prevailing norms, and entrenched patterns of acting. In this frame, teaching is not seen as serving the established social order, but as a subversive activity that should be *empowering* and *liberating.* The point is not so much that learners should be made aware of their oppressions, but that they should be involved in a shared project of interrogating existing structures and co-creating new ones that are more egalitarian. In this sense, teaching is conceived as a matter of *giving voice* and *advocating,* since its goal is to open up spaces for collective action, not to define action that will be taken.

How might an interpretist perspective on teaching be used to interpret Jamie's experience?

Jamie's initial terror might be described as emerging from her remembered and currently lived experiences in the cultures of schooling—first as a student, then as a student teacher in the university classroom, and now as a beginning teacher with her own class of students. The signifying practices that have contributed to her present experience, then, include various narratives of experience about herself and about others. Jamie's sense of identity, in this perspective, emerges not just from what she has directly experienced, but from popular narratives of what it means to be a teacher. Movies that depict the interactions of students and teachers, for example, are signifying systems that may contribute significantly to Jamie's sense of teacher identity.

At the same time, her experience is conditioned by those conceptions of teachers that are assumed in the news and other popular media, in staffroom interactions, in cafeteria gossip, in formal textbooks, by parents, by school board officials, and so on.

Jamie's move from the terrified teacher to the confident one, then, might be described as a resituation. A collection of overlapping semiotic systems that organize her perception in one way has been rearranged into another.

This rearrangement, of course, has as much to do with the way in which "students" are created by signifying practices as with the way that "teachers" are created. As Jamie begins to renegotiate the category of "teacher," so too do her students. When what those students perceive in Jamie begins to approximate what they have come to understand as the teacher's voice, appearance, and manner of acting, they begin to offer responses that fit with Jamie's expectations. These historically effected signifying practices function to create the teaching event that both Jamie and her students can identify as "successful."

Participatory Conceptions. As mentioned in chapter 2, some of the most interesting sites to study teaching are those involving adults with very young children who are just starting to learn language and to develop fine motor skills. While the adults may imagine themselves to be aware of everything they're doing, in fact their actions are too rapid and too finely tuned to those of the children to be the products of conscious decision-making.

Explanations for these exquisite choreographies of action have been offered by neurologists, psychologists, and sociologists. On the level of brain activity, humans are capable of synchronizing certain rhythms while coupling their attentional systems (i.e., noticing the same things at the same time, usually by following someone's line of observation or some sort of verbal cue). On the psychological level, they may be reenacting chunks of behavior that have been honed through years of engaging with others. On the sociological level, such actions might be characterized in terms of scripts (i.e., acceptable patterns of acting) that are called forth in specific social settings.

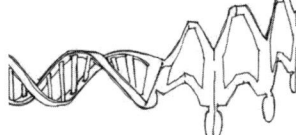

Where do personalities come from?

Studies of similarities and differences among siblings (e.g., biological, adoptive, raised apart, raised together, etc.) have generated two consistent conclusions.

First, about half the variation in personalities among persons seems to be genetic and about half seems to arise from differences in socialization.

Second, the major social influences on one's opinions, preferences, habits, identifications, and so on are not one's parents, but one's peers. Children do most of their experimenting with identity in play groups, cliques, gangs, classrooms, and so on. On this count, given teachers' power to shape the dynamics of peer groups, teachers' roles in affecting children's identities may be as significant as parents' roles.

* See Lyndon Martin, Jo Towers, & Susan E.B. Pirie, "Collective mathematical understanding as improvisation," in *Mathematical Thinking and Learning*, vol. 8, no. 2 (2006): 149–183.
** See Brent Davis, Dennis Sumara, & Tom Kieren, "Cognition, co-emergence, curriculum," in *Journal of Curriculum Studies*, vol. 28, no. 2 (1996): 151–169.
*** See Sylvia Ashton-Warner, *Teacher* (New York: Simon & Schuster, 1963).
**** See Nel Noddings, *Caring: A feminine approach to ethics and moral education* (Berkeley: University of California Press, 1984).

Of course, it is easier to argue that all of these things are happening all at once. Moments of teaching are manifestations of neuronal, personal, and interpersonal coherence all at the same time. Or, phrased in much different terms, the human race is a teaching species. We are biologically enabled and culturally conditioned to teach.

This is the place where participatory theories of teaching elaborate interpretivist theories of teaching. Moving beyond the space of immediate human interest, participatory theories also foreground the role of the biological in human learning, both its influence on human learning and the influence of human learning on it.

With this transphenomenal interest—that is, in the recognition that humans are both biological and cultural beings—participatory theories embrace a complexivist attitude. Another dimension is added to the suggestion that ours is a teaching species. Teaching is a phenomenon encountered in many species, as adults prompt the young toward competencies in, for example, foraging and cracking open nuts. But among humans, teaching is also oriented toward increasing complexity. It is not only about maintaining the existing repertoire of abilities but about presenting opportunities to elaborate that repertoire. It is not merely about maintaining what is known, but about expanding on it.

A participatory mode of teaching, then, is one that is better described in terms of nested, self-similar, scale independent, and recursively generated images of fractal geometry, than in terms of the lines and well-defined regions borrowed from Euclidean geometry.

A popular set of participatory-oriented synonyms for teaching has yet to emerge, although a number of suggestions have been put forward. The list includes *improvising,** occasioning,*** conversing,**** caring,***** and *engaging minds*. To varying extents, these notions are intended to highlight the qualities of contingency, flexibility, emergence, and expansive possibility. Once again, the critical break with entrenched perspectives is in the realization that teaching is not about *telling* or *directing*, but *triggering* and *disturbing*. These sorts of notions point to what might be called a "coupling of consciousnesses"—a uniquely human capacity to coordinate attentional systems and to synchronize brain functioning, in effect presenting the possibility of grander cognitive unities.*

Given this capacity for complex, communal cognition, a potentially useful metaphor is "teaching as the consciousness of the collective." Recalling a topic developed in chapter 2, an important point of elaboration is needed to make sense of this suggestion: personal consciousness is more a commentator than a controller. It does not direct, it orients. What one knows and who one is, then, are not *determined* by consciousness, but they are utterly *dependent* on consciousness, and in very much the same way learning is not determined by teaching, but is dependent on it. The metaphor of "teacher as the consciousness of the collective," then, is a suggestion that the teacher is responsible for prompting differential attention, selecting among and emphasizing the options for action and interpretation that arise in the collective.

So framed, teaching cannot be only about zeroing in on predetermined conclusions. It must be something beyond the replication and perpetuation of the existing possible. Rather, teaching seems to be more about expanding the space of the possible and creating conditions for the emergence of the as-yet unimagined. The emphasis is not only on *what is*, but also *what might be* brought forth. Returning to a point introduced in chapter 5, teaching comes to be a participation in a recursively elaborative process of opening up new spaces of possibility by exploring current spaces.

The last three chapters of the book focus on this conception of teaching—and the intention is to be teacherly, in the sense just described. That is, the discussion is not strictly concerned with rearticulating established knowledge about teaching. It is also aimed at expanding the space of the possible—toward exploring what sorts of things might arise in more generous, productive ways of thinking about the frames that give shape to popular understandings of teaching.

* See Donald, *A mind so rare.*

How might a participatory perspective on teaching be used to interpret Jamie's experience?

If a participatory sensibility could be summed up in a few sentences, it might be, "Everything matters, but we can be aware of only a small part of what goes on around us. We can never know the full consequences of an action and, as such, we must participate mindfully in the unfolding of circumstances around us."

In terms of Jamie's story, then, this perspective would embrace the descriptions suggested by an interpretivist sensibility. However, the scope of interest would exceed issues of explicit interpretation, cultural habit, and social circumstance. In particular, it would prompt attention toward biological constitutions, ecological intertwinings, and relational dynamics. That is, this perspective would look across levels of organization to try to understand the event in question.

Regarding relational dynamics, for example, it is clear that the roles of this classroom have tended to be explicitly defined in oppositional terms: the teacher is *not* a student. In fact, the teacher's role is to manage, to control, to oversee learners and their learning. Such distinctions and definitions, however, are artificial. Teacher and students alike exist as a consensual unity, each specifying the domain of appropriate activity for the other. This is a profoundly cooperative event, although it is often interpreted in terms of competition and conflict. (Indeed, Jamie initially perceived things in just this way.)

A participatory perspective would thus urge that the classroom be seen as a collective of interacting and overlapping unities (i.e., teacher and students), as a unity in and of itself (with its own particular character and established patterns of actions), and as an aspect of grander collectives (e.g., a school, a community, an ecosystem, and so on). In a similar manner, Jamie must be regarded as a complex collective (of biological, historically effected, dynamic and interacting parts), as a coherent whole (i.e., she has an ongoing sense of her own identity and is perceived by her students as having one), and as an element of grander collectives.

More broadly, a complex and situated theory of self also prompts attention to larger phenomenological, cultural, biological, and more-than-human matters. It would be of interest, for example, to know whether this event took place in a cold or warm climate, whether it was morning or afternoon, how active the students had been that day, and so on. The particulars of the students—their ages, their sexes, their levels of sexual and social development, their friendships and intimate contacts with others—would also be of interest, as all these details contribute to the character of the collective. Similarly, Jamie's physical appearance, her health, her age, her physiological responses to stressful situations, her sexuality, her gender, her dreams last night, her spiritual beliefs, and so on, all contribute to the unfolding situation.

The point here is *not* that all these sorts of details must be considered. It is that they all matter. Such a realization would shift one's efforts away from attempting to do "the right thing" and toward finding an appropriate pattern of acting in this setting. It is not a matter of exerting control—the dynamic complexity of the situation makes that impossible—but of being attentive to the effects of one's actions.

Jamie, then, managed to establish a rhythm that fit in with the flow of those around her—and, in the process, helped to constitute a grander collectivity. She, in fact, noticed the sudden harmony of action. Although her role was differentiated from her students' roles, she knew that she had become part of the classroom body.

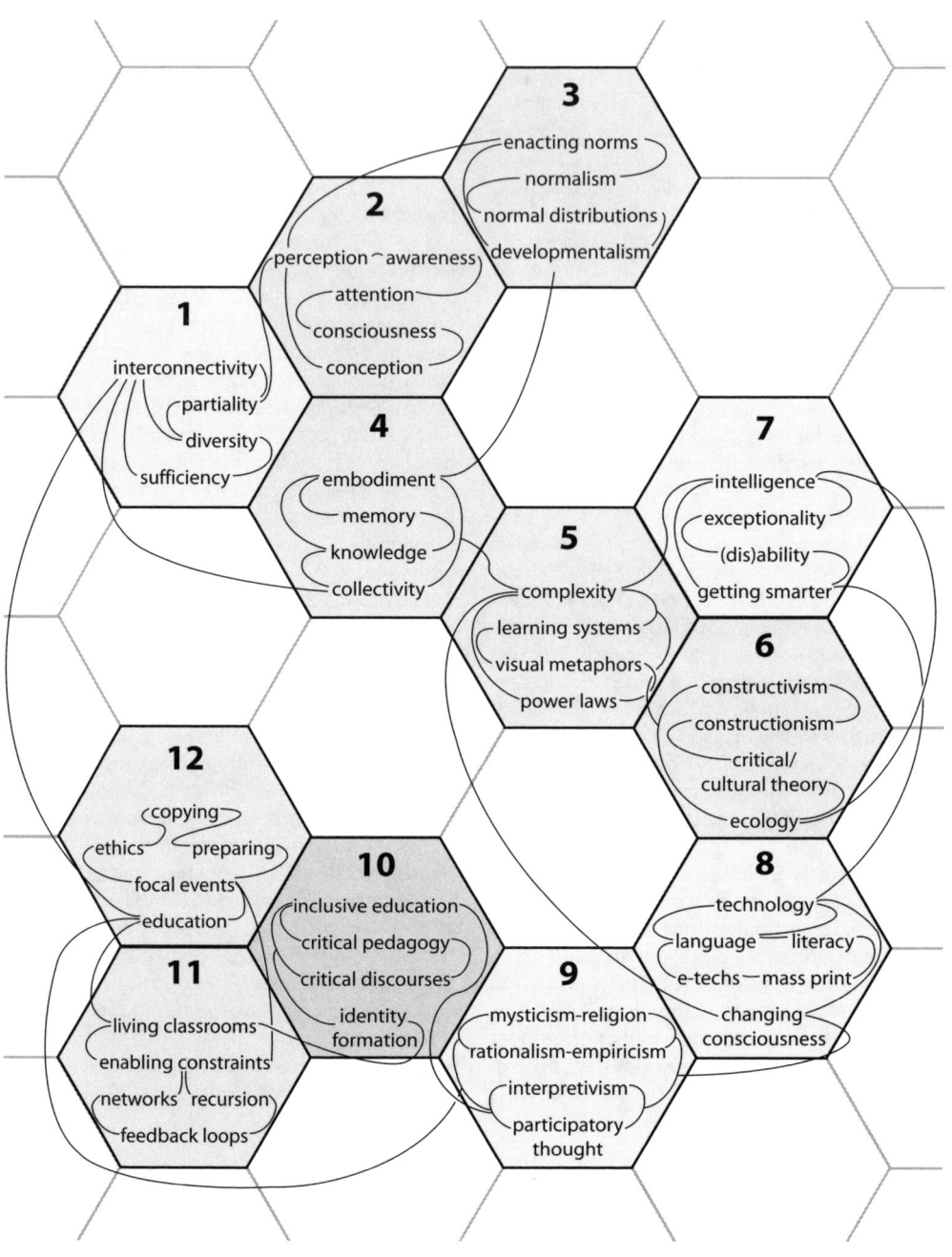

10 Teaching Challenges

The novel *Stitches*** seemed like an ideal choice for the course on English language arts at the secondary school level.

Winner of the 2004 Canadian Governor General award for Young Adult Fiction, the story is developed around the experiences of twelve-year-old Travis, who lives in a small town with his Aunt Kitaleen and Uncle Mike. Travis has never known his father and sees very little of his mother, who travels a great deal in her capacity as lead singer in a country and western band. Travis's best friend is a physically handicapped girl from his class named Chantelle. He experiences considerable psychological and physical abuse from several of his male peers, largely because he is perceived by them to present traits associated with gay males. For example, he prefers sewing, puppetry, and drama to sports and cars. Although he has a positive relationship with his mother and his Aunt Kitaleen, he experiences considerable psychological homophobic abuse from his Uncle Mike, who believes that Travis is not "manly" enough. At the end of the novel, following a brutal physical attack by several boys from his school, Travis moves to a nearby urban center, where he attends a school specializing in Arts education.

In short, the book met several major criteria for selection: it was current; it had received a major literary award; its characters were in the same age range as middle school students; it dealt with a number of social issues that teachers might be expected to face. And so it was chosen for the two-week unit on "how to teach a novel" in the final year course for pre-service secondary school English teachers.

---

* The image is a woodcut depiciting a school from the 11th century in Hungary (artist unknown).

** Glen Huser, *Stitches* (Toronto: Groundwood, 2003).

10.1 Inclusive Education

"Inclusive education" has been a prominent movement in discussions of schooling over the last few decades. As might be interpreted from the phrase, *inclusive education* is concerned with the accommodation of difference in the classroom. Inclusive education is oriented by the question of how *all* children might be meaningfully included in formal educational settings. In principle, this approach is intended to encourage students who are doing well to take on leadership roles and students who are achieving at lower levels to have better access to emotional, social, and academic supports. There is some evidence that the strategy is successful, with indications of higher academic achievement, enhanced self-esteem, better physical health, higher likelihood of graduating, and increased probability of attending college and finding employment.*

The two main categories of discussion within the movement might be characterized as the philosophical (i.e., *why* do it) and the pragmatic (i.e., *how* to do it). On the former, major orienting themes include that all children can learn, that any child can benefit from education under appropriate circumstances, and that differences among children should be treated as a rich source of possibility, not as something to be overcome or ignored.

To state it concisely, the orienting assertion of inclusive education is that every child has a right to an education and should therefore have equal access to the same sorts of opportunities and protections. More directly, a guiding principle is that no individual should be excluded or experience discrimination on the basis of race, ethnicity, social class, gender, sexual orientation, religion, ideology, age, (dis)ability, or other trait. The principle is informed by recent realizations that intelligence and identity are neither genetically determined nor fixed in the early years of life. The focus here is *not* on the qualities that make a child (or a group of children) "special," but on the identification of conceptual and physical barriers to participation. In other words, it locates "problems" in the social, institutional, and cultural realms, not in the individual.

SELF *versus* SOCIETY?

Collective possibility is anchored in individual enablement and empowerment, and, hence, schools must attend to the **self**.

The school is one of the principal means by which a culture preserves itself. Hence it should serve the needs of **society.**

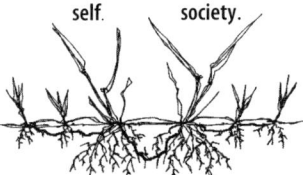

COMMON ROOTS: Self and society are popularly seen as contrasting and necessarily opposed phenomena. From that assumption it follows that human co-activity is a "zero-sum" game (i.e., someone else's gain is my loss).

---

* See National Research Center on Learning Disabilities, "Twenty-five years of progress in educating children with disabilities through IDEA." Retrieved September 05, 2006 from http://www. nrcld. org/resources/oesp/historyidea.shtml.

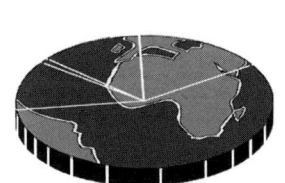

If we could shrink the world's population to a village of only 100 people, it would look something like this:*

Demographics:
    60 from Asia
    14 from the Americas
    13 from Africa
    12 from Europe
    1 from Oceania

Identifications:
    50 female / 50 male
    80 non-white / 20 white
    67 non-Christian / 33 Christian

Educations:
    17 are unable to read
    2 have attended college

Wealth:
    25 live in substandard housing
    13 suffer from malnutrition
    4 own a computer
    20 control 89% of the wealth—mostly male, white, college-educated, from North America, with Christian backgrounds

These sorts of disparities and inequities are a major prompt for more critical attitudes within educational theory and practice.

* Research by Rekha Balu, Christine Engelken, & Jennifer Grosso. Based on statistics collected prior to 2002. Data obtained from http://www.fastcompany.com/articles/2001/05/email2.html.

Several factors have been identified that contribute to the success of inclusive classrooms. These include: well-informed teachers, carefully conceived individual education plans fitted to the particular needs and abilities of each student, access to a team of professionals, adequate classroom support, and ongoing opportunities for teacher development.

A core assertion in the inclusive education movement is that schooling structures should adapt to the particular needs of and variations among children, and not the other way around. Such adaptability entails flexibility around pacing, curriculum, physical access, social organization, pedagogical methods, community participation, and other concerns that arise from the particularity of each child. In some situations, teams that include specialists are needed to address individual needs. Another strong component of the inclusive education movement is the creation and maintenance of healthy relationships across all groups associated with the schooling process, including students, parents, teachers, and other community members. This emphasis on collectivity, coupled with the nature of diversity and the fluid needs of individuals, means that the sorts of adaptations entailed are not one-time events, but highly contingent, necessarily contextual, and always continuing processes. In other words, inclusive education is as much an attitude as a set of practices.

Advocates for inclusive education tend to argue that children should be clustered with age-mates in order to foster friendships and senses of belonging. This practice is one that must be undertaken mindfully, given the human tendency to focus on and amplify difference (see chap. 2). Often teachers need to intervene to nurture relationships among peers through, for example, requesting or assigning individuals to work together on in-class tasks or to accompany one another during out-of-class activities.

For the most part, the rhetoric around inclusive education is decidedly individual-centric, which can be a little misleading. In fact, the movement has a well-articulated community-oriented sensibility. This sensibility is reflected in some specific classroom strategies, including selection of texts that deal with issues of community, direct engagement with issues of difference, selection of activities that build community in classrooms, and prompting students' attentions to ways they can help one another. Indeed, an orienting premise is that the community is stronger when difference is embraced, rather than merely accommodated or tolerated.

Of course, the movement is not without its detractors. Criticisms tend to vary widely, ranging from the worry that inclusive education is too radical to the concern that it doesn't go far enough. For example, at one extreme, some argue that inclusive education can be too resource-intensive, placing unreasonable demands on school budgets, teacher time, and other students' energies. At the other extreme, some argue that the movement is organized around a narrow and constraining definition of "equality"—one that may actually prevent some special needs students from gaining access to most advantageous channels of support. In brief, the argument is that different abilities call for different sorts of educational opportunities; there is nothing so unequal as treating everyone the same way.

Another reason that *Stitches* was chosen for the unit on teaching a novel was that the author, Glen Huser, was actually working in the teacher education program at the time.

He accepted an invitation to visit the class for a discussion of a range of issues around writing a novel—such as what it's like to be a writer, how one develops characters and plots, how other writings figure into stories, the place of personal experience in works of fiction, and the extent and nature of editorial involvement in the publishing industry. Wisely, he refused to get into much detail when asked about characters' motivations and intended themes, noting that it's easy to destroy readers' opportunities to become immersed in others' invented worlds by dictating what they're supposed to "get out of it."

Class participants accepted this suggestion. Unfortunately, however, it seemed to echo through some of the events that followed the author's visit. For example, in a follow-up class discussion of the novel, there was almost no exploration of the literary engagements—that is, of the characters and how students might identify with them. Instead, the focus was on a series of "sensitive issues" that might come up in a class reading of the novel—abuse, bullying, difference, disability, sex-based stereotyping, and gender roles.

In fact, these issues became almost the exclusive topic of discussion. There was virtually no mention of the story itself. Instead, in the normalizing context of this particular teacher education program (which, as it turns out, was the one described in the interspersed narrative of chap. 3), the book was treated as an occasion for raising and contextualizing issues encountered by young adolescents, but not for interrogating the discourses that shape those issues.

10.2 Critical Pedagogy

Critical pedagogy is a movement that is sometimes associated with inclusive education, but is actually rooted in a different set of historical influences and is oriented by quite different theoretical and philosophical emphases.

The common ground between inclusive education and "crit ped" is the desire to improve the educational experience for all students by attending to matters of perceived difference. Whereas the focus in inclusive pedagogy is difference among individuals, the emphases of critical pedagogues revolve around issues of power, privilege, and domination. The orienting imperative is to interrogate the beliefs and practices that prevail within schools specifically and society more generally—interpersonal, economic, cultural, and so on—with a view toward enacting alternatives that are less oppressive and more empowering.

The movement first rose to prominence in the late 1960s, prompted in large part by growing social activist movements around the world.* Critical pedagogy begins with the premise that there is no such thing as a neutral educational strategy. Formal schooling, it is argued, usually functions as an instrument of conformity by integrating young learners into prevailing logics, worldviews, mythologies, wisdom, explanatory systems, and ideologies. However, there is potential for it to become a "practice of freedom" through which one approaches issues critically and creatively.

Critical pedagogy is associated with cultural and critical theories of learning (see chap. 6). As mentioned earlier, one of the more prominent formulations in this movement is Paulo Freire's *conscientização*, a Portuguese word that might be translated as "consciousness raising."*** It is an approach to education that is concerned with noticing and uncovering oppressive political and cultural structures, coupled to an imperative to take action against such structures. Significantly, a major emphasis in the raising of consciousnesses is helping people to understand how they are often complicit in their own oppressions—for example, by their own internalizing of myths of ethnic or cultural difference.

Peace It Together 2006 brought 29 Israeli, Palestinian, and Canadian teens together to hear each others' stories, to develop communication and conflict resolution skills, and to use film-making as a means to break down barriers and transform lives.

The group met for a few days in Vancouver to get acquainted and then traveled to Galiano Island, a 45-minute ferry ride away. In culturally mixed groups of 4 to 5 individuals, participants created brief videos to represent the impact of conflict on their lives. They wrote, filmed, starred in, and produced their own films. The films are now being used as educational tools to inspire youth and adults around the world about collaboration and peace.**

* See, e.g., Neil Postman & Charles Weingartner, *Teaching as a subversive activity* (New York: Delacorte, 1969).
** Visit http://creativepeacenetwork.ca/ for further details, news releases, and the films.
*** Freire, *Pedagogy of the oppressed.*

Freire presented *conscientização* as a practical pedagogical emphasis. First developed when he was teaching poor and disenfranchised members of Brazilian society, the process is oriented toward individual and collective action that is intended to affect the conditions of existence.

The main pedagogical strategy in the movement is the turning of language onto itself—inviting learners into critical examinations of the conventions that frame their experience and into similarly critical examinations of their own complicity in those conventions. As a pedagogical process, it typically begins with one or more identifications (e.g., nationality, cultural norms, religion, gender expectations, social class) that serve as sites for critical study. A preliminary aim of the pedagogy is to participate with learners in recognizing problematic aspects of current identifications. These insights then serve as starting places for articulating alternative beliefs, acting differently, and otherwise altering oppressive aspects of society.

Although developed in the context of work with the underprivileged, Freire's methods are as relevant to the wealthy as they are to the poor. Topics that might be raised to prompt more critical awarenesses of one's situation include the distribution of wealth around the world, the reasons a nation might be at war, spending priorities of governments, the influence of mass media on popular preferences, pervasive conceptions of normality, and the relationships among privilege, cultural exploitation, and environmental degradation. To be clear, the point is not to arrive at a higher truth or a more correct formulation. It is, rather, to maintain an attitude of mindfulness, oriented by the realization that every act of identification is also an act of ignorance—of carving out a focus of attention by discarding a multitude of other interpretive possibilities. The goal is not ultimate truth, but better conditions of existence.

For the most part, critical pedagogues do not frame their conceptions of good teaching in political terms. Teaching is perhaps better described as an attitude that is oriented toward "making the familiar strange"— and, in particular, of challenging what tends to be

Nicole Pageau is a Canadian retiree whose efforts are making an important difference in a small Rwandan village populated mainly by women, their children, and orphans since the 1994 genocide. When she became aware of the extreme poverty and the AIDS-induced devastation of the village, Pageau used her own financial resources to acquire some sewing machines. In addition to providing means to earn incomes, the effort has also created a site for interaction, shared labor, and collective identification.

Pageau's work is part of *Ubuntu* ("Humanity"),* a project to improve the living conditions of the 650 residents of Kimironko by financing micro-projects, sponsoring education for children, and providing health care for the community. All initiatives are aimed at sustainable development and community self-sufficiency.

* The organization's website is http://www. ubuntuedmonton.org/. A videoclip of a newsbroadcast on this work is available at http://www. cbc.ca/newsatsixedmonton/beyondborders.html.

taken-for-granted as normal. To underscore this point, the adjective *normal* is often replaced with *normative* or *normalizing*. For example, as developed in chapter 3, there is no normal child, merely a set of normative standards generated by various assumptions and measurements that are deployed to shape and organize the experiences of all learners. A critical education is thus concerned with the simultaneous tasks of uncovering normative structures and developing counternormative strategies.

Discourses of normality are closely related to and sometimes synonymous with discourses of power. A power structure is a means by which sensibilities are established and maintained. Power structures are both subtle and blatant, both covert and overt, both nonconscious and conscious, both accidental and deliberate. Male privilege, for instance, is asserted through a curriculum developed around the products of dead White males, through a distribution of teachers that is mainly female in the early grades and increasingly male as one moves toward postsecondary institutions, through discourses and social practices that cast males as analytic and rational and females as intuitive and emotional, and so on. The hidden curriculum of male privilege operates simultaneously on all levels, personal through cultural. The same is true of White, wealthy, heterosexual, and other current categories of privilege. Consequently, critical pedagogues argue, these sorts of issues compel responses on all levels, from the pedagogical through the political, simultaneously.

After Glen's visit, the focus of activity shifted toward the development of units of study that might actually be used in a middle school classroom. Students organized themselves into small groups, and the course instructor provided access to the program of studies and other resources appropriate to middle school English language arts classrooms.

A few class sessions were dedicated to working together on this task, and were followed by two more sessions in which groups presented their units to one another. Among the more familiar suggestions were sets of comprehension questions, essay questions, discussion topics, character sketches, and other assessment strategies. Other activities that were less focused on the content of the book included writing a new ending, designing a book jacket, and converting a scene to a play or a screenplay.

In short, the book unit was treated as an opportunity to practice literacy and thinking skills. That is, *Stitches* was seen as an illustrative and generic text. The focus was not on the particularities of the novel and the issues it might prompt, but on the generalities of teaching and the sorts of preparations that must be undertaken.

This focus on the general rather than the particular probably has something to do with the fact that it was unlikely anyone in the class would ever teach the unit they developed—certainly not in the upcoming practicum experience.

But there was something uncomfortable in the ignorance of the specificities of the book. It was with considerable discomfort that one partici-

pant, Marlene, noted in a follow-up interview:

I felt that Travis's sexuality was one of the dominant themes. We went out of our way to avoid the topic during discussions. Let's face it, the reason that this novel might be banned from any school is not the bullying issue; it would be banned because of Travis's perceived sexuality. Unfortunately when we as teachers can't deal with these important topics, students like Travis are the ones who suffer.

10.3 Critical Attitudes

There are actually many different "critical pedagogies." The movement was sparked by concerns for social justice as originally framed by Marxist philosophy. Other discourses have since been taken up, and the current list includes post-colonial, indigenous, feminist, and queer perspectives.* In addition, critical pedagogy has embraced a range of theoretical movements and conceptual domains, including psychoanalysis, post-structuralism,** cultural studies, and ecological thought (some of which were introduced in chap. 6). Consequently, there is a considerable breadth to contemporary discussions. Regardless of the perspective taken, however, education is seen as both a site of struggle and a means to effect change.

A common intention across these frames is to excavate and interrogate habits of interpretation that support inequities and perceived injustices. These are often flagged by the notion of the "hidden curriculum"—a term used to suggest that schools always teach more than what is made explicit in curriculum documents.

As one might expect, different theoretical frames prompt attentions toward different aspects of the hidden curriculum, as will be outlined briefly below. To this end, none of these frames should be treated as unified or single-voiced. Rather, they are characterized by diversities of interest and interpretation, and within each there are persistent (but productive) debates and disagreements.

Marxist analyses, as suggested in the previous section, are mainly associated with concerns around access to resources—including class systems, distribution

What are the *basics*?

This question was taken seriously in an innovative curriculum project in Queensland, Australia.*** Oriented by the realization that "basics" change as cultures change, curriculum developers set out to develop educational structures that are better fitted to contemporary and evolving contexts.

The project was oriented by two key realizations. First, there is a need to address emergent societal problems, such as health care for an aging population, overburdened urban transportation systems, and environmental degradation. Second, these sorts of problems call for complex responses—through which, for example, the civil engineer

* This list is a partial one. For a more thorough review, see William Pinar, William Reynolds, Patrick Slattery, & Peter Taubman, *Understanding curriculum: An introduction to the study of historical and contemporary curriculum discourses* (New York: Peter Lang, 1995).
** E.g., Deborah Britzman, *Practice makes practice: A critical study of learning to teach*, revised edn. (Albany, NY: State University of New York Press, 2003).
*** For more information, visit http://education. qld.gov.au/corporate/newbasics/ (in particular, the introductory texts by Alan Luke).

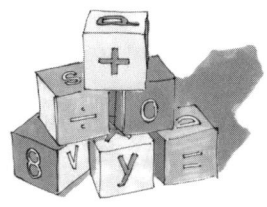

may become attentive to the manners in which roads transform communities.

One change was to redefine literacy to encompass not just functional literacy, but social, political, and environmental literacies. Rather than structuring the curriculum around the traditional disciplines, topics in mathematics, the sciences, English, history, and so on are studied and applied in the context of solving community problems in actual hands-on projects—rich tasks such as organizing a conference to examine a specific environmental issue. Topics of study are relevant, contextualized, and effortful.

* See, e.g., the contents pages for *The Journal for Critical Education Policy Studies* at http://www.jceps.com.

** See, e.g., Bill Ashcroft, Gareth Griffiths, & Helen Tiffin, *The post-colonial studies reader* (New York: Routledge, 1997); Edward Said, *Culture and imperialism* (New York: Vintage, 1994).

*** See., e.g., Madeleine Grumet, *Bitter milk: Women and teaching* (Amherst, MA: The University of Massachusetts Press, 1988); Carmen Luke, *Feminisms and critical pedagogy* (New York: Routledge, 1992).

of wealth, economic policies, and globalization—as they pertain to educational practice. Discussions reach across all levels of educational action, from the topics that define current curricula to policies for international cooperation.*

Those who have taken up post-colonial theory within education tend to have similar emphases on the political and economic dimensions of schooling. Critiques tend to be much more focused on issues that are particular to countries that were once (or are still) subject to colonial rule. These issues include: conflicting worldviews, revitalization of indigenous knowledge, cultural reparation, anti-racisms, and hybridization of knowledge domains.**

The phrase "indigenous education" is often associated with many of the emphases of post-colonial theorists. In many cases, this association is appropriate. There tends to be a strong focus on the recovery and preservation of traditional knowledge of native cultures among indigenous educators. The emphasis is often aligned with the notion of the ethnosphere (chap. 1), through which it is acknowledged that human knowing is enhanced when a diversity of languages and cultural sensibilities are allowed to find expression. Other prominent emphases of indigenous education include attentiveness to place, sustainability, and traditional lore (in particular, with regard to cultural narratives, medical knowledge, and ethnomathematics). The movement has been growing rapidly in recent years and is rising to particular prominence in the English-speaking world in Australia, Canada, New Zealand, and the United States.

Feminist pedagogies present a similar span of interests and are oriented by a desire to understand how education is organized by and contributes to culturally determined gender roles and dynamics. Contemporary topics of discussion include the masculinization of curriculum and the feminization of teaching, gendered differences in subject and career areas, and varied strategies for and approaches to learning—to mention only a few.***

Queer pedagogy is a more recent movement that is organized around a desire to understand not only how educational matters have been *sexed*, but how they have been *heterosexed*—that is, how assumptions of normality associated with straight and (usually) male identities pervade educational policies and practices.*

None of these categories should be understood as a discrete or isolated domain. Most critical educators work across more than one frame and have more than one category of concern.

As researchers, we were interested in students' willingness to comment on the text (see Marlene's comment above) privately, in interviews, but not publically, in class. Neither in whole-class discussions, nor in group planning sessions, was the issue of Travis's apparent gay sexuality addressed in any depth.

Instead, specific issues of homophobia and heterosexism were supplanted by much more general and vague discussions about bullying in schools. In fact, the term *bullying* came to serve as an over-determined signifier, one that was reinforced by discourses of teaching methods under discussion. Rather than trying to unpack and analyze the nested relationships among, for example, sexism, homophobia, and heterosexism as depicted in *Stitches*, the collective (students-and-instructor) was preoccupied with the appropriateness of the novel for use in middle/secondary schools and the ways in which secondary school students might develop literacy skills around its use.

And so, while on the surface it appeared that this teacher education class was addressing important issues of diversity related to homophobia and heterosexism, the failure to engage with these in a specific, deep and committed way meant that stereotypical knowledge was reinforced and reproduced.

No single person was to blame. All of the participants were complicit—a fact that wasn't lost on some. As Yvonne later explained:

I thought that it was too bad that we were not able to really talk about the issues of abuse that were occurring in this novel during class discussions. It occurred to me after I had read Stitches *that the characters most confused about how to have healthy relationships were those that we might call "normal." Travis seemed to have a really good handle on what mattered in a relationship, and so did his friend, Chantelle. I wish that we could have talked about that more in class, because it's something that I'd like to be able to talk about with my students. Instead, we focused on issues of bullying and we made it seem like both Travis and Chantelle were sad and pathetic characters. I hope that I can do better as a teacher, but I can see now that I won't be able to learn how to do that in my teacher education classes.*

10.4 Critiques of Critical Pedagogy

There is an irony with critical pedagogy. It can never prevail in formal education. Critical pedagogy is concerned with interrupting the status quo, deconstructing the structures of dominance, and interrogating how one might limit or be limited, disenfranchise or be disenfranchised. The objects of these concerns are constantly moving and evolving, and a pedagogy that

* See, e.g., Mary Bryson & Suzanne de Castell, "Queer pedagogy: Praxis makes im/perfect," in *Canadian Journal of Education*, vol. 18, no. 2 (1993): 285–305; William F. Pinar (editor), *Queer theories in education* (Hillsdale, NJ: Lawrence Erlbaum, 1998). See also the *Journal of Gay & Lesbian Issues in Education*.

is critical must move with them. It can never fall into a naive belief that it has succeeded in its goals.

It should not be surprising, then, that there are criticisms of the critical pedagogy movement, through which different commentators have attempted to alert practitioners to blind spots and unnoticed biases. In one prominent work, for example, Elizabeth Ellsworth* argues that much of critical pedagogy (in particular, those branches that draw mainly on Marxism) is rooted in the same sorts of rationalist assumptions that underpin the repressive myths it seeks to interrupt. Attentive to the privileges of her role as a white, middle-class woman and professor, Ellsworth critiques notions of empowerment, student voice, dialogue, and critical reflection as she develops the argument that institutionalized engagements with these issues are rife with contradictions and can help to reproduce the very structures they are intended to critique.

Ellsworth's concerns are illustrative of the difficulty of, to borrow from African American poet, essayist, and autobiographer Audre Lorde,** using the master's tools to dismantle the master's house. If theorists limit themselves to the same rationalist and masculinist terms of debate, they are to some extent predetermining the conclusions that can be drawn while, at the same time, they might be setting the stage for the same sorts of hierarchical authority structures that they critique. Indeed, this has been a major criticism of many prominent figures in the critical pedagogy movement: some seem to be well removed from class and other struggles owing to the professional and material benefits accrued from their academic work.

A few commentators argue that this distance from the realities of oppression has prompted some critical theorists to champion ideas that further disenfranchise the already disenfranchised. Lisa Delpit,*** for example, has argued that emphases on cultural heritage, child-centered pedagogies, and individual "voice" can serve to restrict minority students' access to such cultural capital as "basic skills." As troublesome as such constructs of domination might be, they still hold the key to success in modern educational systems.

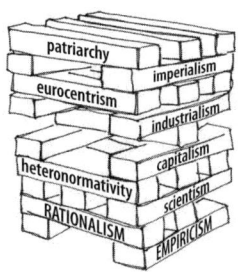

If theorists limit themselves to rational argument and empirical demonstration, they likely won't be able to see past conclusions that are founded in these modes of thinking, even though such conclusions are rife with implicit associations, not all of which are entirely defensible. Audre Lorde highlighted the problem with a metaphor: You can't dismantle the master's house by using the master's tools.

* Elizabeth Ellsworth, "Why doesn't this feel empowering? Working through the repressive myths of critical pedagogy," in *Harvard Educational Review*, vol 59, no. 3 (1989): 271–297.
** Audre Lorde, *Sister outsider: Essays and speeches* (Trumansberg, NY: Crossing Press, 1984).
*** Lisa D. Delpit, *Other people's children: Cultural conflict in the classroom* (New York: New Press, 1996).

The conclusion of this manner of argumentation—that is, that noted educational inequities might be addressed through renewed emphases on traditional structures and processes, rather than on more progressive strategies—may seem paradoxical. However, a more productive interpretation is that any attempt to offer a simple solution is likely doomed to failure. As developed in previous chapters, education is a trans-phenomenon. A prescription that is focused on one level of activity (e.g., teaching practices) and ignores other overlapping, interlacing, and transcendent levels (e.g., curricula, educational policy, and cultural dynamics) is rooted in the same sort of reductionist thinking that it purports to address.

How, then, should we teach?

There are no tidy answers here, but there are some consistent recommendations across different critical pedagogies. For example, there would seem to be an ethical imperative for teachers to be attentive to the ways that classroom dynamics contribute to what can and cannot be said. An important element here is the deliberate creation of spaces for diverse opinions to be represented. When such diversities are stifled or suppressed—whether accidentally or deliberately—the result can be an uncritical common sense that perpetuates and amplifies itself by excluding other points of view.

How do you deal with the culture of the oppressor when it's woven into personal, familial, and social histories?

This question is being asked in many post-colonial nations, where colonizers' cultures cannot be abandoned, simply because of the way they're tangled in daily lives.

As might be illustrated with the example of a traditional basket woven from recycled telephone wire, tactics of deliberate hybridization have emerged—in, for example, art forms (including dance, music, poetry, and theatre) and languages.*

* See Carlotta von Maltzan (editor), *Africa and Europe, en/countering myths: Essays on literature and cultural politics* (New York: Peter Lang, 2003).

Even though our personal interviews suggested that students wanted to probe more deeply into the issues of sexuality and sexual identification, as prompted by the novel, the normalizing structures of teacher education prevented such probing from occurring on a collective level in the classroom. While students' ability to maintain both public and private responses to literary characters may seem sophisticated, we are concerned that it is the public response that is likely to become dominant. Many readers value opportunities to share their responses to novels they have read with other readers. The act of sharing helps readers not only to understand their responses better but also to situate these responses in a larger cultural context.

However, if individual readers feel unable to represent their personal responses to literary engagements, the possibility that renewed collective sensibilities may emerge from shared discussions is likely to be compromised. Learning collectives that do not create conditions for diversity of experience to be represented inhibit the development of both collective and personal learning.

This seems to be what happened within the context of this teacher education program. Because conditions were not created for the students to safely represent their responses and identifications, the collective classroom conversations were developed around the normalized and generic language of bullying. Those conversations contained very little reference to specific acts of homophobia and heterosexism that were depicted in the novel.

To be clear, the issue here is not about assigning blame. It is about taking responsibility. The instructor and the students were complicit in the silence around particular topics—and this sort of ignorance of injustice is as insidious a mode of participation as any overt embrace.

In brief, then, a pedagogical situation was created in which students became obsessed with lesson and unit planning—not as occasions to address issues of social justice but as means to avoid such topics. As one student, Lisa, commented: "I think that many students in our class walked away being reaffirmed with every stereotype that they thought was possible about homosexuality."

10.5 Teacher Identity Formation

Although one's sense of self tends to be fairly stable, personal identity is always evolving. Shifts tend to be small, but there are times when there are dramatic shifts in one's identifications and, hence, in one's identity. Moving to a new city, switching careers, losing a friend, or becoming ill are among the events that can heighten one's awareness of the transitory nature of who one might be.

For most, becoming a teacher falls into this category. Among the most demanding aspects of learning to be a teacher is the need to work across two different settings: the host school and the university. To complicate matters, these profoundly different institutions are not as overtly distinct as most contexts tend to be. By way of contrast, it's relatively easy to keep track of how one is positioned in a department store, in a traffic jam, or at a family wedding. The social and cultural markers are obvious. But the differences between being a student-of-teaching on a university campus and a student-teacher in a public school are usually much more subtle.

There are radical differences between these settings that are rooted in historical, social, political, educational, and structural circumstances. At the risk of oversimplification, the explicit purpose of the modern university is to push out the boundaries of knowledge, which often involves direct challenges to popular assumption and tradition. In comparison, the modern school is most often seen as a place to maintain what is established, not to interrupt it. (As noted in chap. 1, and revisited in chap. 12, this conception of public schooling is not universal. However, it is pervasive.)

Linda Tuhiwai Smith* identifies a series of "projects" that have been taken up by various indigenous peoples in their efforts to preserve their cultures and to become self-determining.

Acts of reclaiming, reformulating, and reconstituting include story telling, celebrating survival, indigenizing, revitalizing, connecting, reading, writing, gendering, reframing, restoring, returning, democratizing, networking, naming, protecting, negotiating, and sharing—thematics have also emerged in discussions of education that are framed by complexity thinking.

* Smith, *Decolonizing methodologies.*

Nowhere is this separation more obvious than in the teacher education programs, where universities are seen as places of theory and schools are cast as places for practice—or in more negative terms, universities offer impractical theory and school's champion un-theorized practice. Small wonder, then, that teacher candidates might feel conflicted as they negotiate their roles. Given their already demanding responsibilities, the added task of having to function as the interpretive bridge between the university and the school can be very troublesome.

Critical discourses, as presented in this chapter and as developed throughout the book (esp. in chaps. 3, 7, and 8), can be helpful in this regard. One of the lessons of these perspectives and theories is that we can be complicit in maintaining the structures that we find oppressive by internalizing the partialities that we explicitly critique (recall the Implicit Association Tests in chap. 3).

And so, for example, if you should find yourself caught up in an "ivory tower versus mind factory" conflict, critical theory offers both an imperative and a means to act. You can choose to be carried along with entrenched assumptions and criticisms, or you can adopt a more critical stance. Where do these sorts of tensions come from? What assumptions are being made? How am I participating in the maintenance of these assumptions? How might I think/act differently? Can perceived tensions be made more productive? In brief: How am I complicit?

Across such actions, it is important to bear in mind that diversities of opinion and interpretation are vital to the health and robustness of knowledge-producing communities. The point, then, is not that tensions must be resolved. It is, rather, that they can usually be productively engaged.

In other words, teaching and becoming a teacher should be mindful acts. Who we are, what we know, and what we are able to do are enabled and con-strained by the possibilities for interpretation that are presented.

In this sense, teaching is challenging, in the twofold sense of "difficult" and "disruptive."

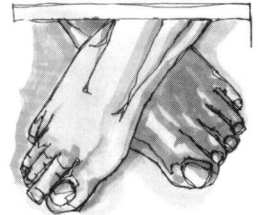

John Uzo Ogbu,* an African-born American anthropologist, offered some important insights into how race and ethnic differences play out in educa-tional and economic achievement.

In particular, he developed the use-ful distinction between "voluntary mi-norities" (persons who chose to move to wherever they are) and "involuntary minorities" (persons born there). Ogbu argued that, because involuntary minorities are raised in contexts where their identities are presented as outside of prevailing norms, they often internalize the biases and oppressions of the dominant culture.

By contrast, voluntary minorities tend not to have embodied the same sorts of disenfranchising, disempower-ing discourses—and, for that reason, are on average much more successful than involuntary minorities (on virtu-ally every measure of success).

Teachers, Ogbu argued, thus have an obligation to uncover, challenge, and offer strategies to overcome internalized prejudices.

* John Uzo Ogbu, "Understanding cultural diversity and learning," in *Educational Researcher*, vol. 21, no. 8 (1992): 5–14.

In the context of the teacher education program, it appears that students were provided with few opportunities to represent and meaningfully use their literary responses, although much attention was given to discussing and practicing the competencies that are typically associated with "good teachers." By focusing on lesson and unit planning, and spending considerable time on effective classroom management strategies, the students were "buying into" the mythic narratives of effective pedagogy. In other words, the rich literary identifications that individual readers had with *Stitches* were eclipsed by the normalizing fictions of good teaching.

It's impossible for us to speculate what might have happened had there been a stronger programmatic emphasis on analyzing student reading. However, we strongly believe that if literary experiences are to be used as opportunities for cultural transformation, deliberate attention must be given to providing students with opportunities both to represent and to analyze the diversity of personal readings within safe and intellectually supportive environments. Without such supportive and focused environments, prevailing normalizing discourses are likely to dominate the perceptual awareness of students. This does not merely have implications for what students might learn; it also has implications for who they might become. As one of the students, Tanya, commented, "Since coming into Education I've been very surprised by how conservative we're expected to be. I'm not sure I can be that kind of person."

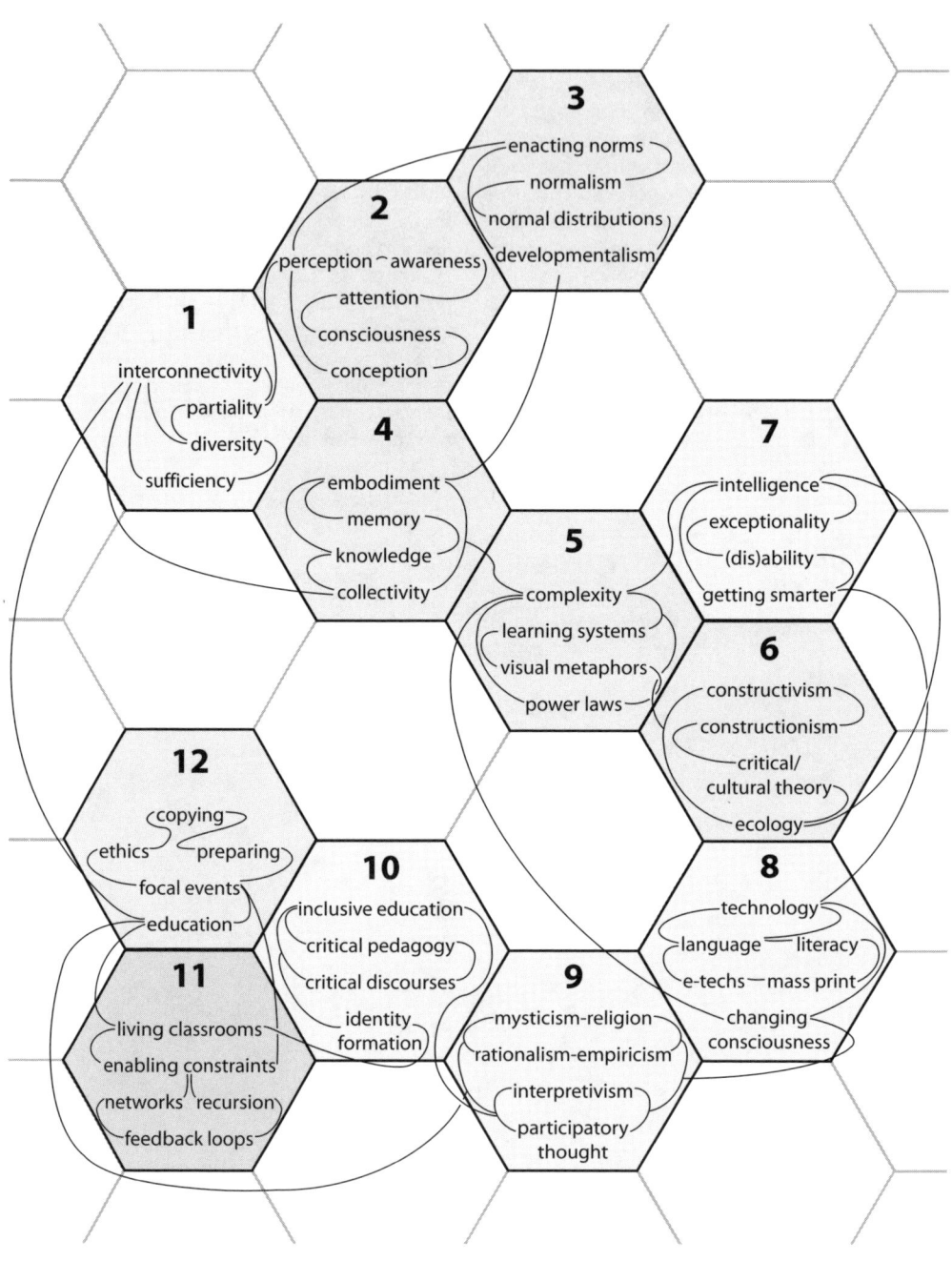

11   Teaching Conditions

It's a bitterly cold day and I'm giving a poetry-writing workshop to 32 pre-service teachers who are enrolled in a course on teaching methods for the middle school English language arts classroom.

To begin, I ask them about their previous experiences with poetry writing. Their responses are familiar:

"We were told to just write what we felt."

"We were told to write a sonnet for our Shakespeare unit."

"I remember writing free verse poems."

"We wrote a lot of haikus and poems with specific rhyme schemes."

From what the students tell me, it seems that poems were seen as artifacts that could either be plucked from the air or extracted from deep inside one's inner being by those few students who had some gift or talent for poetic expression.

I tell them to try to ignore everything that they think they know about writing poetry. Then we begin.

11.1 Enabling Constraints:
Opening Possibilities by Limiting Choices

So far, the discussions in this book have been mostly descriptive. The central concern has been with the identification and interpretation of a range of issues and phenomena associated with the educational endeavor. A few pieces of practical advice have appeared here and there, but the pragmatic issue of how one goes about teaching hasn't been directly engaged in any sustained way.

That changes in these final two chapters, where the emphasis is mainly on how a teacher might enact the complex sensibilities presented so far. However, before proceeding, we want to emphasize that these discussions should not be interpreted as "how-to" texts. Oriented by the conviction that teaching is an enormously complex undertaking that is learned over a lifetime, we offer these chapters more as a set of lenses to recognize and make sense of effective educational practices.

This chapter is focused on what might be called "the conditions of complex emergence." In brief, this phrase refers to a set of elements that complexity researchers have studied over the past few decades in their efforts to restore ecosystems, develop medical interventions, reduce crime, and prompt collective classroom activity—to mention only a few instances in which agents might come together to give rise to more complex, robust, and capable wholes.

This discussion is framed by an assumption that teachers are always and already working to affect different levels of learning systems. In particular, the two foci here are individual understanding *and* classroom collectivity. The orienting suggestion is that effective classroom teaching engages these knowing systems simultaneously. As well, this sort of simultaneous engagement is not a matter of trade-off or compromise. Rather, the successful collective is not just more intelligent than the smartest of its members, it also presents occasions for all of the participants to be smarter—that is, to be capable of actions, interpretations, and conclusions that they wouldn't typically achieve on

CHILD- *versus* **TEACHER-CENTERED?**

Education should foster individual talents, providing opportunities for self-direction and autonomy. That is, schooling should be **child-centered**.

There's just too much going on in a classroom for the teacher to attend to the needs of individuals. So, although not ideal, classrooms must be **teacher-centered**.

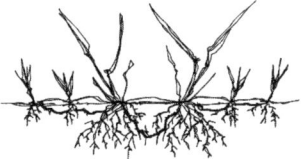

COMMON ROOTS: This popular debate is rooted in an assumption that the individual is the locus of knowing and learning. From that it follows that humans are insulated and isolated from one another—which, in turn, forces a choice in focus in the classroom on either the teacher or the student.

their own. We begin by commenting on "enabling constraints." In education, these refer to the sorts of questions and tasks that support both individual and collective learning.

At first hearing, *enabling constraints* might sound like an oxymoron. However, with regard to complex co-activity, the phrase is intended to flag a necessary tension rather than a contradiction. Complex unities are simultaneously rule-bound (constraining) and capable of flexible, unanticipated possibilities (enabling).

Some constraints are dictated by context, others by the structures of the unities, still others arise in the co-actions of agents. The common feature of these constraints is that they are not *prescriptive* (i.e., they don't dictate what *must* be done), but *expansive* (i.e., they indicate what *might* be done, in part by indicating what must not be done). Familiar examples include the Ten Commandments and the rules of hockey.

To put a finer point on this issue, consider the following learning objectives:

a) By the end of this lesson, students will demonstrate their understandings of some of the core elements of a poem by identifying the rhyme structure, the principal figurative devices, and the core themes of "The Rime of the Ancient Mariner."

b) Students will write original poems in this lesson.

In complexity terms, both statements are flawed. Each is prescriptive and functions to shut down creative possibility, although in a very different way from the other. The first is too constraining. It presumes correct responses and clearly delineated techniques for reaching a pre-specified end—and while these elements might be appropriate to the specific context, the ideas and the competencies might not be applicable to other situations (such as interpreting other poems or composing a short story). In contrast, the latter is probably much too open-ended. Without more structure, students are likely to be frustrated and unproductive.

The rules that define complex systems maintain a delicate balance between sufficient structure, to limit a pool of virtually limitless possibilities, and sufficient openness, to allow for flexible and varied responses.

How many basketballs would it take to fill the school gym?

How many hairs are there on your head?

How much of a tire's tread wears off in one block of driving?

Enrico Fermi, a Nobel laureate in physics, was famous for using a particular sort of enabling constraint when teaching.

These "Fermi problems" are based on everyday situations, but call for sensible approximations and inspired guesses based on very little data.* They are particularly useful for promoting "group think," partly because the questions tend to call for knowledge of many things, and partly because discussion and debate can support more sensible guessing.**

As well, Fermi problems illustrate that enabling constraints should be *expansive*, but needn't be *open-ended*.

* Googling "Fermi problem" will provide access to thousands of questions. On some sites, problems have been organized by grade level and topic.
** See Surowiecki, *The wisdom of crowds*, for a discussion of group think.

These rules are not matters of "everyone does the same thing" or "everyone does their own thing," but of "everyone participates in a joint project." Rephrasing teaching intentions as enabling constraints rather than prescriptions is an important competency—as in, for example, the one that was used to frame the lesson described in this chapter's interspersed narrative:

c) Students will explore poetry-writing processes through inventing characters and plots based on unfamiliar items and unexpected juxtapositions.

A simpler example, and a subcomponent of the lesson described in this chapter, might be that students will be given five minutes for a timed writing on a focused prompt (see the next piece of the interspersed narrative). The critical features are (1) sufficient constraint (accomplished here by using buttons to orient, but restricting decisions to specific characters and contexts) and (2) sufficient openness (occasioned in this case through the introduction of unpredictable combinations of actors and situations).

To be clear, the pedagogical intent here is neither that students will simply *reproduce* established insights (as suggested by objective *a*, above), nor merely *produce* new interpretive possibilities (as suggested by objective *b*). Rather, the goal is a creative mix: to investigate *established knowledge* while engaging in a process of *establishing knowledge*. Again, a key to such an end is a structure that is simultaneously constraining and enabling—imposing rules that delimit possibilities and that allow choice at the same time.

Maria Montessori is famous for the teaching method that she developed nearly a century ago. Originally intended for children of poor families, the method embodies all of the conditions developed in this chapter. For example, it encourages independence and freedom with limits and responsibility (i.e., enabling constraints); the method supports individual interests and talents within contexts of collaborating with others (specialization); ongoing curriculum development is based on the child's interactions with the environment (recursive elaboration).

* Rebecca Luce-Kapler, *Writing with, through, and beyond the text: An ecology of language* (Mahwah, NJ: Lawrence Erlbaum, 2004).

Following some of the practices for teaching poetry articulated by Rebecca Luce-Kapler,* I start by spreading a collection of buttons taken from many different articles of clothing on a large table in the middle of the classroom and then invite students to choose one that is interesting to them. Once seated, I ask each of them to examine the button and decide what sort of article of clothing was previously attached to it and then to write down their decision. Next, I ask them to imagine the person who is wearing this article of clothing.

I try to prompt their imaginations with a few questions: "What interesting place has this button been to? What event has this button participated in?" I follow up with the instruction, "When you think you're ready, take five minutes and write out the details of this place and event. Remember that detail is important. It's more interesting to hear that the button has been in the Tiffany's on Fifth Avenue in New York City at dusk on Christmas Eve amid a throng of busy shoppers than it is to hear that the button was out shopping for jewelry!"

The Division of Urology at the University of British Columbia restructured itself a few years ago by rethinking its sites of redundancy and diversity.

Researchers in the department were once clustered according to their interests in specific organs, but are now organized according to interests in particular medical conditions (e.g., cancers, kidney stones, transplantation). These new, more diverse clusters are transdisciplinary, bringing together different sorts of expertise into more intelligent collectives in which issues are addressed more systemically.*

11.2 Specialization: Redundancy and Diversity

Intelligent unities are simultaneously stable and innovative. On the one hand, they act in predictable ways in varied circumstances; on the other hand, they can behave unpredictably as they transform themselves in response to new experiences. Underlying their steadiness and creativity are two complementary conditions: internal redundancy and internal diversity.

Internal redundancy refers to the extent of similarity among the agents that come together in a complex unity. As demonstrated by the example of neurons in a brain and people in a social collective, typically such agents are much more alike than different—as might be expected. These samenesses enable agents to work together.

Unfortunately, the word *redundancy* is often interpreted in negative terms, since it tends to be associated with unnecessary repetitions or inefficiencies. In the context of mechanical systems, this negative sense is obviously appropriate. Designers of simple mechanical devices usually aim at optimal performances, and extra parts or duplicated processes only reduce efficiency. However, as developed in chapter 5, agents that learn belong to a very different class of phenomena.

Redundancy plays two key roles in a complex unity. First, it makes it possible for agents to work together, as is illustrated by typical redundancies in human social groupings. Samenesses such as a common language, similar social status, shared responsibilities, common expectations, and so on are obviously important for social cohesion. These are the sorts of things that tend to fade into the backdrop unless there's some sort of rupture in one or more of them. Second, redundancy contributes to the robustness of a system, simply because it makes it possible for agents to compensate for one another's failings. When one agent is absent or errs, a system with sufficient redundancy can simply carry on.

None of this is news to public education. Indeed, the modern school could be aptly described as a cultural means to ensure redundancy among citizens. With few exceptions, students are exposed to the same

*Visit http://www.surgery.ubc.ca/urology.html.

curriculum, over the same periods of their lives. They are occupied for the same stretches of the day, and are expected to meet or exceed the same minimal standards … it goes on.

In and of itself, this emphasis on redundancy isn't a bad thing. It is necessary to be able to collaborate on a project of shared interest, and so common curricula, shared texts, and standardized performance assessments can be at least partly justified in those terms. There would be very little possibility of shared work and no reason for collective discussions in a classroom in which everyone was truly progressing at her or his own pace.

The problems arise when redundancy is the *only* ingredient. Redundancy contributes to the stability of a system, but the cost of a highly redundant system is the increased likelihood of an unintelligent system. As it turns out, the source of a system's intelligence is actually the diversity of its agents. Whereas redundancy is inward-oriented, enabling the habitual, moment-to-moment interactivity of the agents, diversity is more outward-oriented, enabling novel actions in response to shifts in the grander context.

The condition of internal diversity has been used to make sense of the tremendous amount of unexpressed "junk" DNA in the human genome, the specialized functions of different brain regions, the range of vocational competencies in any large city, the varieties of cultures in the ethnosphere, and the biodiversity of the planet. In each case, the diversity represented among units/parts/ agents is seen as a source of possible responses to emergent circumstances. For instance, if a pandemic were to strike humanity, currently unexpressed DNA sequences might bestow immunity on a few people, and hence ensure the survival of the species—an intelligent response on the species level. A differently intelligent response, at the cultural level, might arise among a network of researchers in such diverse areas as virology, immunology, sociology, entomology, botany, pharmacology, and meteorology. In both cases, it's impossible to specify in advance which categories of expertise/variation will be needed. What matters most for intelligent response is not an ability to predict the future, but a pool of diverse possibilities in the present.

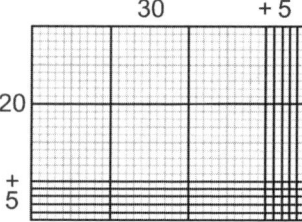

What's multiplication?*

Or, more descriptively, what sorts of interpretations—that is, images, gestures, metaphors, analogies, applications, and other associations—are used to give shape to the concept of multiplication?

These questions were put to a group of teachers (Kindergarten through Grade 12), and their collective response included that multiplication involves:

· repeated addition,
· grouping,
· sequential folding,
· many-layerings,
· proportional reasoning,
· grid-generating,
· changing dimensions,
· undoing division,
· stretching a number line,
· rotating a number line.

In the follow-up discussion, it became apparent that only a few of these interpretations are explicitly developed

The example of a global pandemic is perhaps a bit extreme in the context of a discussion of classrooms, but it is illustrative. With an overarching and pervasive emphasis on redundancy at the classroom level, groupings of students have little opportunity for collectively intelligent action. The tragedy of the situation is that, as with any social grouping, every classroom is filled with diversity, but it can't be manifest in contexts defined by individualized tasks, top-down explanations, inflexible curricula, and prescriptive performance objectives.

x	30 +	5	
20	600	100	700
+ 5	150	25	175
	750	125	875

in most mathematics classes—even though they're all invoked at some point (and, at times, multiple associations are invoked simultaneously).

Why and how does this matter for teaching?

To begin, it interrupts some entrenched assumptions about the nature of knowledge. For instance, there is no absolute, all-encompassing definition of something as *basic* as multiplication. Such fundamental parts of mathematics can be shown to evolve, as new images are created and applications arise.

As such, there is perhaps a need to be explicit about the figurative bases of such notions. For example, ⁻2 × ⁻3 is difficult to understand in terms of repeated addition or grouping. But it is readily interpreted in terms of a blend of stretching and rotating a number line.

An implication is that systems of knowledge—that is, *bodies* of knowledge—are also complex learning forms that adapt to new circumstances.

What if a teacher were to approach each new curriculum topic with the attitude that the diversity of insight needed to address that topic is already present in the collective?

For starters, the pedagogical emphasis couldn't be strictly on ensuring redundancy among students (which, as noted above, is still an important element in co-activity). The teacher would also have to consider strategies to represent diverse insights that are already present. For example, a lesson on multiplying integers might begin with …

What's ⁺3 × ⁻4? Show how you know.

… rather than …

To multiply two integers,
you first look at their signs.

The first is more likely to be an enabling constraint. It provides a narrow focus, yet opens the door to a diversity of explanations.* It is oriented by a faith in the collective intelligence of the collective. In contrast, the latter is merely a technical directive. It isn't about what you *might* do, but what you *must* do—and, in the process, it closes down possibilities for meaning-making. (Notice that this chapter's narrative example is laced with several layers of diversity-generating activities.)

It's important to emphasize that internal redundancy and internal diversity are not opposing, but complementary. They can actually support one another—as commonly happens, for example, when individuals decide to combine efforts in order to improve their

* This question was actually used in a study of integers learning based in a Grade 7 classroom. See Brent Davis & Elaine Simmt, "Understanding learning systems: Mathematics teaching and complexity science," in *Journal for Research in Mathematics Education*, vol. 34, no. 2 (2003): 137–167.

respective situations. For this to happen, they need
to work on establishing greater redundancy between
them at the same time as they exercise their respective
categories of expertise. In other words, working toward
a more intelligent classroom collective does not mean
compromising individual possibilities. On the contrary,
it likely means enhancing them.

But none of this is likely to happen unless the
teacher consciously and deliberately creates structures
and organizes tasks that ensure the development of
necessary redundancies and the expression of diverse
interests and abilities. Some pointers on the creation
of appropriate structures are provided in the next
section.

The next part of the button exercise involves the
introduction of a bit of "accident" to the varieties
of characters and narratives that have already
been created.

I ask students to pair up with someone and,
with their partners, to share what was imagined
and then to create a situation where their two
characters meet.

Once again I remind them of the importance
of detail. I give them another five minutes to
invent the situation where the two buttons
encounter one another.

11.3 Networking Systems:
Neighbor Interactions and Decentralization

It goes without saying that agents within a complex
system must be able to affect one another's activities.
Clearly, neighbors that come together in a grander
unity must communicate. However, what is not so obvious is exactly what a *neighbor* might be in the context
of a knowledge-producing system such as a classroom
collective or an individual student, or in a system of
knowledge, such as language or mathematics.

One of the major insights from constructivist, constructionist, and other coherence theories of learning
is that, to generate new insights, the neighbors that
come to interact are not necessarily physical bodies,
but can be ideas, hunches, queries, images, artifacts,
and other manners of representation. The hope is that
new interpretive possibilities will arise, for example,
when individuals share ideas that come up during
timed writings or when a character based on one button encounters a character based on another.

In fact, the creation of structures to allow ideas to bump together is one of the hallmarks of all progressive human institutions, including higher education, research settings, business, and most governments. (Conversely, preventing ideas from bumping together is a quality of more repressive contexts, such as prisons, authoritarian regimes, and some classrooms.) For example, the academic world employs a variety of mechanisms, including clusters of experts in departments, specialist conferences, seminar series, journals, and visiting professorships, to mention only a few. Options within a classroom are clearly more limited, but might include group interactions, posters that can be hung and organized into clusters, electronic bulletin boards, and "graffiti walls" (e.g., bulletin boards where students can post and arrange thoughts as they arise).

One of the problems encountered early-on by online retailers was that customers couldn't browse. In contrast to shopping in a bookstore, where texts are usually grouped by topic or genre, customers weren't likely to chance across a book when they were shopping for another.

The problem has since been addressed through application of principles of network theory (see chap. 4). By studying the associations made by purchasers, users, and other visitors, sites like pandora.com, youtube.com, and amazon.com have mapped out networks of "similar" writings, singers, videos, and so on—in effect, creating contexts in which neighbors can interact to give rise to new, perhaps unexpected, and likely profitable associations.

Again, the hope here is that the juxtaposition of various representations might trigger other interpretations, which when presented might trigger still others. An obvious caveat is that there must be more than one interpretive possibility to begin with. Clearly, if a lesson on multiplication is based on a single interpretation, such as repeated addition, it's unlikely that rich and farther reaching alternatives will arise. However, if grid-making, area-producing, number-line-stretching, ratio-reasoning, or other interpretations are presented alongside repeated addition, space is opened for emergent possibility.

The critical point is that structures need to be in place to allow ideas to stumble across one another, and this issue is more important than the way the physical system is actually organized. Small group meetings, pod seating, and private conversations may be no more effective than whole class discussions, straight rows, and text-mediated exchanges. Complexity thinking foregrounds the importance of neighbor interactions, but offers little direct advice on means to accomplish the meeting and blending of ideas. These means must be considered on a case-by-case basis, depending on the topic, the context, and the personalities involved.

Given the decentralized network structure (see chap. 4) of complex unities, there is a certain temptation to leap to the conclusion that teacher-led classrooms are troublesome because they're centralized, whereas student-centered classrooms are good because they're not. In practice, however, things seem to be a bit more complex.*

A pivotal issue here is the notion of "center"—or, more precisely, the assumption that the center must be a person or an object. A shift from a centralized structure to a decentralized one (see the diagrams on p. 56) is not merely a matter of shifting attentions from one thing to another. Rather, it is about decentering or displacing such attentions. Think about the center of the action in this chapter's interspersed narrative, for example. That event was deliberately designed so that clusters of people and ideas would come together into grander clusters, reflecting the structure of a decentralized network. More specifically, individuals began by working alone with single artifacts to invent a single character, then in pairs with two artifacts to construct an encounter, and then more collectively with an additional artifact to compose a narrative. Across each of these moments, the center was not the teacher, a student, or an object, but an emerging possibility. The situation was not teacher-centered, student-centered, or curriculum-centered.

And the possibilities that arose did so in the interactions of neighboring ideas, as enabled by a decentralized interactive structure. The teacher certainly couldn't have orchestrated the emergence of the ideas, but he did intentionally organize the activity in a manner informed by his knowledge of complex networks.

"Cooperative learning" is a prominent emphasis in current discussions of classroom strategies.

In cooperative learning settings, teams work on tasks that are deliberately structured to ensure interdependence of participants, individual accountability, and face-to-face interaction within heterogeneous groups. A number of techniques have been developed to meet these aims. Typically, specific roles are assigned to group members and evaluation strategies, intended to ensure individual

* See, e.g., Edwards & Mercer, *Common knowledge.*

As the participants are making their decisions about where and how their characters meet, I move around the room passing out envelopes that contain photographs that I've gathered from different collections.

When the time for constructing the details about the meeting has elapsed, I ask the pairs of students to open their envelopes, examine the photographs, and answer the question, "What happened just before this photograph was taken?"

Giving only a moment to settle on a response, I then ask them to incorporate this event into the situation that they just invented for their two characters. Next, I ask students to work together to write a few paragraphs to summarize their invented plot. Finally, I instruct them to show the buttons and photographs they've used, and to read their paragraphs aloud. Even though they have only been working on this activity for about 15 minutes, the beginnings of imaginative fictional narratives are already appearing.

11.4 Recursive Elaboration: Iterative Processes and Nested Systems

accountability, are set out in advance. In this regard, they tend to be much more ends-oriented than complexivist approaches.

The intention of cooperative learning is that all participants' understandings will be supported. This aim points to a clear difference between cooperation-based strategies and complex approaches. Whereas the former are focused on individual learning within group contexts, the latter are focused on simultaneous elaborations of both individual and collective possibilities.

It's important to underscore that, although there are some philosophical differences, many cooperative learning techniques are compatible with complex understandings of teaching.*

* See David W. Johnson & Roger T. Johnson, *Learning together and alone: Cooperative, competitive, and individualistic learning*, 5th edition (Boston: Allyn & Bacon, 1998).

As developed in chapter 5, learning systems don't progress along linear trajectories. Rather, they unfold recursively by constantly invoking and elaborating established associations. Learning isn't accumulative; it is recursively elaborative. The underlying image here is more cyclical than linear or spiral, calling to mind a process that folds back onto itself.

At the individual level, such reiterative processes are always present in personal sense-making. One's history both enables (and constrains) one's perceptions of new experiences. In turn, the framing of what can and cannot be learned affects one's history.

The same is true on the collective level. A social grouping's history of interactions shapes what will be taken up and how that will affect subsequent interactions. The teacher can actually exploit this natural, cyclical dynamic when structuring learning activities. As illustrated in this chapter's extended example, a series of engagements were structured that drew on, elaborated, and transformed one another. Although it might appear that the lesson consisted of moving through a series of predetermined steps, in fact the important element was not the sequence of tasks, but the manner in which each element of that sequence called for recursive elaboration of already-established products.

For most people, being able to organize these sorts of tasks takes some practice. The image of a growing fractal tree can be a useful mnemonic device for thinking through this type of lesson structure. One begins with a seed (e.g., an enabling constraint, such as "Pick a button, and then imagine the garment it came from and what the wearer of the garment is doing"), elaborates on the product (e.g., "Have that person meet up with another person"), elaborates on that product, and so on. (A useful exercise at this point in your reading might be to examine this chapter's interspersed narrative for the finer details of the elaborative prompts.)

A recursive pedagogical structure is actually anchored in the assertion, presented earlier, that the knowledge needed to deal with a new topic is usually present in the classroom collective, although not necessarily within a single person. Recursively elaborative processes can be a powerful means of representing and knitting together that knowledge, and they can be used across most topics and subject matters.

Let's return to the earlier example of the multiplication of integers. If we start with the seed of "What's $^+3 \times {}^-4$? Show how you know," the next step might be preparation of posters by small groups to present a response and a rationale. When ready for display, the posters might be organized into clusters according to common interpretations. That might be followed by a large-group discussion in which the classroom collective looks across rationales for themes and variations.

This sort of process takes no longer than does a textbook-centered drill-work approach to the topic, and can be shown to contribute to more robust understandings—simply because students have access to a wider range of interpretations.

These two examples illustrate an important point: several different levels of learning systems are operating at the same time within pedagogical structures. Individuals, dyads, small groups, clusters of groups, and the whole class are all knowledge-producing systems (i.e., learners). None is privileged over the others; rather, these nested systems are mutually supportive and intelligent, unfolding from and enfolded in one another.

As mentioned in chapter 5, nestedness is a quality of complex systems. In the classroom, it can be considered a condition of complexity. That is, the teacher can use it as a tool to organize classroom engagements.

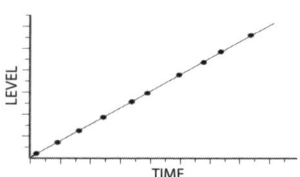

Over the history of the modern school, different images have been employed to describe "curriculum." Most commonly, curriculum has been described in terms of progress along a linear path (always forward, usually upward) toward a prespecified, fully articulated goal.

In the 1950s, the notions of the "spiral curriculum" rose to prominence. The idea was that, rather than proceeding

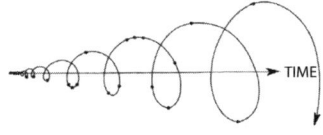

* Lorna Crozier, *Inventing the hawk* (Toronto: McClelland & Stewart, 1992).

Next I present students with examples of several contemporary poems written by Canadian poet Lorna Crozier.* I read them aloud, pausing to draw attention to rhythm, tempo, line breaks, images, and other devices used by Crozier to create poetic effects.

For homework, I ask the students to collaborate with their partners to choose one of the poems that were read aloud. Their task is to use it as a model for a new piece of poetry—one that they are to create together using the plot developed from the button-and-photograph activities.

I re-emphasize to them that they must collaborate with one another throughout the process of creating the new poem.

11.5 Creating Memories: Remembering and Forgetting

It goes without saying that, for a system to learn and to maintain its viability, it must have a means to remember.

We don't need to worry much about these processes on the individual level. For most people, biology provides the selective processes that underlie remembering and forgetting, and culture provides many means to keep track of personal interpretations (see chap. 8). On the collective level, however, we usually have to be somewhat more deliberate.

There are two aspects to memory: selection and preservation.

Regarding selection, a living and learning system must be able to forget/discard as well as to remember/collect. Clearly, keeping track of every interpretive possibility is just as debilitating as keeping track of none.

The teacher has a particular responsibility in this regard. Metaphorically, and as introduced at the end of chapter 9, the teacher acts as the consciousness of the collective—selecting from and orienting towards the interpretive possibilities that are presented.

As for preservation, a variety of tools and artifacts for collective memory are available for classroom use. These include various strategies of writing, wall displays, images and photographs, audio and video recordings, electronic storage devices, and shared rehearsals.

In the metaphorical role of consciousness-of-the-collective, the teacher not only selects interpretive possibilities, but also helps to register them in the collective memory (e.g., through prompts for writing). As with individual consciousness, the teacher does not determine what is noticed and remembered by the grander system. The teacher's role is more that of a commentator than that of a controller. And the teacher has a responsibility to be attentive to emergent possibility. In an intelligent classroom collective, things will arise that the teacher may not have considered previously.

through topics sequentially, students should be introduced to concepts gradually, revisiting topics each year to elaborate understandings. But the path is still defined in terms of convergence onto a prespecified objective.

A complexified conception of curriculum would suggest an image more like a phase space or a fractal tree, in which each event opens up new possibilities for action, which in turn open still other divergent possibilities. There is no particular direction—except, perhaps, toward the expansion of the space of the possible.

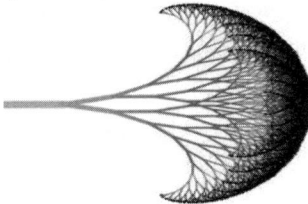

A practical exercise here might be to review some of the teaching narratives in this and other chapters to analyze the means employed to select and preserve insights across different levels of organization.

The next day, I ask students to read aloud the small poems they have created. One poem, written by Margaret and Dwayne, catches our collective attention:

First Date

A sweater with puff sleeves.
A hockey game.

We agree that the poem is not an artistic *tour de force*, yet it seems to hold a certain promise. Upon discussion, it becomes apparent that part of this poem's appeal has to do with its simple form. Very few words are used to vividly depict a situation that is ripe with interpretive possibilities.

Margaret tells the class about her experience of creating the poem with Dwayne:

I began with a small pink button that reminded me of a sweater my older sister used to wear. Dwayne had a button that he said reminded him of a winter coat he used to wear when he was in high school. When we talked about the two buttons, we decided that these two characters could meet on the downtown bus. They would see each other for weeks and not know that one was noticing the other—and then one day they would end up sitting next to one another.

The photograph that we were given showed *a simple church in the background and a snow-covered parking lot in front. When I looked at the picture, it reminded me of going to church when I was a kid—but when Dwayne looked at it he was reminded of going to hockey practice on cold winter mornings. We thought of many possibilities, but eventually decided that our two characters would get into a conversation on the bus about a hockey game that had happened the night before, which would lead to each revealing how much they like hockey and then to a decision to go to a game together.*

Writing the two paragraphs was easy—the plot and the characters were so clear to us. Dwayne and I worked on the poem online last night, sending ideas back and forth using instant messaging. We tried to copy the style of Lorna Crozier, who uses very simple structures with short phrases and everyday images. The poem that we started with was more of a narrative poem. It was a lot longer, telling the story of how these two characters met and so on. As we continued to work on it, though, we kept editing out more and more until we ended up with what we thought was the poetic essence—a poem that announced a lot of possibilities, but one that also had concrete details.

To me, it's interesting how our final poem developed on the screen. I don't think that either of us could say who wrote what.

11.6 Feedback Loops: Positive and Negative

The activities of all living and learning systems—ecological, biological, social, and epistemological—are modulated by a variety of feedback loops, which either amplify or dampen the effects of triggers. As suggested by the term, a "feedback loop" is a continuous and recursive process that takes part of a system's output and feeds it back as input. Note that positive and negative feedback loops shouldn't be confused with the positive and negative feedback of behaviorist psychology, which are conceived in terms of linear, cause–effect mechanisms.

Positive feedback loops are the ones that contribute to amplifications. Unchecked, they can contribute to exponential or explosive increase. Rapid population growth, epidemics, fads, crime waves, runaway bestsellers, and the "rich get richer" phenomenon are some familiar examples. A less obvious example is a conscious thought. Through positive feedback loops that are not yet well understood, certain cogitations and perceptions are amplified in ways that enable them to bubble to the surface of consciousness.

Negative feedback loops are dampeners or stabilizers. The most commonly cited example is the household thermostat that operates to hold room temperature constant. More complex examples include the body's means to maintain a constant temperature and a society's ethical and legal codes to maintain social stability.

There are many positive feedback loops that might be used in the classroom. Two well-researched examples are "wait time" and "emotioning." The example of wait time is especially interesting. A popular topic of research through the 1970s and 1980s, *wait time* refers to how much time is allowed to elapse between asking a question and expecting a response. In most classroom settings, wait time is under one second, and under such circumstances, students typically give either no answer or very short ones that tend not to involve higher-level thinking.

An interesting thing happens when the pause is deliberately extended to more than three seconds or so: students begin to respond more thoughtfully. In fact, if wait times are maintained, students actually begin to pose more involved questions themselves. In brief, the familiar back-and-forth structure of "teacher asks, student answers" can evolve into something more resembling an intense conversation. Questions become more probing; answers become more insightful. These results are consistent across all grades and subjects. In other words, a positive feedback loop is set up. (A worrisome finding of this research is that there is also a prominent tendency for teachers to revert back to

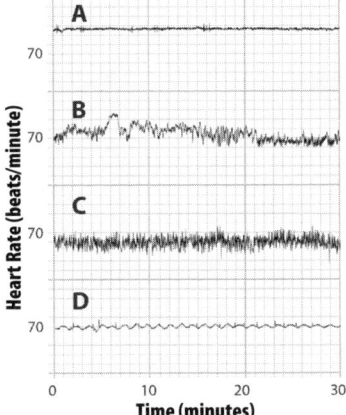

Which, if any, of the electrocardiograms (ECGs) is indicative of a healthy heart?* (The response is on the next page.)

* This image is adapted from Ary L. Goldberger, Luis A.N. Amaral, Jeffrey M. Hausdorff, Plamen Ch. Ivanov, C.-K. Peng, & H. Eugene Stanley, "Fractal dynamics in physiology: Alterations with disease and aging," in *PNAS (Proceedings of the National Academy of Sciences of the United States of America)*, vol. 99, suppl. 1 (2002): 2466–2472. © 2002 National Academy of Sciences of the United States of America. Used with permission.

short wait times and lower level questions. Apparently, the feedback loop can quickly take the discussion to places where some teachers feel uncomfortable or unprepared.)*

Another sort of positive feedback loop, and the subject of considerable current research (thanks to the discovery of mirror neurons—see chap. 4), is emotioning. Humans are biologically predisposed to mirroring and mimicking the emotions they encounter. A teacher who manifests disinterest or distaste for a subject matter (or person, belief, etc.) may well broadcast such attitudes to all present. Similarly, a teacher may broadcase interest and enthusiasm. A positive feedback loop can emerge when attitudes start to percolate through the system, prompting mirrored responses to mirrored responses. The effect can be so powerful that one might argue that teachers have an ethical responsibility to be curious about their subject matter. Certainly, it's unreasonable to hope that students become curious if the teacher isn't engaged!

In a similar vein, a teacher can set up a positive feedback loop by communicating greater confidence in a learner's abilities, and by selecting tasks that are challenging but do-able. Expectation supports greater achievement and, as the saying goes, success breeds success. In turn expectations are heightened. The process can also prompt the student to gain and internalize confidence that is first expressed by someone else. Several provocative studies support this point, one of which was mentioned in chapter 7 (involving black students and the GRE). In another, groups of women were asked to write a math test. One group was primed with accounts of gender differences (suggesting males had superior mathematics abilities), the other was exposed to stories of successful women. The latter group scored significantly higher.**

Of course, not all positive feedback loops are good. For example, we have all experienced how anxiety can cripple mental and physical performance, prompting an increase in anxiety, and so on. It is just as easy to amplify low-level questions, negative emotions, and diminished expectations. As well, an unchecked positive feedback loop can spiral out of control—as

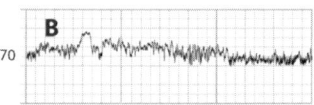

(See the question on page 205.)

The second electrocardiogram indicates a healthy cardiac rhythm. The others suggest severe problems—in particular, worrisome uniformities (which suggest failures to couple with external influences). The first and fourth traces point to severe congestive heart failure, the third to cardiac arrhythmia.

Similarly shaped "healthy" profiles arise in the dynamic interactions of positive and negative feedback loops and can be observed in stock markets, brains, ecosystems—in fact, in any complex learning system ...

... which raises a question: If classroom activity were profiled in a similar manner, what would it look like?***

* Kenneth Tobin, "The role of wait time in higher cognitive level learning," in *Review of Educational Research*, vol. 57 (Spring 1987): 69–95.
** Ilan Dar-Nimrod & Steven J. Heine, "Exposure to scientific theories affects women's math performance," in *Science*, vol. 314 (October 2006): 435.
*** See R. Darren Stanley, "The body of a 'healthy' education system," in *Journal of Curriculum Theorizing*, vol. 20, no. 4 (2004): 63–74.

happens on occasion when a crowd suddenly turns into a mob. Fortunately, such events aren't terribly common in the classroom, in part because there are a number of well-entrenched negative feedback loops already in place in most social systems.

Negative feedback loops are already knitted into the social fabric of the collective and embodied in the individual. Most people know how they "should" behave (i.e., are attuned to social norms) and act accordingly. In cases where a student persistently "misbehaves" (disrupts the collective), positive feedback loops may be at play, amplifying otherwise benign noncomforming behaviors. While it is impossible to offer universal recommendations for responding to such instances, attending to possible triggers and amplifiers might lead to effective responses.

Before leaving this discussion, it is important to emphasize that the list of conditions for complex emergence presented in this chapter is partial and intended only as a brief glimpse into an area that is evolving rapidly. Further, the principles presented here are ones that evolve over the course of a teacher's entire career. The point is not that you should master them before entering the classroom, but that these teaching conditions can serve as powerful tools for preparation, interpretation, and continuous elaboration.

So, what is teaching?

We define *teaching* as any event that prompts a complex system to respond differently. Our definition acts as a rejection of the pervasive anthropocentric assumption that humans are the only teaching species, and against the popular cultural belief that the outcomes of teaching are determinable and deliberate.

This sense of teaching recalls the roots of the word. It posits that the phenomenon of teaching can only be understood in terms of its effects on a learning system. In addition, and to render things even more complex, this conception compels a reconsideration of *learning* and *learners*. As is highlighted in Margaret's final paragraph, above, *who* or *what* is generating new insights and the nature of those insights cannot in many cases be understood in terms of just an individual.

An implication is that the teacher is not only another learner within the classroom, but an integral part(icipant) within a grander learning system. Along with all the other individuals, the clusters of individuals (such as Margaret and Dwayne), and the classroom collective as a whole, the teacher is teaching/learning. The teacher, that is, is constantly perturbing and being perturbed with/in the evolving, self-prompting system of the classroom collective. So far, an effective and familiar vocabulary for this sort of multi-leveled complex choreography has yet to emerge. When it does, it might provide an orientation to the not-yet-imaginable possibilities that are entailed by *teaching*.

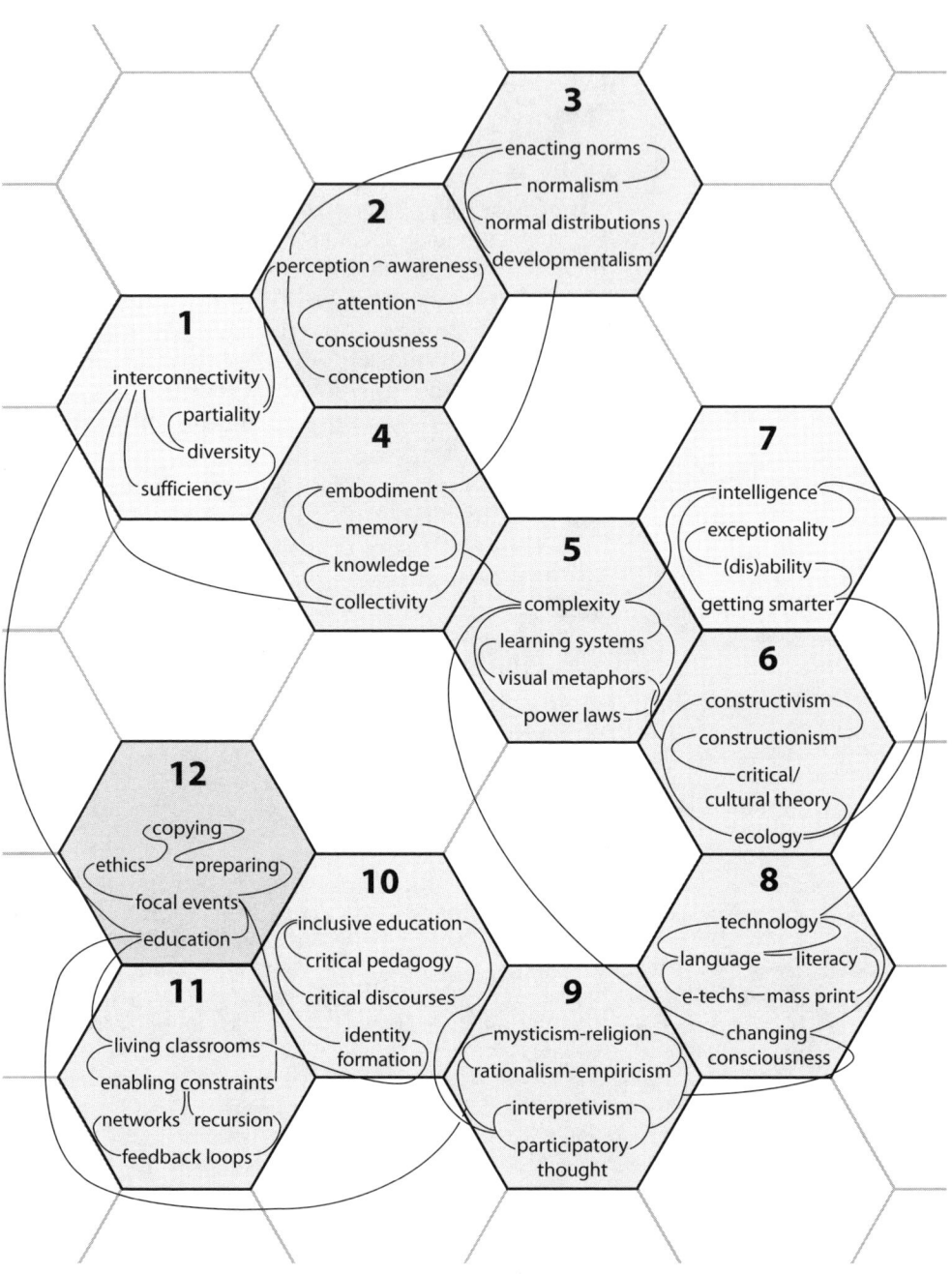

12   Teaching Encounters

The *Intergenerational Landed Learning on the Farm Project* ("Landed Learning")* has taken on the challenge of creating ways to foster environmental care and concern. Its strategy is to bring elementary school children together with community elders, including retired farmers and avid gardeners. Collectively they grow food crops on an urban farm. Children and elders meet at the farm throughout the school year to plan, plant, nurture, and harvest food and flowers.

The project was started in the autumn of 2002 by two university professors, along with one teacher, 18 Grade 7 children, and a small number of retired farmers from the community. Two years later, the project grew to involve approximately 100 children from two schools, 18 home schooled children, and 30 adult volunteer Farm Friends. It continues to grow.

Three intertwining questions frame the project, define the educational approach, and orient the research: Will young people develop care for the environment through working with community adults to grow food crops on an urban organic farm? What role does an intergenerational approach play in inspiring stewardship in children? In what ways does this educational experience impact the health and wellbeing of the children and adults?

* This project was initiated and is directed by Jolie Mayer-Smith and Linda Peterat of the Department of Curriculum Studies at the University of British Columbia. The interspersed narratives in this chapter are drawn from several of their publications, including "Growing together to understand sustainability: An intergenerational farming project" (co-authored with Oksana Bartosh), in *Innovation, education and communication for sustainable development* (ed. Walter Leal Filho; New York: Peter Lang, 2006). Images are drawn (with permission) from their website: http://www.cust.educ.ubc.ca/landedlearningproject/.

12.1 Focal Events

Deliberate efforts at teaching should be developed around focal events—artifacts or activities that are intended to gather and focus learners' attentions.

It almost goes without saying that one of the first steps when preparing to teach is the identification of intentions. What are students expected to know by the year's end? The unit's end? The lesson's end?

For most of the history of the modern school, efforts to express teaching intentions have been framed by fragmented and linearized curricula. By way of specific example, most writers of programs of study and textbooks for middle school students seem to have assumed that, in order to learn to add two fractions, they must learn to name fractional amounts, then to make equivalent fractions, then to identify common denominators, in this specific order. Similar examples could be readily drawn from other subject areas.

The thinking behind this way of parsing and sequencing concepts is actually sound. These practices are anchored in the realization that human consciousness is small. Since learners can deal with only a handful of details at a time, the teacher must narrow the focus. For certain topics, a linearized, one-concept-at-a-time approach might seem like the only logical solution to the limitations of human awareness.

However, a linear curriculum isn't the only possibility. In fact, it might even be argued to be a poor choice. Most human learning happens in sensorially rich, all-at-once situations. Isolated ideas, pre-specified sequences, and artificial boundaries around concepts clearly aren't necessary for students to learn.

What is vital, however, is focus, which is necessary to pull details out of the many and varied sensory possibilities that are always present. Historically, the most common instructional strategy in this regard has been to isolate and decontextualize conceptual bits, hoping that students will be able to reintegrate those bits and generalize their learning when they find themselves in more realistic contexts. (In fact, indications are that there is limited transfer of understandings to other courses and to applications outside of school

AUTHORITARIAN *versus* PERMISSIVE?

Children are unruly and easily distracted so they must learn discipline. A major part of teaching is thus about **control**.	To flourish, the child must be able to develop naturally. The teacher should thus create nurturing contexts that allow for **freedom**.

COMMON ROOTS: Formal education is focused on the development of the individual. Schooling happens within artificial settings, and so it is about *preparation for* (rather than *participation in*) the real world. The role of the teacher and the roles of students are distinct and non-overlapping.

Some research** suggests that social competence and academic achievement are better supported by *participatory* classroom structures than by *authoritarian* or *permissive* structures. In such contexts, teachers typically ...

· develop standards with students,
· use non-controlling talk,
· allow time for thoughtful responses,
· admit their own uncertainties,
· respect *both* independence *and* interdependence.

* See John D. Bransford, Ann L. Brown, & Rodney R. Cocking (editors), *How people learn: Brain, mind, experience, and school* (Washington, DC: National Academy Press, 1999).
** See Rogoff, *The cultural nature of human development*.

under such learning circumstances.)* An alternative is to structure the learning setting in ways that might enable teachers to direct attentions without stripping ideas from the contexts that render them meaningful. Pedagogically, the guiding concerns here are not about parsing up and sequencing concepts, but about selecting and developing objects and events that might be useful in highlighting important distinctions.

In the extended anecdote developed in this chapter, for example, the educators' explicit aim is to affect students' understandings of their connections with and responsibilities to the more-than-human world. It is easy to imagine a linearized, classroom-based set of lessons on the topic, perhaps beginning with key definitions, followed by a study of food webs, leading to academic debate over the relative merits of different means of food production ... all interspersed with regular quizzes to provide students with opportunities to demonstrate their understandings.

That is not what happened in this case. Rather, the teaching intentions were woven through diverse and interrelated experiences that were situated (in a specific place) and engaging (through specific activities). That is, the intentions of teaching were embedded and embodied in *every* aspect of the learning experiences, as opposed to being identified as goals to be met by the end of a sequence of instruction. As the educators worked to point to particular elements, and as students worked to interpret relationships among the various activities, the teaching intentions were realized in a manner that was not just effective, but spilled over into other experiences, within and beyond the school.

The pedagogical activities described in this chapter's narrative—and, in fact, in the narratives across all the chapters—were organized around *focal events*—moments of investigating something general by attending to something specific. Selection and development of these events were anchored in an understanding of perception as something other than a process of "taking things in." Perception, rather, is a culminating event of interpretation, a gathering together of the histories of the planet, the species, the culture, and the individual.

Early in 2000, a small group of students and staff from the Faculty of Agricultural Sciences at UBC learned that the university farm—a 40-hectare property that had once been a thriving research site—had been designated for future housing in the university's development plan. Deeply concerned about the loss of one of the last urban farms in the area, the group began a mission to save it.

Their strategy was to reinvent the farm as an educative site. They invited a few professors from the Faculty of Education to tour the overgrown fields and see the few cattle, sheep, and chickens—all that remained of a once-active animal husbandry and agriculture program. The pastoral space was fresh, green, and alive, and the walk around the grounds provided a welcome break from paperwork and indoor labors.

To the educators' eyes, the site offered a richness of possibility that extended well beyond hands-on lessons about science and food production. Attentive to environmental change and concerned about levels of ecological awareness among young people, the visitors wondered why they were feeling emotionally close to the earth. What experiences influenced their values and beliefs? They concluded that the time they had spent outdoors in youth, contemplating and enjoying nature through play and work on the land, had prompted deep and enduring commitments to the wellbeing of the planet. The question then followed, how might education be reconstructed to create experiences for children that would help them understand nature and develop reverence and care for the earth?

In further discussion, it became clear that two sorts of disconnection were represented: human from environment, and younger generation from older generation. On the latter point, it was clear that, with the modern trend toward urbanization, there is a dwindling number of people with experiences of working with the earth.

These disconnections came to serve as the foci of the project. Adopting a "place-based approach," the coordinators set out to structure a program to support the development of ecological consciousness in children by partnering with community elders with farming backgrounds.

12.2 An Ethics of Responsibility

Throughout this book, it has been argued that there is an ethical imperative for educators to be aware of and explicit about their frames of interpretation. How one conceives of the world shapes how one perceives of and acts in the world.

An example is particularly relevant here: for centuries, the prevailing opinion in western societies has been that the planet is an inert resource, something that is separate from humanity and free for exploitation. Schools have participated in the development and perpetuation of this mindset in many ways, the most obvious of which has been an emphasis on the development of instrumental competencies. The stress has been placed on learning *how* to do things, not on learning *why* things are done or if they are sustainable. More cogently, the emphasis has been on *knowledge*, not *wisdom*.

Until recently, such attitudes and emphases didn't appear to be terribly inappropriate. But a human population that is growing exponentially is placing demands on the environment that are also growing exponentially. The situation is unsustainable. And so, it has become clear that a worldview that has prevailed for centuries must change.

And it is changing. As disasters unfold and crises loom on levels from the cellular to the planetary, there are signs of a revitalized appreciation of the ways that humanity is woven into the web of life. Rhetoric of domination, mastery, ownership, and management—that is, vocabulary that places humanity apart from and superior to other aspects of the world—is starting to give way to sensibilities that are more tentative, participatory, embedded, embodied, and entangled.

What might this mean for teaching?

Clearly, not every event of teaching can be explicitly about ecological responsibility or social justice. However, there is an imperative to be attentive to frames, to their blind spots, and to the ways they might contribute to troublesome actions and attitudes. To this end, there are ample opportunities in every subject area to address social and ecological implications of knowledge. But these opportunities aren't always obvious, and so they must often be made. And they should be acted on in a manner that is sensitive to the ways that curriculum forms contribute to the ongoing production of teachers' and learners' evolving senses of personal and collective identity.

The Landed Learning project described in this chapter is a good example of these sensitivities: activities on the farm serve not only as a focal point for bringing together the full range of curriculum areas, but as a site for contextualizing skills, generalizing concepts, integrating disciplinary knowledge, and extending perceptual frames. Like all curriculum objects, the farm serves as a focus for interpretation. Like all learning experiences, activities on the farm function to alter what students remember, what they notice, and how they read past, present, and anticipated experiences against one another.

The terms *environmental* and *ecological* don't mean the same thing.

Environmentalism is the study of what surrounds us—which, by definition, assumes a separation between humanity and the natural world.

Ecology is the study of relationships. It derives from the Greek *oikos*, household, and is used to draw attention to intertwining webs of activity and meaning. It erases the human/natural distinction and frames discussions in terms of humans within a more-than-human world.

The decision to have groups of students visit a farm for one day each month, then, affects memories and understandings, and not just of farm-related matters. Students' identities are re-formed as students engage with/in grander webs of relation and identification.

One needn't go to an exotic location and engage in unfamiliar activities to affect learners' senses of self, however. On the contrary, the everyday world offers endless opportunities for invention and reinvention. The teacher's role in this regard is to help students think freshly about forms that they already know well. In effect, good teaching is not just about introducing children to unnoticed and unfamiliar aspects of the world, but also about helping them to renotice artifacts and practices that might have slipped into nonconscious familiarity.

This assertion is consistently supported in the biographies of people who are popularly seen as creative. While exotic objects and unusual activities have their places, creativity is mostly a matter of rethinking the everyday and the often-used. The same sensibility can be used to interpret moments of profound learning. For example, in the fractal cards activity (chap. 2), familiarity was interrupted by looking for fractal patterns in common forms. Similarly, in the poetry-writing activity (chap. 11), the familiar was rendered strange by imagining identities that might have worn a garment with a particular button. These sorts of inventive activities can serve to interrupt entrenched habits of thinking (or, perhaps more accurately, habits of not thinking).

There is an important qualification here. To be inventive, one must have achieved a certain mastery of necessary background competencies. For example, the button activity (as presented in chap. 11) could well be disastrous in settings where literacy skills or social relations are not sufficiently developed, such as primary classrooms or at the start of a school year. Similarly, there was a good reason that the two univeristy educators who initiated the Landed Learning project sought out experienced farmers and master gardeners. To be inventive in their pedagogies, teachers must be skilled with the forms that they intend to use.

As the word suggests, *ecopsychology* combines insights from both psychology and ecology, and is organized around the belief that reconnecting with the natural world is a powerful means to address individual and collective pathologies. A core principle is that mental health cannot be understood strictly in terms of the neurological, the personal, and/or the interpersonal. One must also consider relationships with other species and within various nested and overlapping ecosystems.

It is argued, the health of such ecosystems has implications for the health of the human psyche.*

* See Allen D. Kanner, Theodore Roszak, & Mary E. Gomes (editors), *Ecopsychology: Restoring the earth, healing the mind* (San Francisco: Sierra Club, 1995).

The goals for the project were defined in terms of connection—cultivating emotional connections to nature, fostering understandings of human-land-food-environment connections, and nurturing intergenerational connections.

Underpinning the emergent plan was a conviction that eating is an environmental act. That is, decisions on what food we plant, how it's planted, and what we do with it, all impact the resources of the planet. These sorts of realizations were useful in assembling an initial list of discussion topics that could easily be integrated across the curriculum. These included what we eat, why we eat it, where it comes from, the resources needed for its production, and the environmental implications of dietary choices.

In terms of actual work on the farm, initial imaginings were of children tilling open fields, but it was immediately obvious that the project would be enabled by some tighter constraints. The pilot project thus began with 12 raised gardening beds that had been built for other purposes, but that were at the time unused and ready for cultivation. Their clear boundaries suited the team-based approach and supported more explicit identifications with "our plot." As well, their sizes were more appropriate to the small, unskilled hands that would be doing much of the tending work.

A small grant was awarded that, when frugally managed, was enough to purchase supplies and cover travel costs for children and assistants. The first cohort of students wasn't hard to find. The 18 Grade 7s came from a junior high school a 20-minute bus ride away. Finding experienced farmers was somewhat more of a challenge, but in four months, and with the assistance of 4H (a youth agriculture organization), government contacts, word of mouth, and advertisements in community centers, a small number of experienced farmers and master gardeners were enlisted.

12.3 Copying

Teaching is often characterized in terms of conveying explicit information—presenting, telling, expressing, disseminating, transmitting, explaining, and so on.

Such strategies are clearly important, but one must bear in mind that nothing actually moves from one brain to another in moments of explication. Rather, as discussed in chapter 6, such strategies should be understood in terms of triggering associations in the learner. So long as learners have a sufficient mastery of the language and an appropriate repertoire of experience, it is reasonable to assume that they will assemble sufficiently coherent interpretations of what they are told.

Of course, there are at least two major issues announced in that last sentence. The first is around experience. The most brilliant explanation in the world is useless when presented to an unprepared audience. The second (and related) issue, that is not so commonly mentioned, is that not all knowing lends itself to explanation. As detailed in the opening chapters, most of what we know isn't explicit. Rather, it is enacted as we move through the world. On this count, an important but often underappreciated teaching/learning strategy is copying.

As noted in earlier discussions, within a few hours of birth, humans already demonstrate a capacity to mimic those around them. This predisposition contributes not just to the mastery of physical skills, but also to development of emotion and language abilities. In particular, a key feature of infants' learning to speak is the opportunity to mimic more advanced language users—repeating words and mannerisms, practicing pronunciations, and modifying usages in response to expert prompts.

Copying and repetition are valuable and important techniques in the development of "chunks" of knowing (see Part A), which can then be knitted into more complex competencies. However, the copying associated with learning a first language or developing a physical skill often differs dramatically from the copying tasks that are common in school settings. Copying notes, doing repetitive exercises, aping problem-solving strategies, and rote memorizing of procedures are a far cry from the nuanced give-and-take, the rich contextual detail, the ample opportunity to mimic, and the freedom to err without worry of reprimand that are typical of out-of-school learning.

The recognition of the contrasts between these two types of copying practices has prompted some recent and dramatic changes in educational practice. For example, school-based second language pedagogy has shifted from repetition of phrases, memorization of word lists, and completion of pages of exercises. Current pedagogy places more emphasis on mimicking sounds and phrases within more flexible, evolving situations. Rather than aiming at correct answers and rote mastery on easy-to-mark worksheets, current pedagogy is concerned with the ability "to be in" the new language by using and elaborating what has been learned in familiar, yet unpredictable and creative ways.

Such copying practices are not unique to language learning. Many music teachers begin their sessions by performing that week's musical piece—not so much to

Humans are physiologically predisposed to mystical and spiritual experiences—that is, to events of timelessness, boundlessness, transcendence, and oneness that have been commonly associated with the spirit.*

Such events may not be all that unusual. We've all been lost in a book, immersed in an activity, or swept up in a crowd. These types of experience can also be induced and enhanced by repetitive, rhythmic activity. The explicit purpose of most rituals is to lift participants from their sense of isolation into something greater than themselves.

There's a neurological basis for such responses. Certain events affect parts

* See Andrew Newburg, Eugene d'Aquili, & Vince Rause, *Why God won't go away: Brain science and the biology of belief* (New York: Ballantine, 2001).

of the brain that are associated with reason and the imagined boundaries of the self. When the tendencies toward logic and self-identification are relaxed, the sensations associated with mystical experience emerge.

Why might humans be physiologically predisposed to feelings of transcendence? Among the many possible answers to this question, one has a particular intuitive appeal. It happens because there *are* transcendent unities of which we are always and already part. This conviction is at the core of the emergent movement of *ecospirituality*, a defining feature of which is an attitude of respect and entanglement with all living forms.

This attitude is represented in almost every ancient spiritual tradition. An underlying principle of these traditions is *participation*—a word used nearly a century ago to describe the animistic aspects of indigenous people's and oral cultures' worldviews.*

* Lucien Lévy-Bruhl, *How natives think* (trans. Lilian A. Clare; Princeton, NJ: Princeton University Press, 1922/1985).

demonstrate what can be achieved through dedicated practice, but to invite the student into what it means to be a musician. The same emphasis is commonly employed in athletic contexts. Observing, mimicking, and having immediate corrective feedback from an expert is critical when more is involved than simple absorption of information.

This was certainly part of the thinking within the Landed Learning project, with regard to the desire to have children work elbow-to-elbow with experienced farmers and gardeners. There is more to be learned than details about plants and farming techniques; the program is aimed at learning how to *be* in the world in a particular way. And that way can only be learned by having a chance to copy someone who embodies this sensibility.

In fact, peering across the history of civilization, it appears that it was only in the last few centuries that the emphasis on context-rich opportunities to copy was eclipsed by explanation-based teaching methods. For example, copying practices have long been popular among painters and their students. European masters of the 17th and 18th centuries had their students copy paintings that were already made. Once the students had achieved a certain level of proficiency, they were promoted to the task of completing unfinished paintings that the master had already begun. And only when they had demonstrated their own mastery were they allowed to begin work on their own paintings.

Chess masters also use copying practices. Working from transcripts of completed games, apprentices "replay" every move, sometimes several times over. Each replaying can take many hours as the apprentice attempts to "get into the mind" of the original players.

"Getting inside the mind of a master" has been espoused by many professional writers. A common writing practice for beginners is to select passages from their favorite authors and to copy them over and over. Through this repetition, the novice will gradually come to notice particular details of writing, including the "rhythm" of the writer's thinking. Those who have engaged in such practices often report that traces of form from the other writers inevitably appear in their own work. Oftentimes, stylistic elements copied from others become so transparent to the writer that only others can detect them.

Providing students with opportunities to copy already existing forms and processes is a well-regarded strategy for helping them to develop a sense of the mind of the expert. In teacher education, these copying practices are used a great deal, but have seldom been acknowledged as crucial to professional development. In order to help beginning teachers understand how an experienced teacher thinks about pedagogy, it is important to first invite them into the forms that are the immediate products of this thinking.

For example, rather than simply explain to a novice teacher how to introduce multiplication of fractions to a Grade 6 class, or offer a theoretical account of why one might teach fractions in a particular way, an experienced teacher might ask the student teacher to observe and to make detailed notes during a lesson. Then, after an opportunity is provided to question and discuss these observations, the novice teacher might be asked to copy the lesson with another class, armed with the awareness that this sort of *copying* is not a matter of simple *replication*, but of *creative re-enactment*. The aim isn't to duplicate what was done, but to participate in a particular way of thinking—and an important awareness of this way of thinking is that events may well unfold differently in a different setting.

In some contexts, however, pre-service teachers are expected to endure a sort of "trial by fire" by taking full responsibility for whole classes of students. Small wonder that so many beginning teachers find themselves falling into patterns of teaching that are strikingly similar to ones they promised themselves they would avoid. It can take years to overcome practices that are learned in this manner.

By contrast, having an opportunity to copy an experienced teacher can support the development of a rich appreciation for the complexities of teaching. It starts by participating in meaningful but peripheral tasks (e.g., taking attendance, reviewing homework), and then gradually adding layers of responsibility.

The Native American Iroquois Confederacy espouse a "seventh generation philosophy," by which decision-makers are charged to be mindful of the effects of their actions on their descendants for seven generations.

Current ecology-based discussions of *sustainability* have a similar sense. Gro Harlem Brundtland* defined it as development that "meets the needs of the present generation without compromising the ability of future generations to meet their own needs."

Sustainability has to do with the continuity of cultural (i.e, economic, social, institutional, etc.) and environmental aspects of human activity. That is, sustainability touches on every level of organization, from the personal through the planetary.

* Gro Harlem Brundtland (editor), *Our common future: The World Commission on Environment and Development* (Oxford: Oxford University Press, 1987).

The structures for the Landed Learning project that were established in the first year have been maintained and elaborated in the years since. Each year, a group of children—many of whom have never previously experienced a rural environment—meet at the farm in September. They are partnered with members from the community. Each of these "Farm Friend" teams consist of three to five children and one or two adults.

These intergenerational groups work together through all seasons and all stages of the growing cycle. Throughout the program, teachers work with project leaders to plan activities that integrate land, food, and environmental experiences with classroom learning in all school subjects. In the fall, the focus is on preparation for the season ahead. From January to June, teams work together to cultivate and care for plants. Activities culminate in June with a gathering of children, family members, teachers, farmers, project team leaders, and farm management personnel to enjoy the fruits of the Farm Friends' efforts and share in an early harvest meal.

There are approximately 12 visits to the farm throughout the year, and a specific theme is taken up each time. In a recent year, these topics included the harvest, composting, insects and earthworms, preparing for planting, sowing of seeds, observing nature, plant identification, hydroponics, irrigation, First Nations' associations with the land, nutrition, and the harvest celebration.*

In the process, the children learn about where food comes from, sustainable growing practices, food distribution, and security. The children also learn about other activities associated with the urban farm setting, including bee-keeping, chicken and egg production, market gardening, and the ecosystem of the adjacent forest reserve. From these experiences and activities, the children document and share what they're learning by maintaining journals, writing stories, making sketches, and creating PowerPoint presentations.

12.4 Preparing

One particularly striking difference between teacher education programs and other professional programs that are organized around master / apprentice learning structures has to do with sequencing of topics. In the former, tasks such as planning lessons and managing educational programs are typically front-loaded; in the latter, responsibility for tasks that have to do with planning and oversight are left until the end of the apprenticeship experience.** The rationale is uncomplicated: these activities are seen as the most demanding aspects of the endeavor, requiring a deep understanding of all other facets.

How, for example, might a novice be expected to anticipate the sorts of difficulties that learners might encounter, be aware of the range of pedagogical approaches that might be taken, be informed of what students have already covered, be sensitive to the particular personalities present in a classroom, and be attentive to how these and other elements come

* Lesson suggestions and supporting materials are available for downloading at the Landed Learning website: http://www.cust.educ.ubc.ca/landedlearningproject/ideas.htm.
** See, e.g., Lave & Wenger, *Situated learning*.

together in the complexity of the teaching moment? To insist that a pre-service teacher begin with planning of lessons, rather than only gradually assume responsibilities for structuring classroom activities, is to impose a reliance on what is already known or on pre-prepared curriculum materials such as textbooks and worksheets. Very often, the result is merely a re-enactment and perpetuation of the pre-service teacher's own learning experiences. That is, unless something happens to break the cycle, people tend to teach the way they were taught.

Additionally, a too-early emphasis on lesson planning—especially the sorts of decontextualized lesson planning activities that happen on campus—might support a troublesome belief that it is possible to assemble generic lessons that are context-free and suitable for all students. Indeed, the currently popular construct of "best practices" supports the belief that some techniques transcend contexts, personalities, and topics. Anyone who has taken the time to attend to the differences between two individuals or two school subjects will see the problem with such beliefs. There is no *best*; there is only *good enough*.

None of this is to say that the university seminar room is an inappropriate site for studying what is involved in planning a lesson. Rather, the point is that lesson planning is a complex and demanding undertaking and should never be reduced to an academic exercise. It is important to know about some elements that might be appropriate to a lesson, but developing a lesson is not about filling in a template. Rather, a good-enough lesson has to do with wrapping a particular topic around a particular group of learners.

Lesson development also has a recursive structure. It's never a matter of assembling a completed product. There are always aspects that might be approached differently, or that might serve as more appropriate emphases for a different group.

To this end, one of the prominent and promising movements in recent education has been an emphasis on collegial interaction around the preparation of lessons. This emphasis challenges and rejects many of the entrenched assumptions around lesson

There has been a tendency to attribute increases in allergies, asthma, and related disorders to troublesome levels of contaminants in the air. However, this assumption doesn't help account for the prevalence of these phenomena in developed nations

planning, including the notion of generic lessons and the belief that teaching is a solitary endeavor. Within these structures, groups of teachers work together to pool ideas in preparing, presenting, observing, critiquing, and revising lessons. Typically, such exercises in lesson study begin by identifying a problem for investigation, developing a preliminary lesson design, thinking through necessary materials, anticipating student difficulties, and creating strategies for observation, interpretation, and revision.*

In essence, the emphasis in such contexts is not on *planning*, but on *preparation*—and there's an immense difference. The planned teacher has a trajectory of activities; the prepared teacher both has a plan and is able to anticipate the sorts of issues that might arise and digressions that might be taken. In this frame, the lesson plan is a tool for attending to learners, not an obstacle to such attendance.

Phrased differently, the lesson plan is a *thought experiment*. Lesson planning is an occasion to think through some of the possibilities for particular activities with particular students in particular contexts. There are no hard and fast rules for such experiments. They may well involve some sort of lesson plan template, or they might be more freely structured. They might be mostly a matter of adapting lessons taught elsewhere, or they might involve newly imagined activities. The key quality of lesson planning, in this sense, is that it should support a sense of the dynamic and complex possibilities that might arise.

The questions that guide such thought experiments include: Whom am I teaching? Are there any special considerations or accommodations that should be made? How might such contextual details influence what happens? What do I hope will be learned? How might different theories of learning inform decisions? What resources are available? How might these resources influence the learning that occurs?

These are weighty questions—ones that teacher candidates should be considering, but likely not ones that they can always answer on their own. Once again, such preparation activities should be undertaken with experienced teachers.

---

where air quality is often better than in other parts of the world.

A more recent hypothesis is that a lack of exposure to microbes may be contributing to asthma and allergy epidemics. In effect, too much cleanliness deprives the immune system of the experiences it needs to learn—thereby dumbing it down.

Might "over-sanitized" classroom experiences have an analogous effect on children's minds? Tasks that are too clear cut, that lack ambiguity, and that are overly prescribed might reduce demands on (and thereby reduce the flexibility of) student thought.

---

* One such approach is known as "lesson study." See, e.g., Clea Fernandez & Makoto Yoshida, *Lesson study: A Japanese approach to improving mathematics teaching and learning* (Mahwah, NJ: Lawrence Erlbaum, 2004).

Another approach that might be useful in the project of developing one's lesson preparation abilities is to start with only two or three students, rather than an entire class. This sort of arrangement should reduce the demand to anticipate contingencies while enhancing the opportunity to pay attention to the effects of curriculum emphases and pedagogical strategies. That is, the emphasis would be more on students' learning than on the teacher's actions. As well, it is easier to stray from preplanned trajectories or preformulated explanations when working with only a few students.

In the process, one might have more opportunity to attend to the complex relationships between preparing and teaching. As most experienced teachers will attest, there are vast differences between *wonderful lesson plans* and *wonderful lessons*. The best teaching plans can fall flat if the teacher is unable to maintain an environment that supports learners' engagements with subject matter and with one another.

If we, as authors, were asked to summarize what we thought this book is about, one possible answer is that humanity has come to a time when knowing, learning, and teaching must be understood in terms of global citizenship.

Global citizenship is about the obligation to respect and protect the people around us and the world in which we live. It is about ethical and mindful action—that is, a deep attentiveness to one's participation in the unfolding of possibilities. A motto might be: *Everything matters.*

A key quality of successful lessons is flexible responsiveness to events that unfold in the classroom—a responsiveness that is faithful to stated learning aims, but that understands that all complex engagements involve adjustment, compromise, experiment, error, detour, and surprise. That is, as mentioned in previous chapters, teaching is largely a matter of occasioning, of presenting opportunities for things to "fall together" in ways that cannot be fully anticipated. The notion is rooted in the realization, as noted in earlier chapters, that learning is *dependent on*, but never *determined by* teaching. For this reason, teaching should always plan ahead … but in a manner that enables it to select from possibilities as it goes along.

By late June of the first project year, there was a rich early harvest of organic vegetables and an equally rich set of lessons about education for stewardship and sustainability. While not everything had worked as envisioned, important takeaways were evident in the eyes, works, and actions of the participants. The children and their senior mentors had become close, trusting friends who were deeply connected to the farm and committed to their growing projects.

A few elaborations were made in the second year. For example, to bring more of a scientific emphasis to some of the work, students were asked to generate a research question and conduct small experiments with their farm friends. They also participated in more focused conversations within their groups about organic practices and cultivation methods. An emphasis arose in that year on maintaining a meditative, slowed-down pace in the garden by having children write descriptions of all sensory input—hearing, smelling, tasting, seeing, and feeling all parts of the environment. The year ended with an even larger harvest.

The first two years afforded an opportunity to develop a workable model of education for sustainability. The major elaboration in the third year was to work with larger classes of students from more diverse social and economic backgrounds and across a wider range of grades. The manifold increase in the number of student participants presented several issues. More garden beds had to be constructed, the materials for which were donated by a local lumber company; more funding was needed to bring children and volunteers to the site, and these were secured through grants and gifts; more farm friends had to be found, and this necessitated a shift in structure. Not enough seniors could be identified, and so invitations were extended to graduate and senior level undergraduate students at the university.

Few of them had a wealth of farming experience or expertise that could begin to compare with that of the seniors, but they did bring some specialized knowledge, educational expertise, and a desire to learn more about sustainable farming practices.

12.5 What is education for?

Many, and perhaps most teachers begin their careers with the conviction that they will avoid those teaching practices that they found unhelpful or inappropriate when they were students: they will be less directive and more attentive; they will be less technocratic and more innovative; they will be more open to creative possibility and less chained to the textbook.

However, when the demands of full-time teaching are experienced, such resolutions are often pushed aside. How might one sidestep such a fate? Is it even possible to insert oneself into a social institution that is so steeped in unconscious habit and to act in ways that are more faithful to one's espoused goals for teaching? Or are we humans more likely to get caught up in the flow of established patterns?

Fortunately, history has demonstrated that change is possible. But, it has also shown that change is never a matter of individual initiative and rarely a simple matter of conscious decision. Instances of social transformation/learning are complex collective processes that unfold on time scales that are different from those of individual learning, and that involve ongoing interrogations of practices, implicit associations, and so on.

This is particularly true of teaching practice. For the most part, teaching actions are not consciously considered and deliberately selected. There are simply so many demands on teachers' limited attentions that

most of what teachers do has to become automatic—
that is, deeply embodied. Put differently, the moment
of teaching is not really a matter of conscious decision-
making; rather, it is more a situation in which one enacts
decisions that are already made. And these include
decisions that are made by others about, for example,
standards for appropriate action, organization of the
environment, and access to various technologies.

Automaticity isn't a bad thing. As developed in earlier
chapters, it is the necessary complement of conscious
awareness; it enables us to push familiar details and
routines into the background. However, automaticity
does present problems when it comes to changing
entrenched habits of acting and interpretation. This is
why efforts to effect change—that is, to teach—must
operate across layers of complex co-activity.

Of course, teaching has tended to be understood only
in terms of effecting change on the individual level,
and so a more complex take on education presents a
need to interrogate what formal education is all about.
Clearly, education can't be a simple matter of perpetuat-
ing entrenched habits of interpretation or of preparing
youth for adulthood. Complexity thinking reveals such
rationales as not only naive, but impossible—the former because learning is always an elaborative process
(and so attempts to perpetuate necessarily contribute
to transformations), and the latter because the world is
changing so quickly that the best preparation we can
hope for is the capacity for flexible adaptation (and
much of modern curricula and instruction seem to be
pointed in exactly the opposite direction).

One of the important and valuable lessons of complexity is that the consequences of efforts to teach can
never be fully known. Teaching spills over its explicit
intentions, its contexts, its schedules, its rationales. Like
solutions to difficult problems that bubble to the surface
of consciousness only when one has allowed oneself to
be distracted, the most profound impacts of teaching
are rarely if ever realized in the moment of teaching.
Just think about some of the most important lessons
that you were taught: Did you realize at the time how
important they were? One simply cannot judge the
importance of an event of teaching in the moment.

For centuries, most western schools
have been organized along the same
lines as orderly military processions
and factory assembly lines.

New metaphors of group action
are starting to be embraced, however.
As noted in previous chapters, these
are largely prompted by events and
technologies that enhance the human
ability to link minds. With the advent
of instant messaging, blogs, wikis,
chat groups, playlists, online multi-

player games, and file-sharing—and in anticipation of even more dramatic shifts in human interconnectivity—it seems metaphors of jazz ensembles or sports teams are better fitted to emergent possibilities. Participants gather around shared goals and thematics, and then combine their talents and interests into a collective improvisation. It is not about erasing individuality, but about opening possibilities for each *I/me* within the co-laboring *we/us*.

Western culture has embraced this evolution in the means for and modes of collective action. The academic and business worlds have deliberately and explicitly incorporated it into their structures. Few schools, however, have embodied this emergent ecology of knowing and learning.

Unfortunately, discussions and debates around the goals of education and the means of educational reform always seem to get tangled up in the topic of *teaching methods* rather than the *nature of teaching*. Arguments tend to swirl around the specific curriculum topics that should be covered, the levels of proficiency that should be demonstrated, and the classroom structures that are more or most effective.

Underlying these technocratic obsessions is a failure to interrogate what it means to *learn*. Like the word *teaching*, the word *learning* is treated as though it were a matter of common sense—simply about taking things in, or mastering certain competencies, or changes in behavior due to specific experiences. Such simplistic formulations obscure the fact that learning entails structural change on multiple levels. When a student learns, her or his weave of conceptual associations is revised, her or his brain is physically changed, her or his positionings in webs of social activity are affected. Such transformations are so complex that it is simply wrong to suggest that learning is "due to" experience or teaching. Rather, learning is "due to" the evolving structures of an agent-in-context.

Different senses of the goals and purposes of schooling are entailed here. Classrooms are seen not as places of reproduction and replication. Rather, learning and teaching seem to be more about expanding the space of the possible and creating conditions for the emergence of the as-yet unimagined. In this frame, education is not about convergence onto a pre-existent truth, but about divergence. Learning and teaching are recursively elaborative processes of opening up new spaces of possibility by exploring current spaces.

That is, the emphasis is on a sense of *knowing* that understands how it is implicated in all aspects of existence. Knowing is not a matter of inert bits of information, but is inseparable from doing and being. Knowing is the dynamic of existence. When there are changes to knowing—that is, when there is learning—on levels other than that of the individual, they tend to be noticed as moments of evolution (of species, cultures, knowledge domains, social movements, etc.). Teaching reaches through and across the layers of these entangled, evolving forms. Teaching, then, is never simply a personal or an interpersonal act. It touches the subpersonal through the planetary. Teaching is a deliberate participation in what is.

Based on information gathered in the first four years of the Landed Learning project, it is clear that the community-based, intergenerational, experience-rich context of growing food crops in a farm setting can support powerful learning for sustainability.

Children indicate that the hands-on farming and gardening experiences create lasting understandings that they expect will stay with them in their adult lives. They realize that outdoor learning is distinctly different from classroom learning. They indicate that a community context supported by adults makes the learning more authentic, memorable, and transferable. Opportunities to make decisions and to take control in an educative setting are recognized as influential and as contributing to significant learning.

Both adults and students value the opportunity to meet and talk about real issues and life experiences. Intergenerational work is a way to foster appreciations of diversity, a principle of both sustainability and complex collective action. The bonding and friendships that develop within farm friend groups can foster the kind of relational knowing essential to sustainability and complex co-activity.

Nurturing and caring relationships among elders and children provide a context to develop the children's nurturing and caring practices for plants and the land. The community farm-based intergenerational context enables ethical and environmental issues to become real and relevant for students. The gardening experience challenges students in tangible ways about their responsibility toward the environment and how they might participate in sustainability practices around such immediate and practical matters as managing weeds and controlling pests that might damage crops. The children indicate that strategies that allow for autonomy and self-direction can shape new self-identities that promote personal responsibility in the more-than-human world.

How can we live together well with the earth that sustains all living forms? This question is a complex one, and it requires a complex educational response. The Landed Learning program provides one example of how teaming community farmers and young people can be effective, not only in promoting understanding of land-based traditions and concern for the environment, but also in integrating all aspects of school curricula.

The Landed Learning project is an illustration of the ways that knowing, learning, and teaching can and should spill past the official times and places of formal education. It is an example of what can happen when education is oriented not by the desire to predetermine what *must* be mastered, but by a willingness to participate in what *might* be taught, learned, and known.

Across the issues that confront individuals, cultures, and the species, then, the issue that presents itself for teaching is not how to control what happens, but how to participate mindfully in the unfolding of possibilities. It is about maintaining an awareness that we, individually and collectively, are constantly enacting our knowing and always learning.

That is, teaching isn't something that is *done*. Teaching is *lived* as one encounters self and other, individual and collective, past and future, actual and possible.

References

Abram, D. *The spell of the sensuous: Perception and language in a more-than-human world* (New York: Pantheon, 1996).

American Psychiatric Association. *Diagnostic and statistical manual of mental disorders*, 4th edition (New York: American Psychiatric Association, 2000).

Arbib, M. "From monkey-like action recognition to human language: An evolutionary framework for neurolinguistics," in *Behavioral and Brain Sciences*, vol. 28 (2005): 105–167.

Ashcroft, B., G. Griffiths, & H. Tiffin. *The post-colonial studies reader* (New York: Routledge, 1997).

Ashton-Warner, S. *Teacher* (New York: Simon & Schuster, 1963).

Azar, B. "How mimicry begat culture," in *Monitor on Psychology*, vol. 35, no. 9 (October 2005): 54–57.

Ball, P. *Critical mass: How one thing leads to another* (New York: Farrar, Straus and Giroux, 2004).

Barabási, A-L. *Linked: How everything is connected to everything else and what it means for business, science, and everyday life* (New York: Plume, 2002).

Bell, G. & J. Gemmell. "A digital life," in *Scientific American*, vol. 296, no. 3 (March 2007): 58–65.

Berlin, B. & P. Kay, *Basic color terms: Their universality and evolution* (Berkeley, CA: University of California Press, 1999).

Bloom, B.S. *Taxonomy of educational objectives, Handbook I: The cognitive domain* (New York: David McKay, 1956).

Bransford, J.D., A.L. Brown, & R.R. Cocking (eds.). *How people learn: Brain, mind, experience, and school* (Washington, DC: National Academy Press, 1999).

Britzman, D. *Practice makes practice: A critical study of learning to teach*, revised edition (Albany, NY: State University of New York Press, 2003).

Brooks, R.A. *Flesh and machines: How robots will change us* (New York: Pantheon, 2002).

Brundtland, G.H. (ed.). *Our common future: The World Commission on Environment and Development* (Oxford, UK: Oxford University Press, 1987).

Bryson, M. & S. de Castell. "Queer pedagogy: Praxis makes im/perfect," in *Canadian Journal of Education*, vol. 18, no. 2 (1993): 285–305.

Buchanan, M. *Ubiquity: The science of history ... or why the world is simpler than we think* (London: Phoenix, 2000).

Bunge, M. "Ethics and praxiology as technologies," in *Techne*, vol. 4, no. 4 (1999): 1–3.

Burdick, A. "The truth about invasive species: How to stop worrying and learn to love ecological intruders," in *Discover*, vol. 26, no. 5 (May 2005): 34–41.

Cajete, G. *Look to the mountain: An ecology of indigenous education* (Asheville, NC: Kivaki, 1994).

Calvin, W.H. *How brains think: Evolving intelligence, then and now* (New York: Basic Books, 1996).

Carper, J. *Your miracle brain* (New York: Quill, 2000).

Cobb, P. "Multiple perspectives," in *Transforming children's mathematics education: International perspectives* (eds. Les P. Steffe & T. Wood; Barcombe, UK: Falmer Press, 1990): 200–215.

Counternormativity Discourse Group. "Performing an archive of feeling: Experiences of normalizing structures in teaching and teacher education," in *Journal of Curriculum and Pedagogy*, vol. 2, no. 2 (2006): 173–214.

Crozier, L. *Inventing the hawk* (Toronto: McClelland & Stewart, 1992).

Dar-Nimrod, I. & S.J. Heine. "Exposure to scientific theories affects women's math performance," in *Science*, vol. 314 (October 2006): 435.

Davis, B. *Inventions of teaching: A genealogy* (Mahwah, NJ: Lawrence Erlbaum, 2004).

Davis, B. & E. Simmt. "Understanding learning systems: Mathematics teaching and complexity science," in *Journal for Research in Mathematics Education*, vol. 34, no. 2 (2003): 137–167.

Davis, B. & D. Sumara. "Cognition, complexity, and teacher education," in *Harvard Educational Review*, vol. 67, no. 1 (1997): 105–125.

Davis, B. & D. Sumara. *Complexity and education: Inquiries into learning, teaching, and research* (Mahwah, NJ: Erlbaum, 2006).

Davis, B., D. Sumara, & T.E. Kieren, "Cognition, co-emer-gence, curriculum," in *Journal of Curriculum Studies*, vol. 28, no. 2 (1996): 151–169.

Davis, W. *Light at the edge of the world: A journey through the realm of vanishing cultures* (Washington, DC: National Geographic, 2002).

Deacon, T. *The symbolic species: The co-evolution of language and the brain* (New York: W.W. Norton, 1997).

Deleuze, G. & F. Guattari. *Anti-Oedipus: Capitalism and schizophrenia* (Minneapolis: University of Minnesota Press, 1983).

Delpit, L.D. *Other people's children: Cultural conflict in the classroom* (New York: New Press, 1996).

Dennett, D.C. *Consciousness explained* (New York: Little, Brown and Company, 1991).

Dennett, D.C. *Kinds of minds: Towards an understanding of con-sciousness* (New York: Basic, 1997).

Donald, M. *Origins of the modern mind: Three stages in the evo-lution of culture and cognition* (Cambridge, MA: Harvard University Press, 1991).

Donald, M. *A mind so rare: The evolution of human consciousness* (New York, W.W. Norton, 2001).

Edwards, D. & N. Mercer. *Common knowledge: The develop-ment of understanding in the classroom* (London: Routledge, 1987).

Ellsworth, E. "Why doesn't this feel empowering? Working through the repressive myths of critical pedagogy," in *Harvard Educational Review*, vol 59, no. 3 (1989): 271–297.

Evernden, N. *The natural alien: Humankind and environment* (Toronto: University of Toronto Press, 1993).

Fernandez, C. & M. Yoshida. *Lesson study: A Japanese approach to improving mathematics teaching and learning* (Mahwah, NJ: Lawrence Erlbaum, 2004).

Foucault, M. *Abnormal: Lectures at the Collège de France, 1974-1975* (eds. V. Marchetti & A. Salomoni; trans. G. Burchell; New York: Picador, 2004).

Freire, P. *Pedagogy of the oppressed* (New York: Seaview, 1971).

Gardner, H. *Frames of mind: The theory of multiple intelligences* (New York: Basic, 1993).

Gee, J.P. *What video games have to teach us about learning and literacy* (New York: Palgrave Macmillan, 2003).

Goldberger, A.L., L.A.N. Amaral, J.M. Hausdorff, P.Ch. Ivanov, C.-K. Peng, & H.E. Stanley, "Fractal dynamics in physiology: Alterations with disease and aging," in *PNAS (Proceedings of the National Academy of Sciences of the United States of America)*, vol. 99, suppl. 1 (2002): 2466–2472.

Gopnik, A., A. Meltzoff, & P. Kuhl. *The scientist in the crib: What early learning tells us about the mind* (New York: Perennial, 1999).

Gould, S.J. *The mismeasure of man* (New York: W.W. Norton, 1996).

Greenwald, A.G., D.E. McGhee, & J.L.K. Schwartz. "Measuring individual differences in implicit cognition: The Implicit Association Test," in *Journal of Personality and Social Psychology*, vol. 74, no. 6 (1998): 1464–1480.

Grumet, M. *Bitter milk: Women and teaching* (Amherst, MA: The University of Massachusetts Press, 1988).

Grumet, M. "The curriculum: What are the basics and are we teaching them?" in *Thirteen questions: Reframing education's conversation* (eds. J.L. Kincheloe & S.R. Steinberg; New York: Peter Lang, 1993): 15–21.

Haig-Brown, C. *With good intentions: Euro-Canadian and Aboriginal relations in colonial Canada* (Vancouver: University of British Columbia Press, 2006).

Harris, J.R. *The nurture assumption: Why children turn out the way they do* (New York: The Free Press, 1998).

Hawkins, J. *On intelligence: How a new understanding of the brain will lead to the creation of truly intelligent machines* (New York: Times Books, 2004).

Hayles, N.K. *My mother was a computer: Digital subjects and literary texts* (Chicago: University of Chicago Press, 2005).

Hebb, D.O. *The organization of behavior* (New York: Wiley, 1949).

Hoffman, D.D. *Visual intelligence: How we create what we see* (New York: W.W. Norton, 1998).

Huser, G. *Stitches* (Toronto: Groundwood, 2003).

Jackson, S. *Patchwork girl*. Available at http://www.eastgate.com.

Jaynes, J. *The origin of consciousness and the breakdown of the bicameral mind* (New York: Penguin, 1979).

Johnson, D.W. & R.T. Johnson. *Learning together and alone: Cooperative, competitive, and individualistic learning*, 5th edition (Boston: Allyn & Bacon, 1998).

Johnson, M.H. *Developmental cognitive neuroscience: An introduction* (London: Blackwell, 1997).

Johnson, S. *Emergence: The connected lives of ants, brains, cities, and software* (New York: Scribner, 2001).

Johnson, S. *Mind wide open: Your brain and the neuroscience of everyday life* (New York: Scribner, 2004).

Johnson, S. *Everything bad is good for you: How popular culture is actually making us smarter* (New York: Riverhead, 2005).

Juarrero, A. *Dynamics in action: Intentional behavior as a complex system* (Cambridge, MA: The MIT Press, 1999).

Kanner, A.D., T. Roszak, & M.E. Gomes (eds.). *Ecopsychology: Restoring the earth, healing the mind* (San Francisco: Sierra Club, 1995).

Kress, G. *Literacy in the new media age* (London: Routledge, 2003).

Kurzweil, R. *The singularity is near: When humans transcend biology* (New York: Viking, 2005).

Lakoff, G. & M. Johnson. *Metaphors we live by* (Chicago: University of Chicago Press, 1980).

Lakoff, G. & M. Johnson. *Philosophy in the flesh: The embodied mind and its challenge to western thought* (New York: Basic Books, 1999).

Lankshear, C. & M. Knobel. *New literacies: Changing knowledge and classroom learning* (Berkshire, UK: Open University Press, 2006).

Lave, J. & E. Wenger, *Situated learning: Legitimate peripheral participation* (Cambridge, UK: Cambridge University Press, 1991).

LeDoux, J. *Synaptic self: How our brains become who we are* (New York: Viking, 2002).

Lévy-Bruhl, L. *How natives think* (trans. L.A. Clare; Princeton, NJ: Princeton University Press, 1922/1985).

Lorde, A. *Sister outsider: Essays and speeches* (Trumansberg, NY: Crossing Press, 1984).

Lowry, L. *The giver* (New York: Bantam Doubleday, 1993).

Luce-Kapler, R. *Writing with, through, and beyond the text: An ecology of language* (Mahwah, NJ: Lawrence Erlbaum, 2004).

Luce-Kapler, R., T. Dobson, D. Sumara, T. Iftody, & B. Davis. "E-Literature and the digital engagement of concsiousness," in *55th Yearbook of the National Reading Conference* (eds. by J. Hoffman, D. Schallert, C. Fairbanks, J. Worthy, & B. Maloch; Oak Creek, WI: National Reading Conference, 2006): 171–181.

Luke, C. *Feminisms and critical pedagogy* (New York: Routledge, 1992).

MacKay, D.M. *Behind the eye* (Oxford, UK: Blackwell, 1991).

Martin, L., J. Towers, & S.E.B. Pirie. "Collective mathematical understanding as improvisation," in *Mathematical Thinking and Learning*, vol. 8, no. 2 (2006): 149–183.

Maturana, H. & F. Varela. *The tree of knowledge: The biological roots of human understanding* (Boston: Shambhala, 1987).

Mayer-Smith, J., L. Peterat, & O. Bartosh. "Growing together to understand sustainability: An intergenerational farming project," in *Innovation, education and communication for sustainable development* (ed. Walter Leal Filho; New York: Peter Lang, 2006).

Meyer, M. "The grading of students," in *Science*, vol. 28 (1908): 243–250.

Miller, G.A. "The magical number seven, plus or minus two: Some limits on our capacity for processing information," in *Psychological Review*, vol. 63 (1956): 81–97.

Mithen, S. *The prehistory of the mind: The cognitive origins of art, religion and science* (London: Thames and Hudson, 1996).

Morin, E. *Seven complex lessons in education for the future* (Paris: UNESCO, 1999).

Murphy, M.J. "The relationship of school breakfast to psychosocial and academic functioning," in *Pediatric Adolescent Medicine*, vol. 152 (1998): 899–907.

Newburg, A., E. d'Aquili, & V. Rause. *Why God won't go away: Brain science and the biology of belief* (New York: Ballantine, 2001).

Noddings, N. *Caring: A feminine approach to ethics and moral education* (Berkeley: University of California Press, 1984).

Norman, J. *Living for the city* (London: Policy Exchange, 2006).

Norretranders, T. *The user illusion: Cutting consciousness down to size* (trans. J. Sydenham; New York: Viking, 1998).

Ogbu, J.U. "Understanding cultural diversity and learning," in *Educational Researcher*, vol. 21, no. 8 (1992): 5–14.

Olson, D.R. *The world on paper: The conceptual and cognitive implications of writing and reading* (Cambridge, UK: Cambridge University Press, 1996).

Petrina, S. *Advanced teaching methods for the technology classroom* (Hershey, PA: Information Science Publishing, 2006).

Piaget, J. *The origins of intelligence in children* (New York: W.W. Norton, 1936/1963).

Piaget, J. *La construction réel chez l'enfant* (Paris: Delachaux & Niestle, 1952/1990).

Pinar, W.F. (ed.). *Queer theories in education* (Hillsdale, NJ: Lawrence Erlbaum, 1998).

Pinar, W.F., W.M. Reynolds, P. Slattery, & P.M. Taubman. *Understanding curriculum: An introduction to the study of historical and contemporary curriculum discourses* (New York: Peter Lang, 1995).

Pinker, S. *How the mind works* (New York: W.W. Norton, 1991).

Postman, N. & C. Weingartner. *Teaching as a subversive activity* (New York: Delacorte, 1969).

Ramachandran, V.S. & E. Hubbard. "Hearing colors, tasting shapes," in *Scientific American Mind*, vol. 16 (October 2005): 17–23.

Rogoff, B. *The cultural nature of human development* (New York: Oxford University Press, 2003).

Rosch Heider, E. "Universals in color naming and memory," in *Journal of Experimental Psychology*, vol. 93 (1972): 1–20.

Ross, P. "The expert mind," in *Scientific American*, vol. 295, no. 2 (August, 2006): 64–71.

Sabbagh, L. "The teen brain, hard at work," in *Scientific American Mind*, vol. 17, no. 4 (August/September 2006): 20–25.

Sacks, O. *Seeing voices: A journey into the world of the deaf* (New York: HarperCollins, 1989).

Sacks, O. *An anthropologist on Mars: Seven paradoxical tales* (New York: Knopf, 1995).

Said, E. *Culture and imperialism* (New York: Vintage, 1994).

Simmt, E. & B. Davis, "Fractal cards: A space for exploration in geometry and discrete mathematics," in *Mathematics Teacher*, vol. 91 (December, 1998), 102–108.

Smith, L.T. *Decolonizing methodologies: Research and indigenous peoples* (London: Zed Books, 1999).

Stanley, R.D. "The body of a 'healthy' education system," in *Journal of Curriculum Theorizing*, vol. 20, no. 4 (2004): 63–74.

Starkes, J.L. & K.A. Ericsson (eds.). *Expert performance in sports: Advances in research on sport expertise* (Champaign: IL: Human Kinetics, 2003).

Steele, C. & J. Aronson. "Stereotype threat and intellectual test performance of African Americans," in *Journal of Personality and Social Psychology*, vol. 74, no. 4 (1995): 797–811.

Sternberg, R.G. & E.L. Grigorenko. *Our labeled children: What every parent and teacher needs to know about learning disabilities* (New York: Perseus, 2000).

Stone, J.E. "Developmentalism: An obscure but pervasive restriction on educational improvement," in *Education Policy Analysis Archives*, vol. 4, no. 8 (April, 1996).

Sumara, D. *Why reading literature in school still matters: Imagination, interpretation, insight* (Mahwah, NJ: Lawrence Erlbaum, 2002).

Sumara, D., B. Davis, & D. van der Wey. "The pleasure of thinking," in *Language Arts*, vol. 76, no. 2 (1998): 135–143.

Surowiecki, J. *The wisdom of crowds: Why the many are stronger than the few and how collective wisdom shapes business, economies, societies, and nations* (New York: Doubleday, 2004).

Suzuki, D. & W. Grady. *Tree: A life story* (Vancouver, BC: Greystone, 2004).

Tapscott, D. & A.D. Williams. *Wikinomics: How mass collaboration changes everything* (New York: Portfolio, 2006).

Tobin, K. "The role of wait time in higher cognitive level learning," in *Review of Educational Research*, vol. 57 (Spring 1987): 69–95.

Van de Walle, J.A. *Elementary and middle school mathematics: Teaching developmentally*, 6ᵗʰ edition (Boston: Allyn & Bacon, 2006).

Varela, F. *Ethical know-how: Action, wisdom, and cognition* (San Francisco: Stanford University Press, 1999).

Varela, F., E. Thompson, & E. Rosch, *The embodied mind: Cognitive science and human experience* (Cambridge, MA: The MIT Press, 1991).

von Maltzan, C. (ed.). *Africa and Europe, en/countering myths: Essays on literature and cultural politics* (New York: Peter Lang, 2003).

Vygotsky, L.S. *Thought and language, revised edition* (ed. Alex Kozulin; Cambridge, MA: The MIT Press, 1986).

Walker, S., III. *The hyperactivity hoax* (New York: St. Martin's Press, 1998).

Watson, J.B. *Behaviorism* (New York: Transaction, 1924/1988).

Watts, D. *Six degrees: The science of the connected age* (New York: W.W. Norton, 2003).

Webb, J.T. & D. Latimer. "ADHD and children who are gifted," in *ERIC Digest*, vol. 522 (1993, ED358673).

Williams, C. *Terminus brain: The environmental threats to human intelligence* (London: Cassell, 1997).

Name Index

Topic Index